WREAKING HAVOC

Joseph G. Dawson III, General Editor
Editorial Board:
Robert Doughty
Brian Linn
Craig Symonds
Robert Wooster

WREAKING HAVOC

A YEAR IN AN A-20

Joseph W. Rutter

Texas A&M University
College Station

The paper used in this book meets the minimum requirements
of the American National Standard for Permanence
of Paper for Printed Library Materials, z39.48-1984.
Binding materials have been chosen for durability.
∞

Library of Congress Cataloging-in-Publication Data

Rutter, Joseph W.
    Wreaking havoc : a year in an A-20 / Joseph W. Rutter.—1st ed.
        p. cm.—(Texas A&M University military history series ; no. 91)
Includes index.
ISBN 1-58544-289-5 (cloth : alk. paper)
    1. Rutter, Joseph W. 2. World War, 1939–1945—Personal narratives, American. 3. Bomber
pilots—United States—Biography. 4. A-20 bomber. 5. United States. Army Air Forces—Officers—Biography. 6. World War, 1939–1945—Aerial operations, American. 7. World War,
1939–1945—Campaigns—Pacific Area. I. Title. II. Texas A&M University military history
series ; 91.
    D811.R89A3 2003
    940. 54'25'092—dc21

                                                                        2003007369

"Off we go,
Into the wild blue yonder . . . "

—THE AIR CORPS SONG

To Dick and Fred, whose youthful questions regarding my part in World War II prompted me to write a memoir. This is the story.

CONTENTS

ILLUSTRATIONS

MAPS

PREFACE

This book is an account of ordinary experiences and some outlandish incidents that I observed or in which I participated from 1943–45. It grew from a less detailed account presented to our sons at Christmas, 1969. My wife and friend, Bee, commented that the original was a start—she called it an outline and said it lacked human interest—but I had intended it only for Dick and Fred. Later, usually after reading a book pertaining to the war years, Bee would suggest I have another try at expanding the story. She has suffered through reading three or four or more revisions during the past ten years or so and her candid comments and questions have been most helpful. Thanks to Bee, what once was an outline is now a book, although much changed in scope and style.

The 312th Bomb Group has held annual reunions since 1948 and for the past twenty years I have been able to attend many of them. At these gatherings I was able to talk to others who shared the experiences herein reported and subsequently exchange correspondence with a number of others whose recollections prove that a good memory is not faultless and thus have permitted some correction of details, dates, and names. The notes, logs, and official orders in my files did not always give the full perspective of many events in which the 312th participated when we were in New Guinea and the Philippines. In many instances I have relied upon the recollections of Don Dyer, Cal Slade, Ed Hambleton, Jack Klein, Babe Young, Jim Wylie, Clif Graber, and a host of others.

Volumes four *(The Pacific: Guadalcanal to Saipan, August 1942 to July 1944)* and five *(The Pacific: Matterhorn to Nagasaki)* of *The Army Air Forces in World War II*, edited by Wesley Frank Craven and James Lea Cate (Chicago: University of Chicago Press, 1950, 1953), served as the authority for the dates of events, units involved on certain missions, when units were based at particular airfields, and other details affecting our group.

Russell L. Sturzebecker's *The Roarin' 20's: A History of the 312th Bombardment Group* (N.p.: Russell L. Sturzebecker, 1986) includes escape and evasion reports, the names of casualties (there were 150 in all), and mission activity by squadrons, crews, and month. This valuable history also touches upon a wide range of events in the day-to-day life of a combat unit like the 312th: living conditions, recreation, food, the work of the chaplain, and the logistics of moving men and equipment to new bases.

As it stands now, this account is as factual as diaries, letters, logbooks, official orders, and a dimming memory can make it. It is the story of a young man from a small town growing up and engaging in the serious work of the 389th Bomb Squadron and seeing places and sights the like of which he had never dreamed. The tough times and unpleasant conditions made this experience a broad and still-valued education.

Looking back, sharing in the efforts of the 312th Bomb Group in the Southwest Pacific provides me with some satisfaction. We were, during our youthful days, a part of the history that was made in New Guinea and the Philippines in 1944 and 1945. I am glad I was there, grateful to have survived, and pleased that there is still interest in this story.

Overseas Flight Log, 1944–45

Joseph W. Rutter, o–765096
312th Bomb Group, 389th Bomb Squadron

July 12, 1944	Left Hamilton Field, California.
July 16	Arrived Port Moresby, Papua New Guinea.
July 25	Arrived Nadzab, Papua New Guinea.
July 29	Arrived Hollandia, Dutch New Guinea and assigned to 389th Squadron, 312th Bomb Group with 2d Lt. Grant Peterson.
July 30	Familiarization flight Hollandia. 1:30 hrs.
August 1	Familiarization flight Hollandia. 1:15 hrs.
August 4	Mission 1: To bomb supply dump on Sarmi Peninsula near Wakde Island. Turned back by weather. 2:00 hrs.
August 6	Mission 2: Bombed supply dump at Sarmi. 2:30hrs.
August 9	Mission 3: Native village at Ampus, about 30 miles south of Hollandia; bombed and strafed troops; a rat-race. 2:15 hrs.
August 16	Mission 4: Mount Hakko near Wakde Island; bombed and strafed troops. 2:00 hrs.
August 18	Mission 5: Same as 4. Hydraulic system went out; completed mission but brought bombs back; used emergency system for gear, flaps, and brakes; no damage upon landing. Leon Schnell, gunner. 2:30 hrs.

August 31   Mission 6: Bombed Utarom airstrip, medium
                       altitude. Heavy and intense flak. 5:00 hrs.

August combat missions: 6. Combat hours: 16:15. Local flights on
    August 8, 14, 22, 24, and 28. Hrs/mo: 22:25.

September 3   Mission 7: Bombed and strafed Nabire
                       airstrip. 4:00 hrs.
September 11   Mission 8: Bombed Utarom airstrip, medium
                       altitude. Some flak. 5:40 hrs.
September 12   Mission 9: Bombed Babo airstrip, medium
                       altitude. Heavy and intense flak. 5:20 hrs.
September 14   Mission 10: Bombed Babo, medium altitude.
                       Target covered by cloud; brought bombs
                       back. 5:20 hrs.
September 30   Mission 11: Bombed and strafed Utarom
                       airstrip. 5:00 hrs.

September combat missions: 5. Combat hours: 25:20. Other flights on
    September 1, 6, 7, 10, 17, 18, 21, 22, and 28. Hrs/mo: 41:05.

October 5   Mission 12: Bombed and strafed Sawar supply
                       dump near Wakde Island. One 387th
                       Squadron plane shot down, Capt. Edward
                       Pool. 2:00 hrs.
October 10   Mission 13: Bombed Utarom airstrip, medium
                       altitude. 5:40 hrs.
October 11   389th Squadron B-25 with Lt. Albert Eddy and
                       Flt. Off. Ralph Preston plus ten gunners lost
                       on account of weather on flight to Nadzab,
                       Papua New Guinea.
October 17   Mission 14: Babo airstrip, medium altitude; did
                       not bomb due to clouds. Lt. Thomas Harkey
                       and gunner killed in crash on coast west of
                       Hollandia. 3:35 hrs.
October 23   Mission 15: Bombed Babo airstrip, medium
                       altitude; heavy ack. 5:20 hrs.

October combat missions: 4. Combat hours: 16:35. Other flights on
    October 12, 28, 29, and 30. Hrs/mo: 22:20.

November 5   Mission 16: Bombed and strafed Sarmi. 2:10 hrs.

November 6   Mission 17: Same as 16. 1:50 hrs.

November 10   Lt. Grant E. Peterson (tentmate) killed at Wewak, Papua New Guinea, while flying from Combat Replacement Training Center at Nadzab, Papua New Guinea.

November 22   Lt. Don Murison killed in crash on test flight at Hollandia. Body recovered by Lt. Mel Kapson and native party on Thanksgiving Day; buried in military cemetery, Hollandia.

November combat missions: 2. Combat hours: 4:00. Other flights on November 1, 3, 8, 12, 17, 21, and 23. Hrs/mo: 16:10.

December, 1944   No combat missions flown; 312th Bomb Group in process of relocation to Tanauan, Leyte Island, Philippine Islands

December 6–10   Fat-cat trip in B-25 to Cairns, Australia, with Clifton Graber; stayed at Exchange Hotel, Innisfail.

December 16–30   Ten-day leave to Sydney.

December combat missions: None. Flights on December 3, 6, 9, 10, and 14. Hrs/mo: 16:45.

January 3–4, 1945   312th's move from Hollandia to Leyte Island, Philippines, begins with 389th Squadron led by Col. Strauss. Overnight at Morotai Island.

January 4   Mission 18 (A):ª Morotai to Tanauan, Leyte. 4:00 hrs.

January 6   Mission 19: Bombed and strafed Lahug airdrome, Cebu City; 6 holes. 2:00 hrs.

January 7   Mission 20: Bombed and strafed Clark Field, Luzon. Landed on Mindoro Island after mission with flight led by Cal Slade. Stayed overnight after nosewheel snubber failure; rest of flight refueled and continued to Tanauan. Lt. Harry Lillard, 389th Squadron, lost. 6:00 hrs.

January 8	Mission 21 (A): Mindoro to Panay Island area; got lost and returned to Mindoro. UHF radio hit yesterday and went out on landing today; repaired. Radio compass shot out yesterday. 2:30 hrs.[a]
January 8	Mission 22 (A): Flew to Tananan after getting 200 gallons fuel at Mindoro. 1:50 hrs.
January 9	Mission 23: Strafed roads and railroads south of Manila. Flew wing of Col. Wells. 6:00 hrs.
January 10	Mission 24: Strafed roads and railroads north of Manila. 6:00 hrs.
January 13	Mission 25: Bombed and strafed Marikina airdrome southeast of Manila. Flak. 4:20 hrs.
January 15	Mission 26: Bombed and strafed Puerto Princesa airstrip, Palawan Island. Hit on the head and nose by windshield armor glass after it came unlatched at beginning of strafing run; broke off attack. 5:45 hrs.
January 17	Mission 27: Norzagary, Luzon. Turned back due to weather. 3:50 hrs.
January 21	Mission 28: Strafed roads south Luzon near Legaspi. 3:40 hrs.
January 23	Mission 29: Saint-Nichols (Floridablanca), Luzon. 5:25 hrs.
January 24	Mission 30: Bombed and strafed Bataan Peninsula. 5:20 hrs.
January 26	Mission 31: Bombed and strafed Grande Island, Subic Bay, Luzon. 5:00 hrs.
January 27	Mission 32 (A): Tanauan, Leyte, to San Jose, Mindoro; base temporarily moved until later move to Luzon. 1:55 hrs.
January 29	Mission 33: Bombed and strafed Ipil airstrip, Echague, Luzon. 4:40 hrs.

January combat missions: 15. Combat hours: 68:15. Administrative Flight January 3, Hollandia to Morotai. 5:35 hrs. Hrs/mo: 73:50.

February 5	Mission 34: Bombed and strafed Jamolig Island (Polillo Islands). 3:30 hrs.
February 9	Mission 35: Bombed and strafed Bataan. 2:15 hrs.

February 10	Mission 36: Bombed and strafed Bataan. 3:00 hrs.
February 11	Mission 37 (A): Mindoro to Lingayen, Luzon (Mangaldan). 312th moved to Mangaldan Airfield. 1:50 hrs.
February 13	Mission 38: Bombed and strafed Appari (Dugo); troops. 4:00 hrs.
February 14	Mission 39: Bombed and strafed Tuguegaro, Luzon. 4:30 hrs.
February 15	Mission 40 (A): Mangaldan–Tanauan–Mangaldan, Copilot in B-25 with Cal Slade. 5:30 hrs.
February 16	Mission 41: Bombed and strafed Corregidor Island before invasion. 2:45 hrs.
February 17	Mission 42: Bombed and strafed San Fernando Point. 2:00 hrs.
February 17	Mission 43: Bombed and strafed west of Fort Stotsenberg; ground support. Parachute demolition bombs exploded prematurely. 2:00 hrs.
February 18	Mission 44: Bombed and strafed troops, Infanta, Luzon. 2:30 hrs.
February 18	Mission 45: Bombed and strafed troops, Solano, Luzon. 1:15 hrs.
February 19	Mission 46: Bombed and strafed troops, Carranglan, Luzon. 1:55 hrs.
February 20	Mission 47: Bombed and strafed troops, Calamba, Luzon. 2:10 hrs.
February 21	Mission 48: Strafed Basco airdrome, Batan Island. A C-47 reportedly landed; turned out to be Japanese version. 4:30 hrs.
February 23	Mission 49: Bombed and strafed Bauang, Luzon. 1:10 hrs.
February 24	Mission 50: Bombed and strafed troops, Tangadon, Luzon. 2:30 hrs.
February 24	Mission 51: Bombed and strafed troops, Lapog, Luzon. 2:05 hrs.
February 26	Mission 52: Bombed and strafed Ipil airdrome, Echague, Luzon. 2:10 hrs.

February combat missions: 19. Combat hours: 51:35. Mindoro local flight, February 4. 1:40hrs. Hrs/mo: 53.15.

March 1	Air raid on Mangaldan airstrip this night. Bombs dropped on strip and several water buffalo killed; craters on the strip but other damage minimal.
March 2	Mission 53: Bombed and strafed Kagi air drome on Formosa. Leader (from 386th) missed the target and took us to the unfinished Mato airdrome. 6:35 hrs.
March 7	Mission 54: Bombed and strafed troops at Wawa, Marikina River. 3:25 hrs.
March 8	Mission 55: Bombed and strafed troops, Tangadon. 1:50 hrs.
March 11	Mission 56: Bombed and strafed San Fernando on coast north of Mangaldan. 2:40 hrs.
March 13	Mission 57: Bombed and strafed Solvac Bay. 1:50 hrs.
March 15	Mission 58: Bombed and strafed Dalupiri Island. 2:45 hrs.
March 16	Mission 59: Bombed and strafed Baguio. 1:35 hrs.
March 17	Started for Baguio leading the squadron, but the right engine began throwing oil while joining up after takeoff. Made an emergency landing without feathering the engine; Lt. Maurice Owen took over as leader. (0:20 hrs). Crew Chief Ernie Koch had to change a cylinder; Lt. Omar Potts may have caused the trouble by using the high blower at low altitude while flying the plane the previous day. This is the only mission I had to abort.
March 18	Mission 60: Osboy; turned back on account of weather. Mission considered incomplete (CMI). 2:00 hrs.
March 20	Mission 61: Bombed and strafed San Fernando, on coast north of Mangaldan. 1:30 hrs.
March 21	Mission 62: Bombed and strafed Pattao in Dugo area. 3:25 hrs.
March 27	Mission 63: Bombed and strafed troops and supplies at Manyakan. 1:40 hrs.

March combat missions: 11. Combat hours: 29:15. Other flights on
March 5, 6, and 10. Hrs/mo: 38:20.

April 1	Mission 64: Night medium-altitude, single-ship harassing mission to Belete Pass; dropped flares periodically to illuminate enemy lines for ground troops. 3:45 hrs. Flew to Clark Field and back in the afternoon to pick up passengers. This turned out to be *my last flight in an A-20.*
April 7	Grounded for return to United States.

April combat missions: 1. Combat hours: 3:45. Hrs/mo: 5:15.

Total missions: 64. Combat hours: 215:00. Total hours: 652:55.

Source: Author's informal logbook maintained while flying in the 389th
Squadron; Air Force Form 5 (pilot's official flight record). There is some
variation between my notes and the official name attached to a target.
Where this occurs I have shown both in the above listings.

[a] Flights marked (A) were called "administrative" but they were within
the combat zone. These flights sometimes were dangerous. For example, when I wandered around over Panay on the morning of January
8, 1945, it was dumb luck that nothing untoward happened; the day before that, fighter ace Maj. Thomas B. McGuire, flying with three other
P-38s, met a lone Jap Zeke over nearby Negros Island and lost his life.

WREAKING HAVOC

PROLOGUE

IN EARLY APRIL, 1945, the 389th Bomb Squadron of the 312th Bomb Group was based near the village of Mangaldan on the island of Luzon in the Philippines. We had been flying for the past two months from the dirt airfield, which had earlier been used as rice paddies. Mangaldan was a pleasant campsite, although dusty at times, and our tent, which I shared with three others, was often cooled by a soft breeze blowing in from the Lingayen Gulf about two miles away.

The 312th Bomb Group was one of three Fifth Air Force groups in the Southwest Pacific Area (SWPA) equipped with the Douglas A-20 Havoc light bomber. I joined the 389th Squadron as a pilot the previous July while the outfit was based at Hollandia, Dutch New Guinea, and by this time had accumulated more than sixty combat missions. It had been an interesting eight months. At this point in my tour our work seemed almost routine, with only the occasional unexpected occurrence over a Japanese target providing any excitement.

I was writing a letter when Capt. William T. "Doc" Walsh, the 389th's flight surgeon, stopped by the tent and started a conversation about my views on going back to the states. He commented that I had accumulated a good number of missions—more than any of the others who came into the squadron at about the same time—and wondered how I was doing. To be sought out by Doc Walsh was unusual, for we were not drinking or bridge-playing friends; he had something on his mind. Overall, I had found flying with the 389th interesting and challenging and by now I was comfortable with whatever was asked—

whether it be leading a flight or the squadron or a solo intruder flight at night. The squadron had become my home; returning to the states was just a distant, tantalizing possibility.

Perhaps Doc had seen something that suggested to him I was becoming burned out. As we talked, my indifference to going home may have confirmed Doc's assessment, although he said nothing directly. He was older than most of us by at least twenty years, a crusty character who liked a drink. But he was also a friend, and I appreciated the conversation. On his way out, Doc said, "Go home while the going is good." We left it at that. Doc may have taken the same approach with others who had accumulated a sizable number of missions, but it surprised me at the time.

This is an account of flying in a light bomber group by one of many who volunteered for service during World War II. My attitudes and reasons for enlisting in 1942 were probably not unlike those of most twenty-year-olds back then. Growing up in the 1930s was a life not so easy or as affluent as it was in the latter half of the twentieth century.

This is also the story of a young man being molded and maturing after a few months' exposure to the military; forced discipline alone can be an education. Meeting the challenges of learning to fly in the Army Air Forces' demanding program gave one satisfaction and produced a sense of accomplishing something very difficult. The serious business of being exposed to the Japanese shooting gallery and other hazards of flying combat missions inevitably affected my outlook afterward. I was changed—and, looking back from fully five decades later, I think mostly improved—by my experiences in 1943-45.

I was born on March 14, 1923, at Sewickley, Pennsylvania, which is located about twelve miles down the Ohio River from Pittsburgh. My father, Joseph Armstrong Rutter, left Washington Station near Newcastleon-Tyne, County Durham, England, at the age of nineteen in June, 1903. His steamer passage was paid for by a loan from a family friend (Thomas Furness) who had been living in the United States for some years. Joe's first job was driving a delivery wagon for McCullough's grocery store in Edgeworth, a village next to Sewickley, when a sleeping room above the store was as important for a new arrival as was the small pay. After about six months he moved on to become the horseman/coachman for the Theodore Nevin family on Broad Street in Sewickley.

Emma Nightingale, my mother, was from Wolverhampton, England, and moved to Sewickley in 1909 with the help of an older sister. Private service being a desired first situation for many immigrants from the British Isles because it provided a place to live, Emma succeeded in finding such a position and spent two years working as the downstairs maid for the Burns family in Edgeworth. There was, at the time, a small colony of English, Scotch, and Irish in Sewickley and its environs in similar jobs. She and Dad were married in 1912. By then he was working as the chauffeur for the George E. Tener family, which lived on Grove Street in Sewickley. The Tener's estate took up several acres between Centennial Avenue and the steep hillside above Division Street.

Sewickley was an established village when I came on the scene. Dating back to the mid-nineteenth century, its population was about three thousand and the Pennsylvania Railroad furnished easy commuting into Pittsburgh. After the turn of the century, a number of large estates had been built on the hills above the village. By 1920, they and the houses of the wealthy families in the valley provided employment for a sizable number of gardeners, laborers, and domestic help. We lived in an apartment with a large porch overlooking the wooded hillside above the garage on the Tener estate.

My father had begun working for the Tener family in 1906, first as a coachman and then as the chauffeur when a 1909 Peerless automobile replaced the horses. He had observed closely and assisted to some extent as Mr. Tener gradually built a model farm property and began raising Shorthorn milking cattle about seven miles out in the country. The relationship between my father and his employer apparently became, over the years, close to that of a nephew and a favorite uncle. I can still recall hearing Dad say, "Mr. Tener would have done so-and-so." Following Mr. Tener's death in the fall of 1923, his sons asked Dad to become the manager of the Ardarra Farm, a name derived from Mr. Tener's Irish heritage.

We continued to live in the comfortable apartment in town while Dad worked at the farm every day and also filled in whenever the family's chauffeur was allowed to take off on a Sunday. Two-week annual vacations with pay were virtually unheard of in those days, but dedication in a private service job had its rewards and in the summer of 1926 our family spent almost three months in England visiting relatives. Life was good for the Rutters in the 1920s.

By 1930–31, however, Ardarra Farm was no longer a hobby that the owners thought worthy of their continued financial support. The stock market crash in October, 1929, had not left Sewickley's wealthy unaffected. Some of the town's notables lost their lavish houses and fleets of Packards during this period, and many of their children had to be withdrawn from the private Sewickley Academy and sent to the public school—at least for a year or two. The Teners had to make some changes, too: Dad and the career farmer living on the place would no longer draw wages but would instead become partners in the farm's operation. It was up to them to make a living from the property while the Teners continued to pay the taxes. Ours was not the worst situation faced by families in the Great Depression, but it was certainly a comedown.

Moving to the farm was just another adventure for me, a nine-year-old, with the advantages of having a pony to ride and woods and fields in which to roam. The ways of farm kids were somewhat different from those living in the village, but kids adapt—and besides, the school vacations were longer. The Jenny School, out on Campmeeting Road near where we lived, was for kids in grades one through four. The school had only one teacher, a pot-bellied coal stove for heat, and drinking water had to be carried from our springhouse in a five-gallon milk can. Friday School, located about two or three miles away, was similar except that kids in grades five through eight went there.

The move to the country and the loss of regular wages was a serious change of circumstances for my parents, I am sure. Still, we always had plenty to eat, and the farmhouse, half of which was made of logs, was comfortable and roomy, if a little isolated. Somehow, by hard work and conservative management, the partners were able to weather the worst years of the depression, although cash money was always tight.

In the fall of 1935, however, the partnership on the farm evaporated when the property was sold. Out of a job and with no immediate prospects, we moved back into Sewickley to live in an apartment. The location was 658 Maple Lane—right beside the Pennsylvania Railroad and overlooking the Ohio River, both of which held lots of interest for a twelve-year-old. My brother Jim, who was seven years older and already out of high school, had a job in a small steel-fabricating plant and became the household's only financial contributor.

After less than a year in the apartment we moved back up onto Sewickley Heights, this time to the William Penn Snyder estate, which was known as Wilpen Hall. There we lived in half of a double house. The rent was just $30 a month, $25 less than we had paid for the apartment, and Dad found work as a general handyman on the Snyder estate. After a year in another country school, Blackburn, I entered Sewickley High School in 1937.

Like most boys in those days, I was fascinated by airplanes and flying: men like Lindbergh, Wiley Post, Harold Gatty, Frank Hawks, and Roscoe Turner were my heroes. Most of my friends had similar interests and we built ten-cent model airplane kits by Megow, read "Smilin' Jack" in the Sunday comics and hunted out copies of *Flying Aces* magazine for its stories and photos of planes. I can still see the dramatic picture on the cover of *Battle Aces*, a pulp magazine of the time: red tracers streaking from the guns on a Fokker D-7, just missing the head of a desperate pilot looking back from the cockpit of a diving Spad with the fabric starting to tear away on the upper wing. Joe McMaster and I could quote line and verse from stories by Arch Whitehouse featuring Phineas Pinkham, a wild and improbable World War I pilot whose airfield was near Bar le Duc—or "Barley Duck" in Pinkham-speak.

My brother had shown a benevolent impulse one Sunday and given me a ride in a Stinson Trimotor at the nearby Conway Airport, a high point in the life of a teenager. Later, when we had access to a car, friends Ab Rainbow and Joe and I often went to the Butler County Airport on Sunday afternoons to look at the planes. Whenever we were flush with cash, we would splurge $3 for a ride around the airfield in the front seat of a red Waco biplane.

Copies of *I Wanted Wings* by Bierne Lay Jr. and *Falcons of France* by Charles Nordhoff and James Norman Hall were in the local library and seemed to me to be the greatest books ever written. In recent years I found *I Wanted Wings* again and it is still a good read, but in those far off days of youth, Lay's experience as a flying cadet was the source of daydreams about the seemingly unattainable world of flying.

Growing up in Sewickley in the 1930s was pleasant enough, sheltered as we were from some of the worries of the depression years. We were confident that our parents would always see to it that we had comfortable quarters and food on the table. Although money was in short supply for nonessentials such as new bicycles and swimming pool memberships, my situation was no worse than that of most of my peers. Used bikes could be had for $10 at Cleve Wallace's shop on Division Street. Little Sewickley Creek had a great swimming hole only a couple of miles out of town on Backbone Road, and when we grew older, we swam in the Ohio.

Although we engaged in our share of unauthorized explorations of vacant houses and trespassed upon many posted places, our youthful crowd managed to avoid serious trouble. Occasional chastisement by elders, probably known to our parents, was all that was needed to keep most of us on the straight and narrow. That was just the way it was growing up in a small town in the 1930s.

Yet, unbeknownst to us, very serious events were taking place elsewhere in the world that would soon lead to the more serious experiences related herein.

Chapter 1

WAR! MY WORLD CHANGED, BUT SLOWLY

DAD GOT ME OUT OF BED at 6 A.M. on Sunday, September 3, 1939, to listen to Great Britain's declaration of war on Germany on our Midwest shortwave radio. After the war started—and even before, as Germany began making demands on its neighbors—listening to news broadcasts by the BBC was a nightly ritual in our house. We also discussed the Spanish Civil War in my high school history classes, and I had a student subscription to *Newsweek* magazine. Nevertheless, the diary I kept in 1939 and early 1940 contained few references to the beginning of the war or world events afterward.

This war did not seem to fit the pattern of what we had heard about the 1914–18 Great War. The period beginning in late 1939 and continuing until the spring of 1940 was called the "Phony War," and there was little going on to warrant even passing mention in my diary. An exceptional news event was the pursuit and sinking of the German pocket battleship *Graf Spee* in the River Plate off Montevideo in Uruguay on December 17, 1939. The conclusion of the *Graf Spee*'s encounter with British cruisers was an unusual live broadcast and my family listened intently to the commentary coming directly from South America.

After the war started, my mother and many of her friends devoted several hours each week to working at the British War Relief Society in Sewickley. I frequently discussed the latest headlines in the papers with my high school friends, but even in 1941 the war in Europe had not noticeably affected my life.

In March, 1941, with high school graduation approaching and me very undecided about my future, my dream of flying a plane was still alive. I wrote to Canada for an application to enlist in the Royal Canadian Air Force (RCAF). The U.S. Army Air Corps was then asking for two years of college or the equivalent (whatever that was), whereas the RCAF accepted applicants for flight training at age eighteen with a high school diploma. Canada by then had been at war for eighteen months, but I did not try to analyze why they might be so anxious for pilots.

A daring step such as joining up and learning to fly in that blue RCAF uniform was intriguing, but I also felt the pull of wanting to get a job, buy a car, and spend my free time escorting young ladies. At about the same time, Robert Rogge, a Sewickley classmate, joined the Canadian army. It would have been a solitary step for me to join the RCAF, but I lacked the dedication and idealism to take it. As a result, the Canadian application form remained unmailed.

I graduated from Sewickley High School in June, 1941. By that time the local steel mills were again running strong, rushing to fill the orders coming from the manufacturers of the armaments going to England under the stimulus of the Lend-Lease Act that had passed earlier that year. Perhaps a quarter of my high school class aimed to go to college; it was an indication that the depression years were coming to an end. The possibility of college had not really entered into my planning, what with money seeming to be in short supply at home and there also being a lack of direction on my part. Hoping for something better than a job laboring in the mills and possibly getting help for more education later, I enrolled in an engineering-assistant training program Penn State operated at Ambridge High School.

I had taken typing and some business courses in high school with the hope of getting an office job, and that small bit of foresight paid off unexpectedly. Before the Penn State course was very far along, I landed a job as a clerk-typist in the Federal Bureau of Investigation's (FBI) Pittsburgh field office. This was the result of an almost forgotten contact I had made several months before with the Stenotype Institute in Pittsburgh, which had arranged for me to take a test and interview with the FBI. The idea was to help potential students find a regular job so they could pay for the institute's course in stenotyping, a skill then in high demand. As it turned out, I never did complete the course, although I enrolled in good faith and attended classes for a few months before the overtime required at work became too demanding.

The FBI clerk-typist job paid $1,620 with twenty-six days of vacation per year, which was considerably better than most starting jobs at the time. In fact, my pay was $5 more a month than my father earned, which I imagine had to have been frustrating for him. After two months I was able to afford to buy a used 1934 Ford coupe and attain a measure of independence despite still living at home.

The rent for our house on the Snyder estate was still $30 per month and after my first month of work, my mother started charging me $30 per month for room and board—the same as my brother contributed. After some consideration and a little lecturing, I had to admit that paying my way was only fair. I even found some satisfaction in contributing to the family coffers.

The FBI office was a good experience after the somewhat sheltered life I had led in Sewickley, and served as an eye-opener to many aspects of life and human nature. Most of the employees there were college graduates, including many of the stenographers and clerks. The boss, Special Agent in Charge Joe Thornton, encouraged those of us who had come directly from high school to go to night school at Pitt or Duquesne and start working toward a degree; a number eventually did so.

After becoming acquainted with the people in that office and observing the responsibilities that went with the various jobs, the value of getting more education as a job qualification soon became apparent to me. Being a clerk-typist or even a stenographer—the latter earned $1,800 per year—was not my idea of a lifetime career. The agents had law or accounting degrees and started at $3,600 in those days. Plus there was ample opportunity for promotion. It began to dawn upon me that college was obviously attainable, offered opportunities, and would add much other knowledge that I lacked.

In the summer of 1941, FBI cases involving draft registration and draft evasion were a sizable part of the office's workload. National security cases were also active, and agents spent a good deal of time gathering information on organizations such as the German-American Bund, Communist Party, Silver Shirts, and other subversive groups. My eyes were opened to another side of everyday life as we clerks typed and set up files on "subjects" (members) in these organizations, along with people involved in crimes such as bank robberies, kidnappings, and auto thefts involving the crossing of state lines.

One of the jobs for the male clerk-typists was to type up case reports with details then thought to be too shocking for the female stenographers. Most of these reports involved "white slavery," as prostitution was then called, and revealed human behavior that was educational for those of us who had experienced a sheltered upbringing. This protective attitude toward women even then was amusing to most of the office's stenos and it was not unusual to find one of them shamelessly reading one of the hotter files during her lunch hour. Reading the file on Mae Sheible, reputed to have operated the finest sporting house in Pittsburgh, was better than the innuendoes found in stories in the *Police Gazette*.

The male clerk-typists were assigned to the night shifts in the office as the phone and Teletype lines had to be manned twenty-four hours a day. After receiving some training, new clerks were put on the 11 P.M. to 8 A.M. shift with the prospect of moving to the day or evening shifts as they gained seniority. I spent the fall of 1941 working nights typing reports dictated by the agents, filing three-by-five cards stacked up by the daytime indexing typists, and using an Addressograph machine to send out the wanted-criminal notices (Apprehension Orders) to all post offices in our district. Addressing one to a friend or two sometimes relieved the tedium of hand feeding five thousand Apprehension Orders through the Addressograph.

Then came December 7, 1941, and the Japanese attack on Pearl Harbor. My world, the world of a self-centered youth, suddenly began to change. After the United States entered the war, a lot of overtime was necessary on top of the regular forty-eight-hour workweek that had been instituted. On more than one occasion we worked back-to-back shifts. John Edgar Hoover's FBI did not hesitate to ask employees to work overtime, although there was then no provision to pay us any extra or even give us some time off as a reward. Overtime hours were reported each month for possible future payment and, some years later, after the war, I recall receiving a check—at the regular rate rather than time-and-a-half—for a very small amount of the time I had worked.

Ab Rainbow, my closest friend during high school, had gone off to Penn State at State College, Pennsylvania, and was a freshman when Pearl Harbor came along. We had dreamed about flying for years and now we talked seriously about joining up. Shortly after Pearl Harbor the Army Air Corps had dropped the two-year college requirement for flying cadets, so we laid plans to enlist when Ab's college term ended in the spring. "Woody," Ab said, enthused, "two pilots talked to us about the Air Corps last week. They had sharp uniforms, silver wings, and said it was the only way to fight the war sitting down." I replied, "Hey! We'll go off together, Ab." Yes, we were a little naïve.

It is perhaps worth noting here that although the Army Air Corps officially became the Army Air Forces in 1941, it was still called the Air Corps except when referring to major command designations such as the Third Air Force, Fifth Air Force, and so forth.

Cars were an important status symbol at that time in my life, so when I spotted a used 1939 Ford coupe with a spotlight and gasoline heater for sale I lusted for it at first sight even though its tires were well worn. My

'34 Ford still had good tires, but it had a bad engine bearing and needed a number of other repairs. There was an initial glut of used cars on the market when the war began and men were called up by the draft, so it would have been prudent to control my lust for this particular Ford. I was able to do so at first, but in February, 1942, I impulsively bought the "new" car. It proved to be a bad decision: within a week, recapped tires were placed on the ration list. New tires had been rationed for some time. Now I found it impossible to buy either new tires or recaps with my low priority. Without tires—and nobody was sure when, or if, even recaps would be available again—the car was not at all attractive. I had borrowed $200 from Dad toward the $400 purchase price and now that debt did not seem the least bit worthwhile. Within two months I sold that irresistible '39 Ford at a $100 loss and was relieved to be out of debt—even if it meant being without a car.

Getting by without transportation lasted only a month, however. My brother Jim, who had been using the family's 1941 Mercury club coupe, joined the Merchant Marine on May 1, 1942, and left for training at Hoffman Island, New York. After some family discussions, the Mercury was made available for my use. Intended or not, Dad had given me a valuable lesson in managing money: I had felt awfully uncomfortable while I was saddled with debt after making a purchase that was not strictly necessary.

In order to fulfill my agreement to become an aviation cadet with Ab, I first had to take care of some necessary dental work. My fear of dentists was great, but the traumatic experience could be postponed no longer and Dr. Roger Galey in Sewickley went to work with a will. There was the matter of several long-neglected cavities to be drilled out and filled and then the extraction of three baby teeth that he replaced with a bridge. Perhaps I still had three baby teeth at the age of eighteen because I had fallen out of a barn when I was seven and smacked my jaw against a horse trough on the way down. Although the ordeal with Dr. Galey was not as bad as I had anticipated it would be, he did not complete it until sometime in June.

Ab, who had recently come home from Penn State, got tired of my dilly-dallying and enlisted as an Aviation Cadet on July 29, 1942. I passed the written test on August 3 but ran into trouble during the physical exam because the army would not accept me with the removable bridge Dr. Galey had crafted. The army wanted a fixed bridge. After I told him about the medical examiner's pronouncement, my friendly dentist gave me several reasons why he did not install fixed bridges and I went back to see the army doctor.

The newly commissioned Medical Corps major refused to accept my explanation. He looked at me sternly and observed, "You might have difficulty holding the oxygen tube with those teeth when flying." Obviously, this dentist had grown up reading Phineas Pinkham and his knowledge of flying was limited to World War I Spads and SE-5s.

"Sir, my dentist said that a fixed bridge would damage the good teeth it was anchored to," I replied.

"The hell he did!" responded the doctor. "What was his prognosis?"

For a moment I panicked over the meaning of "prognosis" but then mumbled a guess: "He said it would be about four years."

"Hmm," said the doctor, rubbing his chin thoughtfully. "That seems about right. Okay, you pass."

One last hang-up was my weight. I tipped the scales at 131 pounds and the minimum for a height of five feet, eleven and three-quarters inches was 135. After stuffing myself for ten days, including milkshakes and many bananas, I managed to add the required four pounds. I took the oath on August 18, 1942, and was sworn into the U.S. Army for "the duration plus six months." We were told that we would be called up in about ninety days to begin training.

What a difference a few days made: Because I enlisted just three weeks after Ab, I was placed in a different group when we were finally called up. He shipped out for training in the East and I to the West, so our plan of going off together did not work out. Another important difference became evident later: the awarding of reserve commissions ended on July 30, 1942. Those of us who enlisted after that date were commissioned in the Army of the United States (AUS). The holders of reserve commissions received a $500 per year bonus when they left active duty, whereas those of us given AUS commissions did not. *C'est la guerre!*

The war was not going at all well for the Allies in the Pacific in the summer of 1942 as the Japanese continued expanding their sphere of control to the southeast. Meanwhile, General Rommel and his German Afrika Korps seemed unstoppable as they moved at will eastward across North Africa and on toward Cairo. We prospective cadets had only a vague idea how long our wait would be, but given the numbers signing up, the ninety days they had told us to expect seemed somewhat optimistic—and so it proved. Ab and I could only speculate, but we hoped that we would be needed *soon*.

Ab was working in the American Bridge Company mill in Ambridge that summer and there seemed no point in his going back to Penn State in September. With the buildup of the war effort, jobs in the steel mills were available for almost all who applied. The pay was good, too—even if the work was dirty and hard. Although the high pay was tempting, I continued typing and filing in the FBI field office, fully expecting that the wait for the army's call would be short. Except for the pinch caused by the rationing of items such as cars, trucks, and tires and the disappearance of more and more men from the streets, life in the summer of 1942 did not seem greatly changed.

Harriett, a high school classmate, and I had dated a few times before graduation. She now seemed even more agreeable to my invitations, so we saw a considerable amount of each other that summer. My ideas of entertainment were not very innovative—my social skills did not include dancing—so our dates were usually limited to a Saturday movie and a sandwich afterward. She was working as a legal secretary for a Pittsburgh attorney and sometimes we splurged and ate dinner at Stouffer's Restaurant or the Grant's Hill Tavern followed by a show at the Nixon, Pittsburgh's legitimate theater.

These demonstrations of my sophistication did not noticeably impress Harriett, who wisely held the view that nineteen was too young to become seriously involved. Nevertheless, we continued to date more or less regularly while I waited for the army's call. I found the enforced delay in our inevitable parting to be not at all unpleasant.

Thanks to his high pay as a rivet bucker at the American Bridge Company, Ab was able to take flying lessons on weekends at the Butler Airport. We had talked about getting some familiarity with flying before we left for training, but I only talked about it while Ab went ahead. To some extent, finances were a consideration for me even though dual instruction in a Piper Cub cost only $6 or $7 an hour at the time. Moreover, based on some logic I can no longer recall, it seemed likely to me that the military's approach to flying would be different from the civilian, so I decided it was just as well to wait and let the army provide my training. It thus came to pass that Ab soloed the Piper Cub at Butler Airport on Sunday, September 27, 1942, while I stood watching this milestone. Looking back, I cannot imagine why I was not inspired to follow suit.

Although the Army Air Forces flight-training program was expanding rapidly, the supply of waiting enlisted reservists continued to grow exponentially. Seeing a great opportunity, an enterprising fellow in Pittsburgh started a prep school in the fall of 1942 for cadets waiting to be called up. The school was at least something positive to do, so Ab and I signed up and began attending classes at Fifth Avenue High School. Several hundred cadets responded to the ads for the classes and we met in the main auditorium, with the instructor a small figure down on the distant stage.

Two nights a week we had a refresher math course and on alternate nights we went to a Morse code class in the Grant Building downtown. The code class was new to most of us and we were sure it had great military relevance. Later, my knowledge of the code enabled me to pass a test quickly and be excused from the army class, but that was about the extent of my use of Morse code.

The months dragged on into the gloomy, wet winter days typical of Pittsburgh. Ab and I dutifully attended the prep classes and listened to the rumors of when the next call-up for cadets might come. The war was now changing civilian life with food and clothing rationing leading to shortages or the complete disappearance of items that had once been common.

A wartime measure that seemed silly to me at the time and still does was prohibiting cuffs on trousers, which was then the style. If you bought trousers that had to be shortened, the excess was cut off rather than cuffed. I managed to buy some unfinished trousers, refused the free alterations, and Mom finished them with cuffs. The contribution to the war effort of all those bits and pieces of cloth from uncuffed trousers was never disclosed to the public, but it must have been significant.

By the fall of 1942 women were performing many jobs that had previously been filled only by men, even on the track gangs working in the rail yard outside of Union Station. They looked out of place to me as I peered through the grimy, frosted window of a coach on the Pennsylvania Railroad commuter train to Sewickley each evening. However, there just were not enough men to be found even for such heavy labor. The Union Station waiting room was filled with uniforms as I went back and forth daily in my cuffed civilian suits. The commuter trains between Sewickley and Pittsburgh were always crowded and the coaches were even older and dirtier than before.

Nationwide gas rationing began December 1, 1942. The allotment for an A sticker, the minimum, was three gallons per week. Gas rationing had begun earlier on both coasts, extending from the Atlantic seaboard as far inland as perhaps Hagerstown and Harrisburg, as I recall. In anticipation of the extension of rationing to western Pennsylvania, I had fished a fifty-five-gallon steel drum out of the river. High water often caused empty drums to float off, and this one had once held gasoline, probably floating down from a refinery on Neville Island or Pittsburgh. I started filling the drum by buying a five-gallon can of gas about every other day. My diary entry for November 30 reads: "We have 54 gallons stored." It was a way to stretch the A ration when we were finally hit with rationing, and Dad seemed amused, albeit not entirely comfortable, with my barrel of gas sitting in the garage.

In January, 1943, I began having second thoughts about waiting for the Air Corps to teach me to fly without having at least some background. Other than a few hours riding around in a Piper Cub with Bill Grey, a Sewickley flying enthusiast with a private license, I had no idea of how to handle a plane. There was a seaplane base operating Piper Cubs on floats just below the Seventh Street Bridge on the Allegheny River in Pittsburgh, so I signed up there for instruction. At that late date I had no aspirations of trying to do more than get some familiarity in controlling a plane, but I figured even that might prove helpful later.

The instructor was a young woman who was kept busy by a host of other flying cadets waiting to be called to duty. The yellow Cubs with the ungainly looking floats could be seen flitting over the river almost every day. The instructor sat in front and the student was in back, his feet planted on the rudder bar, which passed just under the front seat. Although she was not a large person, the instructor was just a little wide in the beam for the Cub's seat. Conversely, my size twelve shoes had no place to go inside the narrow cabin. The result was that she would occasionally respond with a yelp of surprise when she called for left or right rudder and my big shoe brushed her ample seat.

The floatplanes started their takeoff run under the Sixth Street Bridge and, once airborne, stayed under the Manchester Bridge at the Point before climbing up over the Ohio River. The instructor had me doing turns, climbs, and descents within gliding distance of the river but we never progressed to attempting landings. Nonetheless, the limited instruction I received in four or five half-hour sessions with her did give me some idea of how to handle an airplane. The long waits for my turn at instruction, particularly on Saturdays, were discouraging and I stopped as soon as I was able to satisfy some of my curiosity. That floatplane operation continued to be a moneymaker as long as the pool of waiting cadets lasted.

By early 1943, the army at last seemed to be getting the backlog of waiting cadets in hand. Joe McMaster, who had joined after me, was called to report on February 5. The day before he was supposed to leave, Joe had several bad teeth pulled so he would not have to face a heartless army dentist. Ab, Fred Way, and I saw Joe off in Pittsburgh and we were a little amused that he was not at all looking forward to the great adventure in the army. Perhaps he had a hangover after his mass tooth extraction that compounded his natural apprehension of the unknown.

As the three of us returned to Sewickley over the bricks of the Ohio River Boulevard after seeing Joe off, Ab wailed: "I feel like a slacker. Joe enlisted after all of us and he goes first." It did seem a bit unusual, but Ab and I were a somewhat mollified when we learned that Joe and the rest of his contingent were going to take college courses for several months before going to the classification center. Those of us who had enlisted earlier would go direct to flight training; we wanted wings, not more textbooks.

Ab did not have to feel like a slacker for long. His notice was in the mail when we got home and on Monday, February 8, Fred and I saw him off for the Aviation Cadet Classification Center in Nashville, Tennessee, happy at last to be on his way. As Fred and I retraced our way down the Ohio River Boulevard in Fred's 1934 Ford coupe, the same one that had once been mine, we talked about our two good friends who had departed for a life far different from our familiar one in Sewickley. Fred was finishing his senior year of high school with the prospect of being drafted by the summer.

My notice to report for active duty arrived on February 23. Dad called me at the office and I quickly cleared my desk and signed out for the last time. The prospect of seeing new sights in the South was an attractive alternative to a smoggy, gloomy Pittsburgh struggling to shake off winter. Whatever apprehensions I had about the mysteries of army life were offset by a sense of adventure in doing something entirely new.

Early March in Pittsburgh is not noted for pleasant spring weather and the evening of March 2, 1943, was no exception. The drizzle drifting down from the low gray clouds changed to snow showers as the temperature dropped below freezing. A gusty wind swirled along the streets between the dark, smoke-stained buildings making the twenty-degree temperature feel even colder. Downtown Pittsburgh looked dreary and dirty. There were six hundred of us leaving that evening for the Aviation Cadet Classification Center in Nashville and the alien world of the military. Fred let me off in front of the Old Post Office Building on Fourth Avenue where the recruiting offices were quartered. We shook hands and wished each other "Good luck!" as Fred turned his '34 Ford around and headed back to Sewickley alone.

Inside, I was ordered to join a throng that was being organized alphabetically. When they finished this process we were ordered back outside. There we straggled down Grant Street toward the arches of Union Station. A dozen or more uniformed military types, their ranks unknown to us but clearly displaying authority, attempted to keep some degree of order as they herded us along. Although we tried to look "military" for the benefit of relatives and friends lining the sidewalks, the wide assortment of civilian clothing and the fact that each of us was carrying a suitcase of some description detracted from our attempts at noble bearing.

At Seventh Avenue and Grant the march paused for some reason. While we were standing there, I spotted my parents, who were there on the corner to say good-bye. Earlier in the day, when Fred Way had picked me up for the ride into the city, my mother had said, "We'll be there to see you off, Woody. Look for us at the station." Although inwardly I felt it would be easier if they were not there, I did not give voice to the thought. My folks had come into Pittsburgh on the train and I am sure they wanted to minimize the uncomfortable parting as much as I did. The large group leaving and the crowd and confusion along our route helped to relieve the pain of the final break with home for the three of us. Several girls from the office where I had worked for almost two years were also there to wish me well. We had time for a little small talk and then Mom gave me a kiss and Dad this admonition: "Take care of yourself, Woody, and drop us a line."

One face was missing. My romance with Harriett had been dormant since Christmas Eve. On that evening, with professionally wrapped and carefully selected present in hand, I had knocked on Harriett's door and found an unfamiliar male was there ahead of me. It was an uncomfortable surprise. There obviously had been a lack of communication on my part, so I left the gift with some mumbled pleasantries and backed out. My plans to make a serious impression had gone awry. Later, suffering alone, I awaited the call to duty and danger. I was comforted by the thought that she would eventually read all about me in the papers.

The gaggle began moving again and we passed through Union Station's high-vaulted waiting room and made our way out into the train shed. We were greeted by the familiar smell of steam and coal smoke and the rhythmic throb of the air pumps on the locomotives waiting on the numerous tracks. After being herded into the assigned day coaches in alphabetical order we settled into green mohair seats that were gritty with coal dust and cinders. Ed "Sonny" Quig from Sewickley was the only familiar face in the group at my end of the alphabet and we sat together at the end of our dingy coach.

After what seemed an interminable wait, the couplings clanked and the wheel flanges squealed as the train slowly moved out of the station into the cold, blustery night.

Chapter 2

I Become an Officer and a Gentleman

FROM MARCH THROUGH DECEMBER, 1943, I tried to keep up with the rigors of the aviation cadet program. All along the way there was a degree of apprehension that I would "wash out" for some undefined miscue or inability to meet the demands of the various planes of increasing complexity. During the course of those ten months there was an attrition rate of about 50 percent—for physical reasons, lack of dedication, failure to learn quickly enough to keep up, or something as simple as a bad day on a check ride.

At the Nashville Classification Center the two big hurdles were to pass the physical and psychological examinations and, for me, to be selected for pilot rather than navigator or bombardier training. We were delayed in Nashville because of the size of our group and apparently the lack of openings at the preflight school at Maxwell Field, Alabama. After almost a month, our end of the alphabet, beginning at the letter *R*, was dropped back one class (from 43-K to 44-A) and shipped off to the Western Training Command and preflight instruction at Santa Ana, California. To see the West Coast and ride a Pullman across the country was not unwelcome as far as I could see.

Following completion of the two-months preflight school at Santa Ana, our unit, Pilot Squadron 72, was sent to Tucson, Arizona, for primary flight training at Ryan Field, about sixteen miles out in the desert west of town. There we learned to fly the Ryan PT-22. It was an easy enough aircraft for the novice to master under the direction of civilian instructor Robert Consaul, who saw all five of his students (Mallernee, Moore, Powell, Rosenzweig, and Rutter) successfully through what was

Cadet Joseph W. Rutter at Nashville, Tennessee, about to begin pilot training after one month's exposure to the army. April, 1943.

more than a little accomplishment. Living in the Sonora Desert at the height of the summer heat added to the challenge of the program, but it was an interesting experience nonetheless.

We got no relief from the heat when in August the surviving 65 percent of those of us who started at Ryan Field moved to the Basic Flying School at Marana, Arizona, about twenty to twenty-five miles north of Tucson. The barracks were divided into three-man rooms and had swamp-box air conditioning that was somewhat effective. Lucky for me, I was assigned to instructor 2d Lt. C. C. Johnson. At nineteen, Johnson was younger than all his students and he had a relaxed personality that remained calm when it came to teaching cadets to fly the Vultee BT-13. He naturally generated our friendly respect.

An unexpected opportunity came when Class 44-A's training was accelerated in anticipation of the invasion of Europe in 1944. Advanced trainers were introduced to part of the class after completion of half the scheduled seventy flying hours. Students selected could opt to fly the AT-6 single-engine advanced trainer or, like me, request the twin-engine Cessna UC-78. The challenge of more complicated planes in Basic was welcome; in Advanced Flying School we would learn to handle combat aircraft: P-40 Warhawk fighters or B-25 Mitchell medium bombers.

The accelerated program obviated the need to go through a two-month transition course flying combat types after graduation from cadet training. That suited many of us—who were curious, if not exactly eager, to go overseas and see the war—just fine. Those who volunteered for the accelerated program had done well enough in the BT-13 to be recommended by our instructors and this, I hoped, meant we would be safe from washing out.

The new flying program seemed to be a success. I do not recall any serious accidents or problems with cadets training in either AT-6s or UC-78s although we were at times very lucky. By avoiding making too many mistakes in flying technique, those of us in Class 44-A who underwent twin-engine training at Marana graduated and were sent to La Junta Army Airfield in La Junta, Colorado, in early November, 1943, to begin training on the twin-engine B-25 bomber.

We were gratified and relieved to be informed on our first day at La Junta: "There will be no washouts in Advanced. Go and order your uniforms." Still, the B-25 was a big step up from the UC-78 in terms of weight, performance, and complicated operating systems—and teaching cadets with just 130 hours total flying time on light aircraft how to fly the B-25 was something new, an experiment at La Junta. A much

smaller group of pilots in Class 43-K and a handful in 43-J had under-
gone training ahead of us.

The fall weather on the Colorado prairie was not always conducive to
flying and there were more students than could be easily accommodated
by the number of instructors. Lieutenant Stoka, our first instructor, was
good in the B-25 but he did not last long with us: After flying one night,
Stoka fell asleep in his Ford on the way back to town, awoke with a start
as the car left the road, and instinctively pulled back on the wheel in an
effort to climb over a brick building.

Our next instructor, Lieutenant Carlisle, was only a month out of the
B-25 program when they assigned him to instructor duty. He was still
leery of the B-25 himself—lacking confidence as an instructor—and
was shipped off to instrument school after a week or ten days. Two of us
were then assigned to Lieutenant Peterson, who already had a full roster of students. Although he was game to try, he focused on getting his
most experienced students to solo before tackling the new ones. From
November 19, when I first went up in a B-25, until December 11, I spent
only about six and one-half hours at the controls.

One afternoon, an experienced pilot, Maj. C. L. Killian, came along
just as Lieutenant Peterson dismissed two of us for the day. The major
asked if Peterson needed help with any students and he pointed out John
Salvin and me as being low-time waifs. Without ceremony, the major
ordered us to follow him out to the flight line where we took off on a
three-hour flight during which he watched more or less calmly as Salvin
and then I sat in the left seat and responded to his orders. We shot three
or four landings apiece before the major ordered a stop at the end of La
Junta's main runway and asked, "Do you two think you can get this thing
up and down without killing yourselves?" When we assured him we
thought we could, Major Killian turned us loose and walked back to the
Operations Office. Lieutenant Peterson expressed great surprise and relief when Salvin and I later reported we had been checked out so quickly.

From then on, we cadets who had been checked out flew whenever
there was a plane available. We needed about seventy hours of first-pilot
time in the B-25 in order to qualify as rated pilots. Completing those requirements would be touch and go. Passing snowstorms closed the field
for several days at a stretch and on January 3, 1944, we went on an accelerated schedule: twelve hours on the flight line and then six hours off.
We flew wherever we chose, night or day, without much oversight by
our instructor, all to build up time before graduation day on January 7.

The only phase of our training that was not short-changed at La Junta
was a ten-hour instrument school that was excellent. In my case, the in-

structor taught me some of the finer points of B-25 technique as he delivered some strenuous instrument flying practice. In doing so, he gave me a much-needed feeling of confidence in handling the big plane.

I put in two hours of night flying on January 6, then logged another nine hours and fifteen minutes during the day before getting supper and falling into bed. It looked as if I would be able to get in the eight and one-half hours I needed the following day to fulfill the 205-hour requirement. The word was out that those of us who failed to complete the necessary flight time would be kept at La Junta after graduation to make it up before going on leave. My roommate, John Schley, had been sent to Fort Sumner a couple of weeks earlier to finish up on AT-17s because he was just a bit slow in picking up the B-25. I momentarily thought about going back to the flight line at 2 A.M. before snapping off the overhead bulb.

Voices in the hall and a light in the next room awakened me. Stumbling out into the study to poke the fire in the Warm Morning stove and to find out who was doing all the talking, I saw it was Salvin and one of his roommates.

"Hey, Rutter, did you get done?" Salvin asked.

"No," I replied, "I need nine more hours today."

"That's tough!" he said, shaking his head. "Nobody's flying after the blizzard last night." Still thinking it was midnight, I mumbled something about going to the flight line and was stunned when they informed me it was eight in the morning and still dark because the blowing snow had covered up all of the windows. There would be no flying that day and for a good while afterward. We got dressed and mushed through the drifted snow to get breakfast in the warm, steamy mess hall.

January 7, 1944, was our scheduled graduation day. I was relieved to learn that those of us who lacked no more than ten hours flying time in the B-25 would be permitted to go on leave while those needing more would have to stay. We trooped around the base to turn in equipment at the supply rooms, pick up our financial records, and have our base clearance sheets initialed at such places as the post exchange (PX), laundry, library, quartermaster, and so forth. For those offices with which I had had no contact or owed no money, it was expedient to write in imaginary initials using one of several different pens to complete the clearance form rather than traipse around.

The arrangements for the graduation ceremony were changed at least three times during the day and finally took place in the base gymnasium at five in the afternoon. A number of enlisted men had gathered by the door and waited to greet us as we came out in our new officer uniforms with shiny gold bars. They saluted with their right hand and proffered the left for the customary $1 for the first salute. I sidestepped this mercenary racket and a little later surprised a private who saluted as we met near the mess hall by handing him a silver dollar. I was an officer and a gentleman with silver pilot wings, at last.

Bob Schwarzkopf and I had dinner in the mess hall for the last time. We had been together since Nashville but he was being posted as an instructor at La Junta while I was ordered to report to the replacement depot at Columbia, South Carolina. John Salvin also was slated to become an instructor and that cold evening was the last we ever saw of each other. Vernon Schrag stopped by for a last talk before setting out in his Lincoln Zephyr for Berkeley, California, but we would meet again at Charlotte, North Carolina. My logbook showed a total of 196 hours and forty minutes, of which fifty-five hours and thirty-five minutes had been flown since November 19—day and night in the winter weather over La Junta's barren prairie.

Some wives and families were on hand for the graduation ceremony and added to the later congestion as we all hustled to get away from the base at the same time. It was 2:30 A.M. before I finally got to town in a cab. I was then lucky enough to get an upper berth in the Chicago Pullman standing in the La Junta station yard waiting to be attached to the 4:30 eastbound train. Much to my amusement, several newly minted officers who had lavished their uniform allowance on Brooks Brothers uniforms suddenly found themselves in straitened circumstances after paying their bills, able to afford only the coach fare. They looked uncomfortable sitting there in the station waiting room while I hunted up the Pullman.

The open-section Pullman car was full of new officers and a sprinkling of wives, one of whom was Mrs. Bob Warner from Hempstead, New York. Bob introduced me as a fellow whom he had first met one afternoon in an altercation on the football field at Santa Ana, an incident that now seemed to me to have occurred in another age. The "First Big Class" was over and we were breaking up after ten months of sweat, tension, laughs, disappointments, and not a little tedium. I was asleep in my upper berth long before the train pulled out of the La Junta station.

Our train was due into Chicago at 7:30 in the morning on Sunday, January 9, but wartime traffic and several unscheduled stops to thaw frozen brake lines made us almost four hours late. For reasons known only to the supply sergeant, we had not been permitted to return our winter flying clothing to the supply room. Each of us thus was forced to lug around a large canvas bag loaded with heavy sheepskin-lined flight pants, jackets, and boots in addition to our officer's B-4 folding clothing bag. It made it quite difficult to look military.

There was a saying in those days that hogs could go through Chicago without changing stations but people could not. Those of us continuing eastward were second to the hogs and had to transfer from Dearborn Station, which was used by the Atchison, Topeka, and Santa Fe Railroad, to Union Station, which was used by the Pennsylvania Railroad. The transfer service had for many years been provided by the ubiquitous Parmelee Transfer Company coaches, so we lugged our bulky bags out to the curb. Later, after checking our luggage in at Union Station, a group of us had lunch together in the Morrison Hotel dining room. Dressed as we were in our new uniforms—some of us wearing the sheepskin flying boots in order to save having to carry them—and probably a bit too loud with our flying talk, we must have stood out as very green second lieutenants.

My inexperience with train travel showed when the Union Station passenger agent informed me that first-class seats in the chair cars had to be reserved in advance and that all were already taken. "But I *have* a first-class ticket to Pittsburgh, and that doesn't mean coach," I said with some agitation. Noting the fresh crease in my uniform and the untarnished gold bars, the agent waved me toward the train and suggested that the conductor might have an empty seat and I could pay him the chair charge.

Unfortunately, there were no empty seats that Sunday and I was roused from several different places when reservation-holding passengers boarded the train in suburban Englewood. Finally, I settled into the only seat that was not considered sellable: the straight-backed chair at the writing desk in the club car. It was not the most comfortable way to ride for nine hours going to Pittsburgh, but at least I was in first class, as my ticket entitled me to be. I hoped that my buddies riding in the coach up ahead were properly envious but privately admitted it was likely that they were more comfortable.

My return to Sewickley after the adventures and travels of the previous ten months was not as grand as I had thought it might be. Most of the males in my age group had disappeared, the majority of them into the service someplace. Shortly before Christmas, my parents had rather abruptly (at least it seemed so to me) moved to Wenham, Massachusetts, so there was no familiar, warm house to go to on Scaife Road—nor was the 1941 Mercury available for transportation.

The Ways, parents of my school friend Fred, had long since become my second family and they welcomed me warmly into their home at 121 River Avenue. For years before and after the war, the Way home was a meeting place for adults and young people alike—with a variety of different interests represented. Steamboats, photography, model building, cars, amateur radio, books—you were likely to find a lively discussion on these and most any other subject when you stopped at Ways, day or night. However, Fred III was off in the army now and the house was quiet, with none of the old gang coming through the backdoor at all hours.

The reception I got when I paid a visit to the FBI field office in Pittsburgh where I had worked was friendly enough. However, I was not the first file clerk to return in uniform, nor was I even the first one sporting pilot's wings. I took some of the office girls out for lunch and we had a pleasant visit as they caught me up on the news of the others who had gone into the service and office gossip in general. Only one or two of the men who had been my contemporaries in the office had taken advantage of the draft-deferred status that was available for some FBI employees. Working in that office was now part of my past; my perspective and interests had grown far away from that once familiar scene.

Only Harriett, whom I had not seen for more than a year, seemed suitably impressed by my accomplishments. We had been conducting a regular and increasingly warm correspondence since shortly after I left home the previous March and my stock with her had seemingly risen. Nevertheless, three evenings was hardly enough time for us to become really reacquainted, even after our frequent letters. More training and an overseas assignment lay ahead for me, so the immediate future seemed much too indefinite for discussion, even given our now more serious interest in each other. All too soon it was time for me to catch the train for Boston to go see my folks and find out about their situation and new life in Massachusetts, a place that was completely foreign to me.

My brother was attending the Merchant Marine radio school at Gallups Island in Boston Harbor, less than an hour by train from Wenham where Mom and Dad had located an apartment. We four enjoyed a family reunion for a weekend, but the rest of my leave was rather unsatisfactory. The Wenham-Hamilton area was not unlike Sewickley. It had a number of private estates and was about twenty-five miles from the center of Boston. However, with no familiar acquaintances around for me and only public transportation (Dad had sold the family car in Pittsburgh) I spent a very quiet, low-key week.

One day, at least, was interesting. Morton Woodason, the son of the family friend for whom I was named, took me to the Squantum Naval

Second Lieutenant Rutter on leave in Wenham, Massachusetts, in January, 1944, following graduation from the La Junta, Colorado, B-25 Advanced School. The trench coat was a real bargain: $39 at Goodman's Clothing Store in La Junta.

Air Station (NAS) south of Boston. I had met Morton and his family in the summer of 1940 during an overnight visit while on a quick tour of the East Coast in the company of my brother and friend Bud Morrison. Mort Woodason, then in his forties, had been a navy reserve officer since his college days. He had been called up just before Pearl Harbor and now was a lieutenant commander serving as the engineering officer at Squantum, a small air base on a peninsula sticking out into Boston Harbor that was being used for coastal antisubmarine patrols.

The navy was using single-engine OS2U observation planes with wheeled landing gear for the patrols and a bit of excitement occurred the day I visited when two of the OS2Us collided over Boston Harbor. The accident damaged both planes but neither went down and the pilots duly reported by radio that they were returning to Squantum. We listened to the radio chatter while the pilots brought the planes back. One had a damaged wing and the other was missing the top of its vertical stabilizer. Both landed without much difficulty and I stood back, listening to the explanations. As a newly minted pilot qualified to fly the much larger B-25, I felt a bit superior. Hopefully it did not show too much.

The formality of the navy mess, with the seating graduated by rank from the captain at the head of the table, impressed me. The white tablecloth and mess men waiting on us was a touch of military class that I had not experienced or anticipated; the navy lived well. We took a leisurely drive along the Atlantic shore on that gray, wintry afternoon, with Mort acting as my tour guide on the way back to Wenham. The entire excursion and conversation with a knowledgeable elder somewhat salvaged what to that point had been a frustrating leave. It was reassuring to talk military shop with Mort, who was a down-to-earth guy with a great sense of humor. We became good friends after the war during my yearly visits to New England and Wenham, where my parents lived out their lives.

The trip by train from Boston to Columbia, South Carolina, is perhaps worth relating because it was typical of the conditions experienced by travelers during the war years. Mom and Dad rode the commuter train with me from Wenham to Boston and we ate lunch together in the South Station dining room before saying our good-byes. I caught the noon train south on the New Haven Railroad. Surprisingly, it ran on time all the way, arriving in Washington, D.C., at 9:30 P.M. I had hopes of getting a berth on the midnight train headed south but one look around crowded Union Station and the line of people waiting for Pullman space killed that idea. Just getting a place to stand in one of the coaches was an achievement that night. I wound up standing in a vestibule until the train reached Richmond before a seat became available. Others who were less fortunate than me stood or sat on their suitcases in the aisle all night.

There was a diner on the train and standing in line for an hour and a half for both breakfast and lunch was just another way to spend the time. Scheduled passenger trains did not have a high priority during wartime and we were shunted onto sidings more than once to clear the way for military freight and troop trains. Equipment breakdowns also caused delays during the trip. With the railroads using every available car, such breakdowns were common. When we finally disembarked in Columbia at 3:30 the next afternoon, two and one-half hours late, we were a rumpled, gritty lot.

The Columbia replacement depot was located at the airport a short distance outside of town. I spotted several familiar faces from La Junta when I checked into the tarpaper barracks that served as bachelor officers' quarters (BOQ). Each of us had a story to tell of our adventures while on leave. Most of the boys seemed to have enjoyed one long party if their stories were factual. Several of them had gotten married while on leave and were now wondering when and where their brides could join them.

We had no idea whether we would be staying in Columbia as part of the B-25 Replacement Training Unit (RTU) operating there or be assigned elsewhere. There were lots of questions but few answers for the first two or three days. New second lieutenants waiting to be assigned did not have great stature in a replacement depot and my impression of Columbia was of a place of great confusion. We were kept occupied to some extent with a few formal classes each day covering topics related to living under field conditions. I remember a demonstration of camouflage techniques that was particularly interesting. Most of us spent ten days in the replacement depot before finally receiving orders to an RTU.

There were B-25 training schools in both Columbia and Greenville, South Carolina, so we assumed that we would be assigned to one place or the other. Then we heard that there was another option: A-20 Havoc light bomber training units had been established in Charlotte, North Carolina, and Florence, South Carolina. None of us, as I recall, had ever seen an A-20 nor did we know much about them, although the plane had been around since the start of the war. The *A* stood for attack, which we guessed meant flying ground-support missions. The crew usually consisted of a pilot and two gunners, with a bombardier-navigator added in some models.

The A-20 seemed to me to be an interesting alternative to the B-25. The question was, how did one go about getting assigned to either Charlotte or Florence? One of my unspoken concerns about continuing to fly B-25s was the possibility of ending up as copilot. I quickly learned that there were others who shared that fear. Given the time we already had logged in B-25s it seemed unlikely that we would be slotted as co-pilots. Yet the idea of having a copilot at my side, someone who might be unhappy with his lot or who might view my flying critically, was not particularly attractive.

After a week or so, sign-up sheets were posted in the orderly room and we were instructed to choose an RTU location. Whether or not one's preference would be honored probably depended on the mood of a cor-poral someplace. Since the A-20 had only one pilot and the training would not be at Columbia (the short time I had spent there did not make a favorable impression on me) I signed up for Charlotte based on those criteria alone.

A day or so after I made my choice we heard there was an A-20 parked on the flight line, so I walked over to check it out. If it was not love at first sight, the A-20 at least made a very favorable impression. It had a trim, jaunty look with a narrow (forty-nine inches) fuselage, a single rudder, and altogether smoother lines than the angular B-25 with its twin rudders. The wingspan was six feet shorter, the gross weight about eight thousand pounds lighter, and the engines practically identical to the B-25's, so I figured its performance should at least be comparable. I was pleased with my choice and delighted when I received orders a day or two later directing me to report to the 46th Bomb Group at Morris Field in Charlotte, North Carolina.

Chapter 3

TO MORRIS FIELD AND THE A-20

SEEING NO REASON to stay around Columbia any longer than necessary, I left by bus on February 4, 1944. Although there were twenty-eight pilots assigned to the 46th Bomb Group at Charlotte on the same orders with me, they evidently were not as anxious to escape since none of them were on the bus that Friday. The only quarters available when I arrived were some temporary ones in a single-story barracks on a rise of ground behind the officers' club, but this did not dampen my enthusiasm for Morris Field. There was always a lot of signing in to do when arriving on a new base, so even though the following day was a Saturday I started making the rounds.

A routine Type 6–4 physical exam was required with each change of station, so I stopped by the hospital and made an appointment to take it the first thing on Monday. The exam, however, turned out to be not quite as routine as anticipated and, at least for a time, caused me some concern. My eyes checked out at 20/15, even better than previously noted, but for some unknown reason my pulse was a hundred when it should have been eighty. The flight surgeon seemed serious as he questioned me and leafed through earlier exams then pronounced, "As it stands now, I'll have to turn you down for flight duty, Lieutenant." In response to my protests, he told me to go out in the waiting room, relax for an hour, and then return for a final decision.

During my enforced wait in the hospital's outer office, a number of newly arrived Class 44-A acquaintances drifted in to schedule physical exams. Among them were Jim Rutledge, Wayne Musgrove, John Ross, Bill Morgan, Bob Mosley, and Maurice Owen. They said they had all been assigned to the 53d Squadron located at the north end of Morris Field. When I mentioned why I was cooling my heels in the waiting room, the always sympathetic Maury Owen, commented, "Don't sweat it Rutter, they'll probably make you mess officer." I grew to expect and appreciate Owen's laconic and sometimes caustic witticisms as Rutledge, Owen, and I would be together for more than a year.

Another recollection from that wait in the clinic was the appearance in the doorway of a huge man in a sergeant's uniform. He was well over six feet tall and had the largest pair of hands I had ever seen. Buddy Baer was a professional boxer and the younger brother of one-time heavyweight champion Max Baer. Buddy was traveling around entertaining troops and that particular afternoon he was making a tour of the hospital, shaking hands with everybody in sight. My pulse, maybe with the help of Buddy Baer, eventually slowed down sufficiently to satisfy the doctor, who judged me fit to fly and sent me on my way.

The living quarters for student officers at Morris Field were in buildings that looked not unlike the standard two-story enlisted barracks of the time. After about three or four days I moved down from the temporary quarters I had been given on the hill overlooking the officers' club. Our BOQ had central hallways with small two-man rooms along either side. Latrines and showers were located at the midpoint on each floor. The furnishings were sparse: two steel cots, two lockers for clothes, a table, and two chairs. Our building was adjacent to and a little below the south end of the north–south runway, a short walk from the officers' club where we usually took our meals. Enlisted men kept the rooms reasonably neat and made the beds. Although it was not exactly plush living, the BOQ was a step up from cadet days.

The 46th Bomb Group had four squadrons that carried out the flying training. The commanding officer of the 53d Squadron—to which Rutledge, Owen, and I were assigned—was Lt. Col. T. B. Summers, an old Air Corps hand who had been awarded the Silver Star in the Pacific and was credited with sinking a couple of Japanese ships. Colonel Summers talked to the pilots occasionally and recounted some of his flying wisdom such as, "When flying over the ocean in the tropics a patch of cloud usually means there's an island under it." He warned us that pilots were in charge and should not rely on the abilities of "boy navigators," as he called them, without question. The colonel seemed to limit his appearances in the squadron office mainly to signing orders and such and was not otherwise involved in our training.

The squadron's day-to-day operations were left to Capts. George C. Farr and William W. Neel—both veterans of the early days in the

Southwest Pacific, where they had flown A-20s with the 3d Attack Group in New Guinea. Several other instructor pilots, all of them veterans of combat in either the Pacific or with the 47th Bomb Group in North Africa, were assigned to the 53d Squadron. These men had a rather relaxed attitude toward the details of the formal training program but recognized that they had lacked proper knowledge when they had been sent out and so tried to share their experiences with us in a helpful way. On rare occasions Farr or Neel would tell a "war story" to illustrate a point or a particular bit of flying stupidity. I think most of us took the directions from our instructors seriously.

Captains Farr and Neel had created a reputation for coolness under pressure around Morris Field by their performance a month or so before we arrived in the squadron. They were in a B-25 starting out on a cross-country flight when an engine caught fire shortly after takeoff. Copilot Neel alerted the tower to the sudden problem while Farr smoothly circled around to make a quick landing as the crash trucks screamed out from the fire station.

"Farr was doing the flying and was too steep on his last turn, too damned fast and not lined up with the runway," Neel told us. "Then Farr says, 'We'll go around for another try.' I yelled back, 'George, you're crazy!'

"'No sweat, Bill! Feather the goddam engine,' says Farr.

"The plane was now trailing a big plume of black smoke as we went around the field a second time and everybody was out to see the crash. Farr was again off to one side of the runway when he announced, 'Hell Bill, we'll have to go around again.' That's when I pulled back the throttle and jerked the landing gear handle up. He was going to kill us."

Those watching said the burning plane dropped flat onto the grass and slid along beside the runway as the crash truck raced to the scene. The rescue crew desperately searched the cockpit for Neel and Farr but found no sign of them. Then someone spotted them sitting on the grass well away from the excitement, puffing on cigarettes as they watched the B-25 burn.

Captain Farr would at times remark for the benefit of any pilot listeners, "Neel's a good pilot, but awfully nervous."

Since the A-20 had room for only one pilot, the checkout procedure consisted of several rides in a B-25 and four landings with an instructor. There was a written test on the systems and other matters contained in the A-20 pilot's handbook and then a blindfold test in the cockpit to see if we could readily find the various handles and instruments: landing gear, flaps, cowl flaps, mixture and throttle controls, fuel tank switch and indicator, airspeed indicator, altimeter, radio controls, and so forth. Most of us were checked out in the B-25 by one of the instructor pilots within a week or two and judged ready to try the A-20 on our own.

Getting into the cockpit of an A-20 required some rather strenuous gymnastics because the only access was to step down into it from atop the narrow fuselage. It was about a ten-foot climb to the top of the fuselage using a series of steps and handholds located behind the trailing edge of the left wing. The handholds and steps had spring-loaded covers and a retractable bottom step extended below the fuselage. It was easy enough if you got started properly by placing your left foot in the bottom step. If you started with your right foot, the sequence of steps and handholds was all wrong and you wound up clinging to the top of the fuselage with no place to go. The climb was even more difficult if attempted while wearing the seat-pack parachute that we used, so we usually threw the chute up onto the wing.

A hinged hatch about eight feet long was positioned on top of the forward fuselage and extended beyond the wing's leading edge. A shelf behind the cockpit provided a walkway and could also hold a five-man life raft, although we never carried one during training. A piece of three-eighths-inch armor plate was located just behind the pilot's seat, with the top hinged so that it could be folded flat onto the shelf. However, most of the armor plating had been removed from the planes we used at Charlotte.

The inside of the cockpit was snug, about thirty inches wide at the windows, and all the controls and switches were within easy reach if you knew where to look for them. The landing gear and wing-flap controls were positioned low on the bulkhead behind the left side of the seat. The seat could be adjusted vertically and the rudder pedals could be adjusted fore and aft to accommodate long or short legs. The seat-pack parachute also served as a seat cushion. With the hatch cover down it was a very snug cockpit. The main source of ventilation was the side windows, which could be opened by pulling in and sliding them rearward.

If there was one concern about the layout of an A-20 it was how the pilot went about bailing out if that became advisable. The seat was positioned ahead of the two props, there was no way to escape through the bottom, and the high tail had a sharp pitot tube (used to measure airspeed) at the top that was a hazard too awful to contemplate. The best option seemed to be to roll the plane over, drop out, and hope you cleared the props and vertical stabilizer. Another option was to slide back along the shelf to get aft of the props and then drop down off the wing. Some of the early models had a rope anchored along the shelf to

Flight line of the 53d Squadron, 46th Bomb Group, Morris Field, Charlotte, North Carolina. The A-20J in the foreground had space for a bombardier, whereas the A-20G beyond it had six .50-caliber machine guns in the nose. Either, or any, A-20 was a delight to fly. The large "buzz numbers" on the nose discouraged overly low flying by making it easy to identify the culprit.

facilitate this method of escape. One was left to wonder about the wisdom of hanging onto the rope and then sliding over the wing in a 150- to two-hundred-mile-per-hour breeze.

Before my first flight in an A-20, Captain Neel crouched on the shelf behind me, ran through several pointers regarding the landing approach speed, and reminded me to go easy on the brakes when taxiing. I was ready to go. The Wright R-2600 engines were almost identical to those on the B-25, so starting and other procedures were very similar. Still, the cockpit was not completely familiar, and there was no copilot reading a checklist and taking care of part of the routine. I felt both a little concern and excited anticipation as I prepared to make my first takeoff in the plane.

The takeoff run was from southwest to northeast that morning, and I can still clearly remember the pleasure and surprise of the experience. The plane seemed to accelerate down the runway at a much faster clip than the heavier B-25. The nose lifted quickly with just a little back-pressure on the wheel and she flew herself off at about 110 miles per hour just as smooth as could be. I yelled out an exuberant, "Hot dog!" as we climbed away from Morris Field. The controls responded to much lighter pressure than did the B-25. Everything in those first few minutes of flight felt just perfect. My later experiences with the A-20 under a variety of situations did not alter that first impression: it was a pilot's plane and a joy to fly.

The training program for replacement crews was divided into thirty-seven segments or missions over about 150 flying hours. We also attended a ground school for half a day for about four weeks. The classes covered details of the various systems on the plane, maintenance, local flight procedures, armament, bombing, gunnery, and so forth. The ground school's sergeant instructors were dedicated and most had served an overseas tour. While fresh second lieutenants were not always the most receptive students, I do recall paying considerable attention to the peculiarities of the A-20's fuel and hydraulic systems and learned to strip and reassemble a .50-caliber machine gun blindfolded.

Often we were able to divert the instructors from the subject at hand and get them to tell us war stories. One example of the flip attitude of new second lieutenants with which the enlisted instructors had to contend began with a sergeant telling us about some of his experiences in B-25s in the South Pacific. Perhaps not realizing that we were all familiar with the plane, the storyteller portrayed the B-25 as being outstanding in every respect, the backbone of the Pacific war, and far superior to anything else, even the A-20. After too many superlatives, Jerome Potter of Waco, Texas, raised his hand. When the noncom called on him, he said with a straight face, "Sergeant, do you think that the B-25 will ever replace the airplane?" That ended all serious discussion. Although I laughed with all the others, I thought the ridiculing remark was a bit unkind.

The first six or eight flying hours were devoted to becoming acquainted with the feel and characteristics of the new plane and also getting to know the area around Charlotte. There was rolling farmland surrounding the city, then about eighty-five thousand in population, with the Catawba River to the south and west making a good landmark. The layout of the railroads and highways and the look of the smaller towns in the general vicinity were useful signposts for locating Morris Field. Off in the distance to the west were the rising foothills of the Blue Ridge Mountains, with the higher peaks beyond usually hidden by the hazy atmosphere.

The planes assigned to the training squadrons were a mixture of several variations of the Douglas A-20, although most were the later G and J models then being used in combat squadrons. The plane had started out as a privately funded Douglas design to meet the needs of the French and British, who were building up their air forces prior to 1939. Designated Douglas Bomber 7 (DB-7) for export, we had several DB-7Bs built to British specifications with some peculiarities in the cockpit arrangement. There was one A-20B in the 53d Squadron, conspicuous in its natural aluminum finish and lacking self-sealing fuel tanks.

The A-20C model was similar to the DB-7 with a multipaneled glazed nose for the bombardier and two hand-held machine guns for a gunner in the dorsal position. The G model had six forward-firing .50-caliber machine guns in the nose and a Martin power-operated turret with twin fifties in the rear dorsal position. The J model had a glazed nose made of formed Plexiglas for a bombardier-navigator in place of the solid gun-nose but was otherwise similar to the G. There was also provision for a gunner in the rear to fire a single .50-caliber machine gun out of the access hatch in the bottom of the fuselage, but the position was used for an automatic camera on low-level missions. Each model flew a little differently and the earlier versions, being lighter, were faster.

An example of how small differences in the arrangement of the controls could cause momentary confusion for the pilot occurred the second time I attempted to fly an A-20. The first plane had been an A-20G, which had a landing gear handle shaped like a large cube. Both the landing gear and flap controls were mounted low on the bulkhead behind the pilot's seat on the left side. The cube-shaped handle could readily be distinguished by feel from the smaller, rounded flap handle. To retract the gear, the pilot pulled the cube handle out and then moved it upward to the halfway point, then horizontally through a solenoid actuated gate in a cross slot, and then upward again. On the C model, the landing gear handle was rounded like the flap handle and the mechanism was simpler, with a manual latch at the halfway point to permit sideways movement before coming up to the gear-retracted position.

My second takeoff, a few days after the first, turned out to be anything but a smooth climb away from the runway. The takeoff was north on the north–south runway and the A-20C quickly accelerated. As before, the ship became airborne almost as soon as the nosewheel lifted. The airspeed rose toward 150 miles per hour and my hand dropped to the vicinity of the landing gear handle, found it easily, and then moved it upward until it was stopped by something very solid. The gear remained down as I safely crossed over the telephone wires along the railroad at the end of the runway. Meanwhile, my tugs and wiggles on the handle failed to produce any results. I glanced down and to the rear and saw that there was a spring-loaded catch that kept the gear handle from moving beyond the halfway point in its travel. It took only a flick of the thumb to raise the latch and then the handle came up the rest of

The cockpit of an A-20. The fuselage was forty-nine inches wide, narrowing to about thirty inches at the cockpit windows, making it an extremely tight fit for the pilot.

the way and retracted the gear—a simple enough procedure when you knew the drill.

All of this seemingly took only a few seconds, but it was probably more. Meanwhile, the plane continued to accelerate at a high power setting in almost level flight at about five hundred feet. When I looked up I was startled by the sight of two Piper Cub trainers about a half-mile straight ahead: a yellow one diving out of the way and a red one clawing for altitude. During the few seconds that I had been distracted, I had been heading straight into the traffic pattern of the small civilian airport located a few miles north of Morris Field. My only hope was that any witnesses in the area were too startled to catch the large "buzz numbers" painted on the A-20's nose. At least three pilots would not forget that particular morning.

Something should be said about the one weakness of the A-20 compared to the B-25: the brakes. The brakes on the two main wheels were of the multiple disk design, with half of the disks fixed to the wheel hub and the remainder interspersed and rotating with the wheel. The A-20 had only one set of disks in each hub and these tended to overheat with overuse. The B-25, on the other hand, had two sets in each wheel and overheating never seemed to be a problem. On the ground, the pilot steered the plane with the brakes. Hot pilots liked to roll down the

The cockpit of the A-20G at the U.S. Air Force Museum at Dayton, Ohio. The fuel mixture, throttle, and propeller controls are on the left. Radio and trim tab controls are on the right.

taxiways at a fast clip while appearing suitably nonchalant as they tramped heavily on the brakes.

It seemed that every A-20 pilot made the mistake at least once of setting the parking brake on red-hot disks only to find that the metal plates had welded themselves together as they cooled down. The stuck brakes usually could be broken loose by manipulating the throttles to free one wheel and then the other, but sometimes it took a tractor sent out from the ramp to loosen them. The secret was to avoid riding the brakes when taxiing in the first place and then to allow the plane to creep a bit while running up the engines at the end of the runway. Setting the parking brake after a fast trip down the taxi strip was a formula for pilot embarrassment as planes backed up waiting to use the runway. It happened once to me and only full power finally broke the disks loose just before the tractor reached me. Once was enough.

Many of our flying assignments included the instruction, "At minimum altitude." Up to this point, we had been consistently admonished about the dire consequences of being caught flying low or buzzing, but now it was legal. Speed was most evident to the pilot when flying low, while the startling effect upon people going about their business on the ground was sometimes amusing and made buzzing all the more attractive. To our instructors in the 53d Squadron, veterans that they were, minimum altitude meant three hundred feet or lower—and that was low enough to suit most of us. Inevitably, there were pilots who got carried away and ran into such things as wires, trees, and even barns. Fortunately there were relatively few such instances.

Navigating at low altitude with few landmarks beyond those directly ahead was difficult and there were several instances of off-course pilots running out of fuel, which was always embarrassing and sometimes amusing. Bill Morgan of the 53d Squadron ran into navigation difficulties on a minimum altitude mission one afternoon and, after reading the name on the water tank of some small town in South Carolina, he headed directly for Charlotte. As he came within sight of the city, his fuel gauges were reading "empty." When the engines stopped there was nothing he could do but put the plane down in a farmer's plowed field. Thereafter, Bill's face bore a prominent scar across one cheek as a souvenir and some of his crass friends dubbed him "The Face."

Another of the 53d Squadron boys (was his name Wright?) decided to slip away one afternoon to play a round of golf. That same afternoon an A-20 ran out of gas and the pilot used one of the country club's fairways for a belly landing, which caused considerable damage to both the plane and the fairway. Our golfer was a close observer and, naturally, ran over to lend assistance to the pilot, who had been banged about a bit. After rendering assistance he beat an anonymous retreat just as an officious colonel appeared from another foursome and began collecting the names of witnesses. The pilot claimed that he did not know the golfer who had pulled him from the plane. Wright had by then disappeared and he was always discreet when later discussing the incident. "I was having a good round until that happened," he would say, shaking his head.

The early spring weather in the Carolinas was not always the best for the type of training we were doing and there were many days when thick haze or rain caused us to sit around the ready room without getting off the ground. One morning I took off and saw a solid bank of fog rolling toward Morris Field from the west. Before I could make a single circuit of the field to get back down, the fog had moved across and blanked out the runway. A number of other A-20s were also milling about when the tower announced that Columbia was still open and we should head south promptly. After an overnight stay in Columbia (with our trim A-20s lined up beside those solid B-25 trucks) we all flew back home to Morris Field.

A few days later the field was again closed down suddenly, this time by an afternoon rainsquall. As the squall line moved in from the west there seemed to be planes approaching the field from all directions as the pilots attempted to get back on the ground. We watched the excitement from the shelter of the ready room doorway as first one and then another plane attempted to land on any open runway and seemingly without the formality of a traffic pattern. Several of the wiser pilots pulled up and headed for Columbia, but two of the A-20s came to grief on the field. Jim Rutledge, making a last attempt to land, touched down in the downpour at an angle to the runway while still moving much too fast. His A-20 skidded off the left side of the pavement into the wet sod in a cloud of mud and spray with the landing gear collapsing before the plane slid across an intersecting runway. Still moving fast, it made a half-rotation before sliding backward over the wet grass and down a slope to stop on the edge of the Morris Field junkyard. Jim was not scratched, but the plane was a total loss and left to be dismantled where it had come to a stop.

Most of the veteran A-20 instructors who had returned from their combat tours were very sharp flyers if at times a bit reckless. There was one fellow who stood out as not fitting the mold, however, whether from just being burned out or not having flown for several months I do not know. He had been in the 47th Bomb Group in Africa and Italy, joined the 53d Squadron, and I was asked to ride copilot with him in a B-25 while he became acquainted with the area and shot some landings. He was the veteran in my eyes, but a remark he made as we settled into the cockpit seemed a bit unusual: "Rutter, it's been a long time since I flew a B-25, so keep an eye on me."

The takeoff may have been a little ragged, but we went off to look around Charlotte and Gastonia, Rock Hill, Monroe, and elsewhere. The pilot wanted to shoot some landings and it was then that I became somewhat apprehensive as he misjudged his turns in the pattern and was erratic on the final approach. After making two rough landings, he was smoother on the third approach. However, he leveled off much too high—it seemed like fifty feet to me—and the B-25 shook with a tremendous jolt when the main gear hit the runway. The struts went to the stops with a bang and the plane made several great leaps but stayed on the runway.

Even my worst landings had not been like that one. I was surprised that the B-25 seemed to be intact, but the pilot was noncommittal and we taxied back to the parking ramp. The pilot made no comment to the crew chief about that hard landing and failed to note it on the Form 1A

Flight Report, so I later went back and reported it to the crew chief. The incident proved to me that B-25s were indeed rugged: the sergeant found no cracks, bends, or buckled bulkheads.

Later, that same fellow flew a B-25 through a hailstorm on a trip from Florida one weekend and came back with most of the glass in the nose gone and large dents in the leading edge of the wing. Captain Farr gathered the student pilots together and gave us a serious lecture about hail and airplanes with the damaged B-25 as exhibit number one. That instructor disappeared after the hail incident and the plane was sent to the repair shop for a complete overhaul.

About halfway through our training schedule we were formed into crews consisting of a pilot and two gunners. The enlisted gunners had also had training in either aircraft maintenance or armament. A few crews destined to fly the A-20J also included a commissioned officer as bombardier-navigator. Assigned to my crew were Sgt. George R. Millson and Cpl. Leon D. Schnell, both about my own age and fresh from gunnery school. Millson was from Utica, New York, and an extrovert interested in beer and girls, whereas Schnell was a quiet, smiling boy from the farming community of Tyler, Minnesota. Lacking much experience as the leader of a crew, my demeanor was no doubt somewhat stiff and more formal than necessary when dealing with my two new subordinates. Some pilots seemed to encourage a first-name basis with their gunners; others thrived on overly correct military courtesy. Hopefully, my style was somewhere in between. In any event, we three got along well together.

After our crew was formed, one or the other gunner and sometimes both flew on the training missions when they were not engaged in their own gunnery training or details such as kitchen police (KP) or guard duty. When we flew together, there was little for gunners to do except become acquainted with the plane's equipment and systems and acclimated to the sensation of low-level flight. The gunners assisted in the armament shop and Millson also worked with the crew chiefs on inspections and maintenance. The gunner could be vital to an A-20 in a combat situation, but his lot was not to be envied—his fate depended largely on the competence of his pilot, from whom he was separated by the bomb bay.

The weeks passed quickly and the early spring weather improved. My time at Charlotte was really the most pleasant period of my military experience. We did a great deal of flying, often as much as six hours a day, but we also had the freedom to come and go when away from the flight

The Rutter crew comes together at Charlotte: Cpl. George Millson of Utica, New York (left), and Cpl. Leon Schnell of Tyler, Minnesota (right).

line. Most of the married pilots had brought their wives to Charlotte and lived off the base in furnished apartments. Occasionally, Maury and Rosalie Owen took pity on a youthful bachelor and invited me for dinner at the apartment they shared with Wayne Musgrove and his wife. Charlotte was large enough to provide some entertainment and it was sufficiently remote from other military bases not to be overrun by soldiers. Fort Bragg, outside of Fayetteville, was 125 miles away and sometimes a few paratroopers would find their way to Charlotte on Saturday nights, but the military was a relatively small presence there.

Perhaps Charlotte made a favorable impression upon me because of a young lady named Nancy Ann. We met on a Sunday afternoon in early April at the Mint Art Museum, where one of the Morris Field meteorology officers and I were sampling the culture. The museum was about to close and we were looking for a cab to take us downtown when Nancy and another girl offered us a ride. After accepting the invitation and going to Nancy's home to be properly introduced to her mother, we found that we were also going to dinner at a sorority house at Queens College. The two of us survived the experience of being the surprise guests at the all-female dinner party and the food was good. It was their southern hospitality, of course.

Nancy subsequently invited me to Sunday dinner to meet the rest of her family, who lived with her grandmother in the Myers Park section of Charlotte. Nancy was attractive, rather tall and blond, and always well dressed, but that was the fashion during those more formal days. She was attending Women's College at Greensboro, and her mostly serious outlook was modified by a touch of amusing foolishness. With her southern ways, sense of humor, intellect, and pleasing aura of assurance, I found Nancy to be very entertaining company. The fact that she showed some interest in me was also flattering.

There was one unexpected twist to this new friendship when, while out on a later date, Nancy informed me that she was engaged to a pilot who had been shot down and was a prisoner of war (POW) in Germany. This called for some ground rules that Nancy set down very directly: our relationship would not become too involved or serious. I agreed—it was fair enough.

Nancy's grandmother had a '36 Studebaker and an uncle in the used car business always had some extra gas ration coupons. We attended dinners at Queens College, basked by the pool at the country club, and took her mother to the Myers Park Church on Sunday mornings. On one particular evening, the unpredictable Nancy decided we should walk home to Myers Park from the movie theater downtown, a distance of four miles or so—and she did it barefoot. We engaged in serious discussions on many subjects, laughed a lot, and enjoyed the springtime weather. Small wonder that I enjoyed life in Charlotte.

When ground school ended we started spending the full day on the flight line. The improving weather also permitted more flying, both day and night. We had, of course, practiced formation flying in the B-25 at La Junta. Now we got even more practice in the A-20, at both medium and low altitude. The combat veterans serving as our instructors had some different ideas about formation flying than we had previously been exposed to: closer, and with some rather wild evasive action thrown in. When they said low level, they did not mean five hundred feet. The leader would take three- and six-ship formations over the countryside in a manner that required the wingmen's full concentration. On that subject, my diary records: "Flew low level formation this afternoon that was REALLY low. Had a good time doing it."

One practice medium-altitude formation flight included perhaps too realistic a portrayal of what we might experience in combat. Two of the instructors who had been with the 47th Bomb Group in North Africa were to intercept a six-ship formation being led by another instructor. We had been forewarned that this interception would take place— sometime—and that the attackers would be flying A-20s since no P-40s were available. The fighter pilots put on a good act as they warned us to be alert, and I was a little worried when we saw them sitting at the bar in the officers' club drinking from tall glasses during lunch.

During our mission that afternoon I was flying on the wing of the in- structor leading the lower flight in the six-plane box. Just when it seemed that perhaps the fighter pilots had stayed in the bar, our leader called out, "Bandits at six o'clock high!" We wingmen stayed glued to the leader while our gunners shouted excited warnings over the intercom. Over- taking the formation from the rear over Lake Murray, South Carolina, the two A-20s, flying in echelon, cut between our flight and the lead flight above. I saw a flash as the planes passed by much too close for comfort and then they were gone. Later, our flight leader admitted that he knew what they were planning to do and had purposely left enough space (he hoped) between our flights for the attackers to slip through. Never- theless, the demonstration was unnecessarily realistic for my taste.

In April, John Ross, a member of the La Junta group in the 53d Squadron, invited me to go along to visit some relatives of his who lived on a farm near the village of Turbeville, Virginia. Turbeville is about twenty miles east of Danville and John wanted some company, for this was a "duty visit" to an aunt and uncle he hardly knew. We took the train one Saturday afternoon from Charlotte to Danville, stayed in a hotel overnight, and found a USO dance in progress for our entertainment.

The Wilkins family met our bus at the small community of Turbeville the following morning and we all attended Sunday services in the little country church near the highway before traveling out to the family farm. The house was old, roomy, and comfortably furnished in a style I equated with a time when the family might have been more affluent. The outside of the house and barns had not seen paint for a number of years, but that was not unusual in the rural South in those days.

The traditional southern Sunday meal featured a huge fish on a large platter and was served in the dining room from the detached summer kitchen. John had not seen these kinfolk for a considerable time, I gathered, but they made us most welcome and the huge dinner and conversation are still a pleasant memory. Later, we rode the fam- ily horse and explored the farm under the guidance of John's cousin, Louise Wilkins, who was attending Women's College at Greensboro. I found talking with Mr. Wilkins about the farm work to be interesting, but John came from Los Angeles and was unfamiliar with serious agriculture.

Late in the afternoon, John and I caught the bus from Turbeville and then the evening train from Danville back to Charlotte and got to bed at midnight. The duty visit with John Ross's relatives had turned out to be an enjoyable excursion all around and exposed me to another facet of the South, which was still a distinct culture in 1944. Most people during the war years went out of their way to make servicemen welcome and the Wilkins family of Turbeville, Virginia, was particularly gracious.

According to the schedule, each pilot had to put in fifteen hours of night flying and fifteen hours of instrument time. Much of my night flying consisted of following along the lighted airway that extended from Atlanta to Richmond. Lighted beacons were located about every fifteen to twenty miles along designated major air routes and each rotating white beacon had a red flasher giving a Morse code letter to identify the position. From north to south and from east to west the beacons were coded W, U, V, H, R, K, D, B, G, and M. We remembered them by memorizing the phrase, "*W*hen *U*ndertaking *V*ery *H*azardous *R*outes *K*eep *D*irections *B*y *G*ood *M*ethods."

These lighted airways dated back to the late 1920s and by 1944 could be followed to major cities throughout the country. They were still useful for night flying, although the low-frequency radio navigation range system had by then become the major navigational aid. On a clear night, navigation by the light line was simple, and I spent hours in the still, cool air flying between Spartansburg and Danville while listening to popular music played by station WBT in Charlotte. The radio compass would home in on WBT from a considerable distance and I occasionally used it for navigating back to the field just for the practice.

On Friday, April 14, the assigned mission was a low-level cross-country flight. The route was supposed to be southwest to Greenwood, South Carolina, north to Spartansburg, and then back to Charlotte. There was no lighted airway between Charlotte and Greenwood, so navigation was by compass course and time. Half an hour after takeoff we spotted clouds moving in from the west with some lightning. Meanwhile, the radio traffic indicated that other pilots out that night were turning back to Charlotte. There was light rain on the windshield by the time I got to Greenwood, but all seemed well since the ceiling remained above a thousand feet and I could still see the lights of towns in the vicinity.

My next heading would take me north and a little east to Spartansburg and back into clearer weather, so I decided to carry on with the mission. Unfortunately, my course plotting turned out to be not very accurate. When the clock said we should be approaching Spartansburg and I could make out the lights of a town up ahead there was a sudden confusion of red and green aircraft navigation lights all around. I was in heavy traffic! There was no commercial or military field at Spartansburg at that time, so I reacted with great surprise. The large, red, leading-edge wing lights identified the planes as B-25s, and I could hear radio chatter calling attention to a strange plane in the pattern of "Greenville Army Airfield!" I was, for whatever reason, about twenty-five miles west of my intended course and chose not to respond when the tower asked for the identity of the plane then crossing over a runway. Having somehow missed the gaggle of B-25s practicing night landings at Greenville, I slipped off in the dark and onto the friendly light line toward Spartansburg and then home.

By this time my confidence was high when it came to flying the A-20, although I did show a little prudence—at least most of the time. With most of the armor and guns removed, the planes we flew were comparatively light, so the recommended speed when making a landing approach was 120 miles per hour or even a little less. The power-on stall speed of the lightened planes was about a hundred miles per hour with gear and flaps down, and with some practice, the A-20 was easily controllable at 110 miles per hour or less when there was no disturbed air.

My newly discovered landing technique was to stay higher than usual on the final approach, well above the prop wash from planes up ahead, and then kill off speed down to what felt like the minimum needed for maintaining control. By holding the nose up, the rate of descent increased dramatically with just enough power to keep the plane headed toward the intended spot on the runway. Releasing backpressure on the wheel at just the right position and altitude resulted in picking up a little speed for a smooth touchdown. After some experimenting and practice I gained considerable confidence and could usually hit my intended spot on the runway—a hot-rock pilot, without a doubt.

Such unorthodox approaches were, of course, noticed by personnel in the control tower and on one occasion the female operator directed: "Six-three-four, you are too high. Go around." Being well occupied at the moment with keeping ahead of the airplane and dropping fast, I did not respond but instead touched down nicely within an acceptable distance from the end of the runway. That was hot! I thought. Moreover, when the tower operator did not remonstrate any further, I figured I was home free. Captain Farr may have heard the call from the tower or witnessed my newfound skills. In any event, he looked me up a day later and pointed out that I was asking for trouble. Keeping a straight face, he directed, "Knock it off, Rutter." All I could do was say, "Yes, Sir," for he was right.

We flew a number of training missions to the Sand Hill Gunnery Range in South Carolina, always at low level. After becoming accustomed to low-level flying and the problems of navigation we students were involved in surprisingly few accidents. High-tension power lines were potentially the most serious hazard, and I can recall only one fatal accident involving wires. When the map showed a power line in the vicinity it was wise to allow a little extra altitude, although most lines were not over a hundred feet above ground level.

Flying close to the ground gave a great feeling of speed and there was a sense of anticipation as you watched for the next landmark and excitement when you avoided the next obstruction. Mules were still common on Carolina farms in 1944 and the animals invariably made a dash for the nearest cover whenever an A-20 surprised them. A farmer on a spring-toothed harrow pulled by a team of mules was fair game as you came over the pines on the edge of a cotton field. He was always assured of a fast ride toward the nearest trees.

One of our training missions at Sand Hill involved laying a chemical smoke screen from two tanks suspended from bomb racks on the wings. There are photographs of A-20s performing this function to screen a parachute drop zone in New Guinea's Markham Valley in November, 1943, so there was a very practical application for the technique. The tanks held several hundred gallons of the chemical mixture. The devices had a ram-air inlet in the front sealed by a glass disk and a discharge pipe at the rear. When a pilot reached the desired area he triggered an electrically fired charge that broke the glass seal over the ram-air inlet. Laying an effective smoke screen over a target was no great problem as long as the air was still and you were not flying too fast.

The day I was assigned the smoke mission the winds were reported to be erratic at Sand Hill. The operations officer warned that reports from the range on previous smoke missions that day had been unsatisfactory. After an uneventful run from Charlotte and locating the target on the rolling terrain, I checked the wind direction and sized up how best to lay the smoke. After receiving clearance from the range officer I made a low turn around a clump of pine trees, followed the contour of the ground at about 160 miles per hour and fired the first tank in the shelter of a hollow upwind of the target.

When I pulled up I could see that the target was well hidden, but my satisfaction in the accomplishment under adverse conditions was quickly punctured. "Three-five-four," the ground controller commented sternly, "the minimum altitude at this range is fifty feet!" After making my second pass at a somewhat higher altitude, he carpingly remarked, "Three-five-four, that was fair." Oh, well. When I got back to Charlotte I could at least cross off one more mission on my training chart.

There were two or three primary flying schools in South Carolina that were not far off our usual course from Charlotte to the Sand Hill gunnery range, so we often saw the slow-moving biplanes floating around or practicing stalls and spins. Unsuspecting cadets in Stearmans at Lancaster or Camden could be startled by sneaking up on them from behind with flaps and wheels down, dragging along at about 120 miles per hour. However, the dangers posed by the unpredictable reactions of suddenly startled cadets dawned upon me and caused me to discontinue this game.

It did seem particularly worthwhile to inspire the primary school cadets with a low pass across the flying field now and then. While heading home late one afternoon I buzzed the parade ground at Bennettsville when everybody was lined up for the retreat formation—it must have been inspiring. Shaw Field at Sumter, South Carolina, was the site of a basic school and although those cadets also needed some inspiration, the place looked just too military to risk a buzz job; some overeager "ground-pounder" would surely report the large numbers on the nose if he could read them.

If there was ever a single incident that dramatically affected an individual it occurred one afternoon when Allan Showler, another Class 44-A graduate, was returning from Sand Hill Gunnery Range at the usual minimum altitude. He became overly enthusiastic while pursuing a team of mules across a field and his plane took the top out of a pine tree, damaging the wing and stopping one engine. After struggling for several miles to keep his plane in the air, Showler had to put it down in the first open space he could find. The aircraft hit the ground going fast and bounded along, shedding wings, the engines, and the rear of the fuselage before coming to a stop between two trees in a cloud of dust and shower of pine branches. All was quiet. Showler was only banged up a bit, but there was little left intact of the A-20; even the forward fuselage section containing the cockpit's instrument panel was gone. Allan unsnapped his belt, ducked under the remainder of the cowl and windshield, and stepped out.

As he looked back at the trail of wreckage and the little of his A-20 that remained intact, a change suddenly came over the amusing, fun-loving Showler we knew. Although there was no fire, the noisy crash into the grove of pine trees on the edge of the small field brought help in short order. Showler, who was uncharacteristically quiet and serious afterward, said it was a miracle when asked about his spectacular crash and would display eight-by-ten photos of the A-20's remains to prove his point. After seeing his collection of photos, the change in Allan's personality was as understandable as it was dramatic.

One afternoon Col. Robert L. Scott, author of the popular postwar memoir *God Is My Copilot*, was scheduled to land at Morris Field for a well-publicized war bond rally in Charlotte. The colonel and his wingman were flying P-40s sporting the colorful shark design on the noses of their planes that was the trademark of the famed "Flying Tigers," a group of American volunteers who flew in China before we went to war with Japan. The two fighters landed just ahead of our B-25. As we turned left to taxi over to the 53d Squadron flight line, the tower operator calmly announced, "Colonel Scott, your wing man is on fire."

The engine on the second P-40, which had stopped on the nearby taxiway, was belching smoke and flame. We watched as the pilot jumped out, slapped his cap on his head, sprinted ahead, and climbed onto the wing of the colonel's plane. Leaving the burning P-40 where it sat, Colonel Scott advanced the throttle on his shark-nosed P-40 and continued along the taxiway with his passenger to where a reception committee stood waiting to welcome the celebrities on the main ramp. The crash truck arrived a few moments later and put out the fire, but the second P-40 was a total write-off. I thought the colonel's matter-of-fact handling of the situation was amusing, but one of our older cynics, who claimed to know him, commented dryly that Scott had always been a grandstander.

A landing incident involving Thomas A. Murphy of Laurel, Maryland, and John B. Murphy of Emigrant, Montana—nicknamed Big and Little Murphy because of the difference in their heights—was also cause for amusement. One evening, those lounging at our squadron heard that one of the planes was having trouble lowering its landing gear. Word quickly got around and those of us who were in the area gathered to watch the outcome. It turned out to be an A-20C, one of the variants with a Plexiglas "greenhouse" to accommodate a bombardier in the nose, flown by Little Murphy. Big Murphy had gone along to ride up front in the bombardier's seat just to experience the sensation. The only way for Big Murphy to get out was to jump through the lower hatch. Finding that idea unappealing, and trusting in Little Murphy's flying ability, he elected to ride the plane down.

After circling around the field to burn off fuel, Little Murphy finally was able to get the main gear down and locked. He would, however, have to bring the A-20 in with its nose gear still dangling loose. The landing was perfect and Murphy held the nose up as long as possible before it eventually dropped onto the runway. The plane was still rolling at fifty or sixty miles per hour and we could hear the screech of tearing metal and see smoke rising from melting Plexiglas as the bottom of the nose was ground off on the asphalt. As soon as the A-20 came to a stop, the escape hatch above the bombardier's compartment popped open and Big Murphy's head and shoulders popped out. He was facing the windshield and shaking his fist at the laughing pilot in the cockpit. Nobody was hurt, but it was obvious to all of us watching that being a bombardier in an A-20 could be dangerous.

The Murphys, both members of our La Junta class, were later killed in separate incidents while flying in Europe.

One day toward the end of our training, Capt. Bill Neel scheduled me to fly as his copilot in a B-25 on a run to the parts depot at Middletown, Pennsylvania, near Harrisburg. Bill was from Philadelphia and I suppose he thought I might like to visit Pittsburgh. We got to Middletown in time for lunch and, not unexpected, we were told we would have to wait overnight for the parts order. Bill wasted no time catching a train to the east and I took one headed west.

I considered the five-hour train ride each way a fair exchange to see Harriett, who met me at the station. We had only about four hours to visit before I had to catch the train back to Harrisburg, but such is young love in wartime.

The following morning, after getting very little sleep, Bill and I were back at the airfield by nine o'clock anticipating an early afternoon takeoff for our return flight to Charlotte. The weather was bad to the south so, after waiting around most of the day for it to clear, we went into Harrisburg and got a room at the Penn-Harris Hotel. That evening, Bill told me a little about his experiences flying in New Guinea in 1942–43. The 3d Attack Group was one of the first units operating in the Southwest Pacific at the beginning of the war. It was a desperate time. The Japanese threatened to take Port Moresby on New Guinea's south coast and push on to Australia. Neel had had some close calls, but he told his stories with gallows humor and all of them were interesting to me.

Bill was awarded the Distinguished Flying Cross (DFC) for flying across the Owen Stanley Mountains from the north coast on one engine while returning to base after a mission. He described how he tried twice to get up to a low pass through the mountains only to have the remaining engine overheat before he could gain enough altitude to cross over. On his third and last attempt, Bill flew parallel to the ridge in order to judge his rate of climb better and was able to get high enough to slip through the pass before the overheated engine lost power. "It was Thanksgiving Day and a turkey dinner was waiting at Port Moresby so there was an incentive," Bill said, smiling.

He surprised me later by saying, "I hope they don't send me over for another tour because I'll never come back." The thought of not coming back had occurred to me, too, but I always quickly dismissed it. Bill's comment was totally unexpected and out of character. He was very serious that evening as we talked over dinner and his fears later proved to be prophetic.

Our last training exercise was an air-to-air gunnery mission conducted at Myrtle Beach, South Carolina. The 46th Bomb Group had a half-dozen or so A-20s based permanently at Myrtle Beach, so we had to endure a long, hot trip by truck from Charlotte through largely rural and poor farm country. My impression of rural southern life gained during that trip was of a procession of unpainted shacks built on posts or rocks, unscreened windows, shoeless and overall-clad forms sprawled on front porches, and a few scattered country towns—with hardly a white face to be seen.

The village of Myrtle Beach was small. Several small hotels were scattered through the area and there was a tacky amusement park with only half of its concessions open. There were few vacationers in sight. The airfield was on the beach to the south of town and we were housed in a typical one-story tarpaper barracks. It was a short walk from the barracks across the coast road to the beach. The sand stretched southward into the distance with hardly a building or person to be seen. A weekend at the beach was not hard to take, even if there were no vacationing females, or civilians for that matter, frolicking about.

A number of Negro fighter pilots were also undergoing training at Myrtle Beach. It was my first encounter with black pilots, although we knew the army was training a number of them at Tuskegee, Alabama. The army was segregated in 1944, particularly on southern bases, but we all shared the same chow line at Myrtle Beach's small officers' club. The fighter pilots were flying P-39 Airacobras and displayed an air of self-confidence as they rolled fast along the taxiways with the side windows rolled down, their fingers drumming on the top of the canopy in time to music coming through the radio compass.

The training missions, all of which were relatively simple, consisted of both aerial gunnery and dropping bombs on floating targets not far offshore. On some of the gunnery flights only the gunner in the dorsal turret fired, while on others the pilot fired his fixed forward guns at the towed target. It was the middle of May, and my strongest impression is of the heat in the cockpit while we waited at the end of the runway for our turn to take off.

The lone night mission involved making a single pass over a lighted floating target and dropping a hundred-pound practice bomb. The real challenge was not scoring a hit on the target, but taking off at night over the beach toward the dark ocean with no visible horizon. A "dim-out" was being enforced along the coast at that time, so even looking back toward land gave no pronounced reference point. Heading down the runway toward the darkness with no horizon showing brought back the words of Lieutenant Gunnarson at Marana: "When you come off the runway at night, *always* go on the instruments." After reaching five hundred feet the horizon could easily be detected on a clear night, but the transition from the ground to flying visually required some care.

Two members of our squadron, Jim Pelton of Grand Rapids, Michigan, and John Higgins of South Somerset, Massachusetts, lost the horizon and their lives that spring at Myrtle Beach. The Owens and Peltons lived close to each other in Charlotte, perhaps in the same building, and I well recall Maury Owen trying to help Jim's wife make arrangements to get back home to Michigan. The pregnant Mrs. Pelton was having difficulty dealing with her sudden loss and Maury expressed his disgust for the army, which did little to help the young widow.

On Thursday, May 18, after flying three gunnery missions, I left Myrtle Beach in a truck at about 5 P.M. and rode back to Charlotte, arriving at midnight. My diary notes the heat in general and mechanical faults in the planes in particular at Myrtle Beach. It was not a vacation. I spent the afternoon on May 19 in the Link Trainer and thus completed the last of my requirements for the Replacement Training Unit. My flying time while in the RTU—166.35 hours, including test hops and cross-country administrative trips—was somewhat higher than the 136 hours required to complete the scheduled training sessions.

I was given a ten-day leave, part of which I spent in Sewickley and the rest visiting my folks in Wenham, Massachusetts. I returned to

Charlotte on June 5, ready to move quickly on to "The War." A number of the crews scheduled to make up the next shipment to Hunter Field outside of Savannah, Georgia, for overseas assignment had not yet completed their training, so I would have to wait.

On the morning of June 6, a radio down the hall in the BOQ interrupted my sleep with the announcement of the invasion of Europe. The big show we had been expecting was started and I thought of Ab and others from Sewickley who undoubtedly would be there. What were they facing? Who among them would not come back?

My time was now mostly my own except to put in a daily appearance at the flight line as evidence that I had not left the base for parts unknown. New planes were as intriguing as new cars and Bill Neel asked me to do the test flying on planes then being delivered to the squadron. The new H and K models were equipped with engines developing 1,750 horsepower, identical to those on the B-25, and gave noticeably better performance compared to the sixteen-hundred-horsepower engines in the G and J models. Flying the A-20 was becoming increasingly pleasurable. I felt completely at home in its cockpit and the plane responded to the controls like they were an extension of my hands and feet, at least most of the time.

One day, while flying in a new A-20H with a six-gun nose similar to the G model's, I elected to see how the ship would feel at the 412 mile-per-hour redline speed. Diving from about eight thousand feet, I watched the airspeed indicator quickly roll around the dial past the redline. When the arrow reached 425 miles per hour there was a loud *bang!* beside my head. At first I thought something had parted company with us, although the plane responded readily when I pulled out of the dive. The scare turned out to be only the side windows snapping inward on their tracks because of the buildup of air pressure at high speed.

Amongst the reading material scattered around the 53d Squadron's ready room was a flight safety bulletin with a discussion of how much altitude modern fighters lost recovering from a split-S maneuver. The figure of six thousand to ten thousand feet cited in the article seemed excessive, given my limited experience with aerobatics in the PT-22 and BT-13—but I really knew nothing about flying fighters. Other pilots loafing in the ready room seemed equally surprised and we speculated as to how much altitude an A-20 might lose. The consensus was much less than six thousand feet, but how much?

The A-20 pilot's manual contained the following quaint note: "The aircraft is designed for the duties of a medium bomber. Aerobatics and intentional spinning are not permitted." Mindful of the allegations regarding fighters, I decided to allow at least seven thousand feet above ground level before attempting a split-S and reminded myself that an A-20 should not pick up as much speed as a fighter in a dive. Then, trusting the plane to remain responsive, I rolled it over onto its back and pulled back on the control wheel. The plane dropped like a stone, the altimeter winding down rapidly. The pine trees were getting much, much larger than I had anticipated and the g-forces rather high before it finally began to recover. I remember wishing that I had started the maneuver with more altitude before the nose finally came up to the horizon. It was in this manner that I learned an A-20, even one that was lightly loaded, took most of six thousand feet to recover, and that once committed, the only way out was to continue through the half circle. The safety article was just about right!

On another afternoon, while putting some time on a new A-20H, I headed north to see if it was possible to locate the Wilkins farm near Turbeville, Virginia. The geography was easy enough to unravel and I located the unpainted Wilkins house and outbuildings in the midst of the fields without difficulty. All looked very quiet. There was nobody in sight as I dropped down and made a pass over the house low enough to be noticeable should any of the family be at home.

I looked over my shoulder as I climbed away and saw what appeared to be the entire family pouring out the back door. That called for another demonstration. Sweeping around just over the pasture fields to the east, I came up low over the chicken house, across the backyard, and then pulled up at full power with the right wing raised so it would clear the big pine trees in front. Louise Wilkins later wrote a very descriptive letter of her impressions of the flyby and the noise raised by the engines at full cry. Among the other dramatic effects of the buzz job, Louise alleged that the hens did not lay an egg for a week afterward.

On another occasion I was out putting in time with a new plane when I found myself in the vicinity of Greensboro. The Women's College buildings stood out clearly (Greensboro's population was then about fifty thousand) and, especially since the buzz numbers had not yet been painted on the nose, there seemed little reason not to impress the young ladies. I was sure that all those watching would be suitably astonished to see an A-20 roaring across the athletic field beside the dorms a hundred feet off the ground. Nevertheless, I was cautious enough not to swing around after making the one pass and I also headed toward Florence for a while rather than go directly to Charlotte.

In the officers' club that evening I was called to the phone. It was Nancy calling from Greensboro. "Did y'all fly through here this afternoon?" she asked. How sweet of her to think that it must have been me. Life was all fun and games with expensive toys during those bright days in June, 1944.

Our overseas destinations, either Europe or the Southwest Pacific, were a deep secret that would not be revealed until we reported to the assignment center at Hunter Field. I had no preference as to where I went; either place would be a totally new experience and what would happen would happen. It seemed to me that survival was mainly a matter of luck. I was comfortable with whatever the military decided to do with me. Now that the training program was over I was ready to move on, although not particularly anxious to give up the pleasant life at Charlotte.

Harriett and I had seen each other for only brief visits lasting a few days in January and again in June. However, our correspondence had been regular and lengthy for more than a year. Our feelings and intentions toward one another had become mutually serious, but I refrained from making a formal marriage proposal. The prospect of a year's separation and the unknown fortunes of war and their affect on each of us were daunting, at least to me. After discussing our circumstances, Harriett and I parted with an understanding of commitment until I returned and the future seemed more stable. A year's separation seemed likely.

As for Nancy, she firmly adhered to the ground rules she had established early on in our friendship. We thus had been able to enjoy each other's company without too many serious overtones. Although she said little about her fiancé languishing in the German POW camp and no longer wore his ring, she would continue to wait for him. Nevertheless, we had become attached to each other over the past several months of lighthearted association, so we agreed to meet when I came back and see where our personal lives stood. Who could predict what a year would bring?

On June 30, our shipment consisting of twenty-seven three-man A-20G crews and seven four-man A-20J crews reported to Hunter Field after an overnight train ride from Charlotte. Some of the G crews and all of the J crews were going to Europe, where the Ninth Air Force used A-20s mainly for medium altitude bombing missions. John Ross and Vern Schrag were assigned to fly planes across the North Atlantic, an interesting challenge. We three from Class 44-A had a last beer, shook hands, and wished each other "Good Luck!"

On July 2 the crews assigned to the Southwest Pacific, which included mine, boarded a troop train destined for Hamilton Field just north of San Francisco. We were going to New Guinea and the war experienced by Bill Neel and George Farr, our dedicated leaders in the 53d Squadron. The die had been cast. I had faith that events would somehow play out in my favor.

Chapter 4

ACROSS THE BROAD PACIFIC

AIRCREWS WERE DISPATCHED to the Pacific war zones by both sea and air. I suppose that the method was dictated by the urgency for getting replacements out to the combat groups. Our A-20 crews had Air Priority and our stay at Hamilton Field was less than a week.

There was just time enough for one afternoon and evening in San Francisco. We had received a stern briefing against loose talk but any spy in those times had only to wander into the Mark Hopkins Hotel and hang around the bar and listen. Thousands during the war years had a last drink at the Top of the Mark before shipping out, usually with exchanges of solemn promises to meet their drinking friends back there in some future year—someday.

Departing pilots traditionally left their calling cards stuck on the ceiling as evidence for their buddies that they had been there. The Mark was crowded. There was hardly any elbowroom and it was thick with smoke when we looked in, so, tradition or no, we went someplace else to have a beer or two. Mainly, though, I remember the ride into San Francisco in the back of a six-by-six truck and the surprisingly cold temperature for July. It was a long-lasting impression of the climate in San Francisco.

Shortly after sunset on the evening of July 12 our crew loaded into a four-engine Douglas C-54 transport plane for the overnight flight to Honolulu. The passenger list included six A-20 crews (eighteen personnel) and three or four colonels, plus the plane's four crewmen. The C-54, the military variant of the Douglas DC-4, was a cargo transport with a metal trough along each side of the cabin for seats. The troughs were designed for passengers (paratroopers) wearing seat-pack parachutes.

Since we had neither chutes nor cushions, they did not lend themselves to comfort on our long flight.

Our luggage and some priority freight was stacked and tied down in the cabin's center aisle. A Red Cross lady presented each of us with a small cloth bag containing shaving materials, writing paper, a sewing kit, and other odds and ends, and a sergeant checked off our names as we clambered aboard. Surely we deserved a band playing as we went off to war, but such departures were just the usual evening routine at Hamilton Field in those days.

Hamilton Field was located a short distance north of San Rafael and as the C-54 climbed into the dark sky out over San Francisco Bay there was still a red line marking the sunset on the western horizon. The hills surrounding the west side of the bay were in deep shadow with only scattered lights showing like stars on black velvet, while San Francisco was easily visible even with the wartime coastal dim-out in effect. We climbed out from the Golden Gate over the featureless ocean and each of us probably thought briefly that some on that plane would not be seeing San Francisco again. I wondered how long it would be until I would be coming back, but I had no regrets about starting out on this big adventure.

There was little to be seen through the cabin window once we were out over the open ocean. The moon came up early and outlined some fair-weather clouds above us while the path of moonlight far below indicated the surface of the sea. Our colonel passengers had obviously made the trip several times and were engaged in conversation among themselves about places and people they had just seen while in the States. There was no reason for them to pay particular attention to a bunch of green second lieutenants heading toward the active war and the unknown.

Several card games were started on blankets spread out on the cabin floor and some of us tried to read by the weak illumination of the cabin lights. By midnight, most of us had followed the colonels' example and were wrapped up in blankets asleep on the cabin floor. The creak of the plane and the steady roar of the engines in the uninsulated cabin did not keep me from falling asleep on the hard metal with only a thin blanket for a pad.

The first signs of daybreak were showing through the cabin windows when I woke up. The rest of the passengers still seemed to be asleep as I made my way forward to see what the flight deck looked like. The C-54 belonged to the Air Transport Command but was being flown by a TWA airline crew consisting of two pilots and a navigator who had been contracted for the flight, with a military crew chief riding along to oversee the plane's servicing and maintenance. Dawn was breaking behind us and I knew we should be approaching Honolulu and Hickam Field before long.

All was relaxed on the flight deck. The pilot was sound asleep with his seat pushed back and his head cradled on his rolled-up jacket. The plane was flying on autopilot and the copilot had his seat pushed well back, his shoes off, and his feet propped up on the control pedestal. The navigator greeted me and the copilot looked up from the paperback he was reading, glanced at the instrument panel, and went back to his book without comment. The clouds to the west were beginning to turn to pink while the ocean below was still in the dark of night. The C-54 hardly shuddered in the smooth morning air and the navigator offered the information that we should be seeing the ten-thousand-foot volcanic peak on the island of Maui shortly.

For me it was an impressive sunrise, looking out over the trackless Pacific that until then had been only a description in a book. In the Sewickley High School library I had read everything available about the islands of the Pacific: *The Cruise of the Snark*, *Seven Seas on a Shoestring*, *Mutiny on the Bounty*, and stories by Conrad, Villiers, and Von Luckner. Those were much more interesting than the dry assignments for Old Lady Kerr's English class. Now, somewhere ahead lay Tahiti, the Marquesas, the ghost of Richard Halliburton, and perhaps native maidens resembling Dorothy Lamour, supine of course. My anticipation for the sights in a part of the world that had seemed so out of reach pushed aside more serious thoughts about the purpose of the trip.

Suddenly, the outboard engine on the starboard side backfired loudly and the prop slowed before picking up again as the C-54 gave a shudder. The copilot's feet hit the floor and the pilot was suddenly awake and alert. We all looked out the window toward the right side but there were no ominous signs from the engines. One engine was running a little rough, but an adjustment of the mixture control smoothed it out.

The pilot stretched, inquired as to our location, and moved his seat up into position with the observation that we might as well lose some altitude. The cone of the mountain on Maui was now clearly visible, its brown shape poking through the puffy white clouds to the south of our course. In my simple tourist's view, our trip was off to a good start.

We landed at Hickam Field in Honolulu about breakfast time and were warned not to leave the field: as soon as the plane could be serviced we would be off on the next leg. Most of the airfield damage had been erased in the two and one-half years since the attack on Pearl Harbor, but some of the hangars still showed chips out of the walls and broken masonry.

We wandered around the tarmac while waiting for the plane to be readied, each with our own thoughts about this place where the war with the Japanese had begun on December 7, 1941. What a dramatic event! How had it happened? Two friendly ladies running a Red Cross canteen handed out doughnuts and coffee and responded to our questions. They had probably answered the same questions about the attack from every new arrival that came their way.

It turned out to be more than just a short stop for fuel and minor service: we were on the ground for about six hours before the crew chief finally announced that we were nearly ready to go. It was past noon and box lunches were loaded aboard for the second leg of our trip. The colonels had left us after being overheard discussing their chances of spending at least a week in Honolulu. One of them was overheard saying, "Good old George can arrange a delay for us."

We looked out the windows at Pearl Harbor as the plane climbed away from Hickam Field. There was still some wreckage in the water, and streaks of seeping oil could be seen here and there. The mountains in the background rose into the scattered, low-hanging clouds. Soon the island was lost in the humid haze.

The plane was now on a southerly heading and the early rumor was that we were heading for Christmas Island. It was a meaningless location to most of us as we had only a vague idea of the geography and distances involved. After a while the word came back from the cockpit that the winds and fuel would permit us to fly direct to Canton Island. That was another meaningless location, so one of the lieutenants went up to the cockpit and checked the chart. He reported back that Canton was somewhat farther west of Christmas Island and below the equator in the Phoenix group. We caught a glimpse of one or two small reefs in the vast expanse of water that afternoon, but it seemed to us a remarkable feat of navigation when the small patch of sand that was Canton Island finally appeared. I held our navigator in considerable respect.

It was twilight when we took off from barren Canton after only a brief refueling stop. Our next stepping-stone was Tarawa in the Gilbert Islands, about twelve hundred miles to the west and just north of the equator. Tarawa had been in the headlines the previous November when the marines captured it after a ferocious battle that was a predictor of the way the Japanese would fight for the other islands they held.

We reached Tarawa a little after midnight. Even in the darkness, the total devastation of the island was evident in the shattered stumps of palm trees and huge mounds of broken equipment. The warm air carried a combination of the odors of rotting vegetation and the bodies still entombed in pillboxes that had been covered over with a thin layer of sand. We had had nothing to eat since the box lunches, so we piled into several trucks for a ride to the mess hall. The meal was an introduction to the fare we would come to expect in the Southwest Pacific: C-ration stew, thick-crusted bread, and coffee with canned evaporated milk. In one long afternoon we had flown from civilized Honolulu to a place that was unquestionably in the war zone.

The stop at Tarawa was short, not much longer than was needed to re-fuel the plane and stretch our legs. The moonlight sharpened the outlines of the broken palm trees, and we were able to see the hulk of a ship caught on the reef offshore. The smell of decay was everywhere. The crew chief added a little excitement for the next leg when he pointed out that we would be passing within sight of Nauru Island, which the Japanese still held. Later, the outline of Nauru could be made out some distance off the starboard wing and we all tried to catch a glimpse of it. After learning that we would be landing on Guadalcanal in the Solomons chain in the morn-ing, we sacked out on the floor of the plane for a second night.

At sunup, as we were crossing over Malaita Island on the northern edge of the Solomons, we looked down into the clear water between Florida Island and Guadalcanal. They called it "Iron Bottom Sound," and here and there we could make out the shadowy outlines of sunken ships. Sev-eral wrecked ships were visible nearby and on the shore of Guadalcanal itself as we approached Henderson Field.

Guadalcanal had been much in the news in the fall of 1942 and early 1943—until the Japanese army was finally forced to evacuate. By mid-1944, Henderson Field was a rear area of the war, a large support base and refueling stop for air transport traffic. Once in the newspaper headlines, it had been cleaned up and enlarged while the war moved on to the next en-emy strong point. We were becoming accustomed to the warm, humid air that greeted us when we stepped down from the still cool cabin. Ground personnel directed us to a nearby camp area. After two nights of sleeping on the floor of the C-54's cabin, few of us were feeling very frisky.

One recollection of that flight across the Pacific in 1944 deserves mention: I was introduced to DDT—the then-new miracle insecti-cide—and aerosol spray bottles. Before each landing, the crew chief would appear at the front of the cabin holding a steel, olive-drab-painted canister in his hand and announce: "I'm gonna disinfect the airplane. Try not to breathe the mist from this thing." Then, with the canister spewing out an impressive fog, the crew chief would walk the length of the cabin. By the time he was done, you could hardly make out the win-dows on the opposite side. This performance was apparently an edict of

Air Transport Command since it was carried out before every stop. As I write this, the use of DDT has long since been banned in the United States. More than three decades ago it was discovered to be deadly to animals, fish, and people as well as insects—all of which is a bit amusing in light of what we inhaled in that C-54. Later we were issued our own "bug bombs" with which to spray our tents, mosquito bars, and in general slathered DDT around liberally. More than fifty years afterward, I have yet to experience any ill effects of note.

We were supposed to continue our flight to New Guinea about mid-morning, but upon returning to the flight line after breakfast we learned that there would be a delay. The crew chief and several other mechanics were poking around the nosewheel well trying to locate the source of a hydraulic leak. We stood around watching the investigation for a half-hour or so and then were told to make ourselves comfortable at the nearby replacement camp until called. The repairs might be done by noon. I found an empty cot in one of the transient tents and was soon oblivious to the enchantments of our tropical surroundings.

We lounged around the transient camp all afternoon as the problem with the hydraulic system proved to be elusive. We could see a line of low, green hills across Henderson Field and we speculated about the possibility of there still being any Japanese out there. All now seemed peaceful on Guadalcanal, at least from our viewpoint in the tent camp, but there really were some stragglers out there in the jungle. A few of them did not come out until several years after the war ended. Some of the men in our group took a walk over to the beach where the hulks of sunken ships could be seen. I decided to lie down and try to get some more sleep.

There were five or six veteran B-24 pilots in the transient camp waiting for transportation back to the States. They inquired about the destination of our C-54 and speculated about the chances of catching a ride to someplace where they could take a ship home rather than wait for air transportation. We eyed these veterans with interest and some respect while noting that they seemed a little reserved toward us. Their uniforms were faded almost white and frayed around the edges. Their complexions had a uniformly yellow tint that was not hidden by their tans. These old-timers were undoubtedly amused by our innocent questions about what we might expect in New Guinea, but they did offer us some pointers that seemed honest. One thing we learned from them was that the bright yellow Atabrine pill taken daily to ward off the effects of malaria was the cause of their yellow skin. Dissolved in water, Atabrine made a good dye, intentionally or not.

While the veteran pilots seemed to give us more or less straight answers and advice, we quickly found that the enlisted men running the
transient camp could spin more than a few wild yarns. They told us
about strange lights over in the distant low hills and warned us that we
would probably hear a few shots after dark. One annoyance reported to
us with straight faces was the habit hungry Japanese stragglers had of
joining the chow line when it was dark. However, we were assured that
this happened only once or twice a week. As we lined up for dinner and
the shadows of the palm trees started to lengthen, I made sure that the
face of the man behind me belonged to a GI.

While the work on the hydraulic system continued under lights, most
of us wandered over to watch the evening movie. Sitting under the stars
on rough benches and watching the movie (enemy stragglers supposedly
enjoyed watching movies, too) was unexpected civilization in the tropics and a daily event in most units of any size. Whatever the feature
might have been that evening we did not get to see the conclusion as an
announcement at about 9 P.M. directed us to report back to the flight line
for loading. The B-24 pilots joined us for the ride to our next stop: Milne
Bay on the eastern end of New Guinea. There they hoped to catch a
troopship headed home. They really did not trust airplanes (or so they
said) for the long flight over water, especially if it was to be made in a
war-weary bomber being flown back to the States.

The night was clear when we left Guadalcanal but clouds began to
build up as we proceeded toward the west. By the time we reached the
vicinity of Milne Bay, the plane was in an area of heavy rain and the pilot sent word back that we would not be attempting a landing. The B-24
veterans took the announcement philosophically. One of them commented that he really was not looking for any exciting flying such as instrument landings. The rain finally ended before we landed at Port
Moresby at about 2 A.M.

It had been a long trip, but we were on New Guinea where there was
fighting going on somewhere to the north and west. Most of us had an
unclear idea of the size or geography of this large island. It is the second
largest in the world, covering 306,000 square miles. Only Greenland is
larger. Counting the day we had lost crossing the International Date
Line, it was July 16 when we arrived in New Guinea. The B-24 pilots
wished us luck and went off in search of the next plane headed for Milne
Bay. The C-54 flight crew had had a very long day and gave us a tired
wave as they slumped off toward the operations shack to check in and find
a bed. We transients were instructed to load our baggage into several GI
trucks that had arrived to take us to the replacement camp located several

miles from the airstrip. My curiosity was aroused, but all we could see of this new land was the dirt road and a blur of dense, lush jungle.

It was 3 A.M. by the time we checked into the 268th Replacement Company. The duty sergeant there directed us toward a row of tents dimly visible in the gloom. "Take any empty cots you can find and come back in the morning." Some of the men in our group proceeded to go in search of beds; others elected to sprawl out in the orderly room and wait for daylight. I sat down at a typewriter and proceeded to write a letter home while the duty sergeant retired to his cot in the corner of the office.

The Port Moresby replacement camp was not a pleasant place to spend any length of time. The entire area had the appearance of months of neglect, probably because those in charge knew that the camp would be moved to the north side of the island sooner rather than later. The tents assigned to us were rotten, there was a shortage of usable cots, and mosquito bars without holes were hard to find. The mess hall was a screen-enclosed building, but the flies had little difficulty getting inside through the holes—and they were of a variety not easily intimidated. Only the thick-crusted army bread and the murky coffee steaming in a fifty-gallon drum made the menu of C-Ration stew or Australian corned beef (bully beef) palatable for me. The latrines were full and noisome, even from a distance, and there was no apparent effort to dig new ones. The 268th Replacement Company camp was a mess.

The war had been carried to the Japanese on New Guinea's north coast, across the Owen Stanley Mountains, by the landings at Nadzab and Lae the previous September. A number of airfields were built north of the mountains in early 1944, and the once dominant Japanese airpower in the region had largely been eliminated. In April, Gen. Douglas MacArthur initiated his strategy of bypassing the larger Japanese troop concentrations, in particular the large base at Wewak, by landing at Hollandia some one hundred miles farther west. By the midsummer of 1944, the Allied advance was reaching toward the western part of New Guinea, with airfields operational at Hollandia and a hundred miles beyond at Wakde Island. More airfields were under construction on Biak Island, some 330 miles west of Hollandia, and plans were under way for an invasion even farther to the west, at Noemfoor Island, Sansapor on the New Guinea coast, and nearby Middleburg Island. With the Fifth Air Force's three A-20 groups all now located along the north coast and far from Port Moresby, we hoped that our stay in the replacement camp would be short.

Port Moresby was a place that had been much in the news early in the war, so one afternoon I decided to catch a ride into town to check it out.

The road from the camp skirted along the shore on a narrow shelf beside a steep hillside with here and there a palm tree overhanging—just as a tropical island was supposed to look, I thought. The buildings that made up the town seemed to be grouped along three or four streets ranging back from the sizable land-locked harbor. Well out from the docks was a ship lying on its side but still very much intact. It was the MV *Macdhui*, which had been sunk by bombs in June, 1942. Out on a reef on the ocean side was the hulk of a ship that had been used for skip-bombing practice.

Port Moresby fulfilled my romantic expectations. The place had a lazy air about it and there was little evidence left to suggest that it had once been the key port for the Allied forces barely hanging on as the Japs pushed over the mountains. I sat on the veranda of an Australian officers' club overlooking the blue Pacific. Canned tomato juice, the only drink available in the afternoon, was served by a fuzzy-wuzzy in a lap-lap. One could well imagine that Trader Horn might appear at any minute.

One day I was sitting in the mess hall keeping the flies in flight with one hand and spooning C rations with the other when a familiar face appeared. It was Jerry Shannon from Ford City, Pennsylvania, whom I had not seen since we parted company at the Marana Basic School the previous October. The quiet, retiring, serious Jerry, whom I had first met in the barracks at Nashville trying to look military in his oversized uniform, had changed considerably during the intervening months.

Jerry had been selected for the AT-6 program at Marana—evidence that he really could fly, although he had continued to worry incessantly about check rides. The self-effacing Jerry had become a confident fighter pilot type, and he regaled me with his adventures at Luke Field flying P-40s and later P-39s, P-63s, and finally P-38s. Jerry said he had been stuck in the replacement camp for two weeks and was still waiting for his next assignment. We spent a long afternoon reminiscing. We exchanged news about the western Pennsylvania area and wondered what had become of Dick Slaeker, the third member of our cadet trio at Marana. Afterward, I reflected on the noticeable change the Air Corps experience had made in Jerry Shannon and wondered if I looked as different to him.

A Combat Replacement Training Center (CRTC) was operating at Port Moresby. Its purpose was to indoctrinate newly assigned pilots in the procedures used in the combat squadrons. The schooling for A-20 and B-25 pilots usually lasted one or two weeks and included a refresher in skip bombing using the hulk out on the reef outside of the harbor plus some exposure to New Guinea's seemingly endless, jungle-covered terrain. Several A-20 crews that had arrived a week or so earlier were en-

Snapped shortly after my arrival at the 268th Replacement Company, Port Moresby, Papua New Guinea, in mid-July, 1944. Our stay in the rundown camp there was fortunately short, and we moved on to the 312th Bomb Group at Hollandia, Dutch New Guinea, where the veteran pilots called us "fresh meat."

rolled at the CRTC and I wondered how much longer it would be before we were assigned. After a week dragged by we were told that the CRTC was being transferred to Nadzab on the north side of the island and that we would undergo our precombat training there. This probably meant a delay before we started flying, but at least we would be getting out of the replacement camp and the poorest living conditions I had thus far experienced.

Most pilots had prejudices against various types of planes, usually based on rumored idiosyncrasies or perceived flying performance. Such attitudes were often adopted after listening to stories around the bar rather than any personal experience. In transports, the Douglas C-47, affectionately known as the "Gooney Bird," was considered to be as safe as a church, whereas the newer Curtiss C-46 Commando, notwithstanding its better performance, was viewed as unreliable and not to be trusted. In heavy bombers, the B-17 was believed to be strong, stable, and safe, compared to the B-24, which had a wing that looked to be too skinny to fly and an electrical system that was rumored to be completely unreliable. We who had never been close to a B-24 viewed it as a dubious proposition and had comments aplenty when we learned we were going to fly to Nadzab in one.

Bombers make poor transports, and it seemed almost dangerous for fifteen passengers and their luggage plus the plane's regular ten-man crew to attempt the trip over the rugged Owen Stanley Mountains in a fully combat-equipped B-24. The first nine passengers to board found seats in the waist behind the bomb bay or crawled up into the bombardier's compartment in the nose. Six of us had to line up on the narrow catwalk running through the bomb bay, wrap an arm or leg or both around a vertical brace to steady ourselves, and hope our pilot was a smooth flyer. None of us passengers were provided parachutes.

The B-24 (fortunately it was a new one) waddled out to the end of the runway at Seven-Mile Drome with its poorly secured load and the pilot paused to check the engines. One of the members of the catwalk crowd loudly commented, "If this sonofabitch doesn't fly I'm going to be pissed off!" His wisecrack helped relieve our apprehensions somewhat.

After a successful takeoff I noticed that the top turret behind the flight deck was unoccupied, so I climbed up and claimed it for the rest of the trip. This was as good an observation post as could be desired and offered a seat and safety belt, too. The Owen Stanley Mountains form New Guinea's rugged spine and there were jungle-covered peaks rising up to twelve thousand feet in the area over which we flew. What an impressive sight! I could now appreciate Bill Neel's story about the difficulties he had experienced flying an A-20 on one engine through one of those high, narrow passes. He deserved the DFC they gave him.

Although our flight was fairly early in the morning, clouds were already forming around the mountains. By afternoon the weather would most likely be solid at the higher elevations, but for the time being our B-

24 was able to weave between the gathering clouds and soon the Owen Stanleys were behind us. The engines kept running, the skinny wings did not break, and the pilot eventually began to let down on the north side of the island to land at the collection of landing strips known as Nadzab.

Nadzab, located in the wide valley formed by the Markham River, was about fifteen miles inland from a coastal village named Lae. The land was mostly covered with coarse *kunai* grass that grew three to ten feet high. The thick jungle was restricted to the sides of the mountains in the distance. Until a month or so prior to our arrival, Nadzab had been the main U.S. base with a number of bomber and fighter groups operating from several airstrips. It was now a supply dump and staging area and soon would be home to both the replacement camp and the CRTC. The tents we were assigned were not much of an improvement over those we had left, but the camp was clean and a steady breeze through the valley moderated the heat.

It was understood that we would go though the training center's course of instruction before being assigned to one of the three A-20 groups: 3d Attack Group (a prewar designation), 312th Bomb Group, or 417th Bomb Group. There was talk that the indoctrination program was to be expanded to four weeks for A-20 crews, a discouraging rumor if true. Most of us felt that we had been trained to the eyeballs and that any additional training would just be repetitive. Moreover, the training unit's move from Port Moresby would take a week or so. In the meantime, we would just have to wait for the planes and personnel to arrive.

None of us expressed any regrets when, after only a week, we received orders to proceed to our combat groups without additional flying training. On July 27, the crews led by William Cornelius, Bill Montgomery, Grant Peterson, Thomas Riggs, Robert Irvin, Robert Spencer, and me were ordered to the 312th Bomb Group at Hollandia in Dutch New Guinea. That same afternoon, three crews were instructed to meet a 312th Bomb Group B-25 at the airstrip for the flight west. Our luggage was loaded into the plane's bomb bay while the nine of us crawled aboard and found places to sit, stand, or lie in the tunnel over the bomb bay. By now we took the lack of parachutes and Mae West life preservers (or seats) as a matter of course.

Our sudden assignment to a combat unit did not seem strange to me at the time, but the 312th had lost five crews during its July operations and replacements were urgently needed.

From Nadzab we flew to the northwest and made a stop at an airstrip called Gusap. It had been the 312th's base until early July and a small group of men were still dismantling the camp and packing equipment to be flown up to Hollandia, some four hundred miles farther west on the coast. After a brief stop we were again on our way and climbed up from the Ramu River valley and over the ridge to the coast. The pilot flying the B-25 that day considerately stayed low and gave us a sightseeing tour, probably understanding our curiosity and desire to see this strange land.

Not all of the ground was covered with dense jungle. There were a number of large areas covered with seven-foot-high *kunai* grass and only an occasional tree. We saw a C-47 that showed little damage sitting in a large patch of grass having made a belly landing sometime earlier. Flying along a hundred feet over the sea, our pilot turned west and stayed less than a mile off the Japanese-occupied coast east of Wewak. We could see an enemy truck moving along the shore road with two or three soldiers standing on the running boards, probably keeping a wary eye on our B-25 and ready to jump should it begin to turn toward them. Wewak was still dangerous. It was the headquarters for the enemy's Eighteenth Army and home to upwards of eighty thousand troops. Our sightseeing pilot took a prudent turn out to sea and around the offshore islands before continuing along the coast. That trip to Hollandia is still a vivid memory.

Hollandia was in western New Guinea, which had been part of the Dutch East Indies. The Japanese seized the area in 1942 and it had served as the main base for Japanese air force units in New Guinea after the base at Wewak had become unusable for air operations after the Allies began bombing it in 1943. The large main harbor and town of Hollandia were located on Humboldt Bay. Tanahmerah Bay was thirty miles or so in a direct line to the west on the other side of Mount Cyclops. The Hollandia complex consisted of three airstrips located in a valley between the two bays. From east to west they were: Cyclops, Sentani, and Hollandia. Lying south of the airstrips was Lake Sentani, a sizable body of water dotted with several islands. The Cyclops mountain range, with peaks up to seven thousand feet, ran between the valley and the sea.

Construction was still going on and there seemed to be plenty of mud and considerable confusion on the Hollandia strip as our B-25 picked its way along the dirt taxiway to a hardstand. We crawled out, unloaded our luggage, and began to survey what was to be our new home. It was a rough-looking place with piles of wrecked Japanese equipment and planes scattered about as evidence that the enemy had been gone for only three months.

Jeeps soon appeared to take us to the 312th's camp, which was several miles away in the direction of Tanahmerah Bay. We had arrived in the war zone at last.

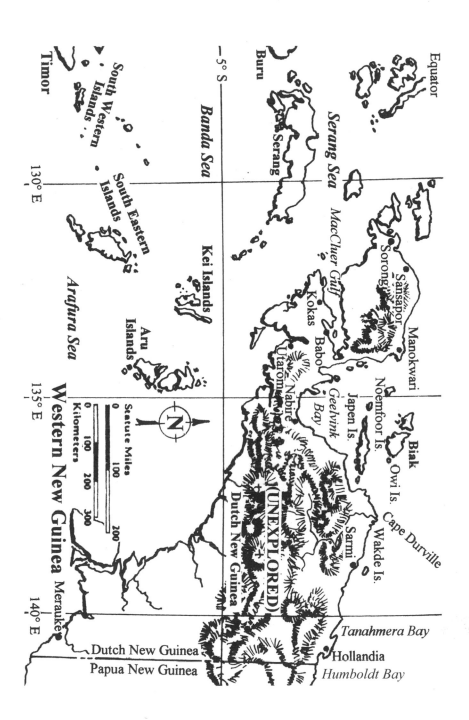

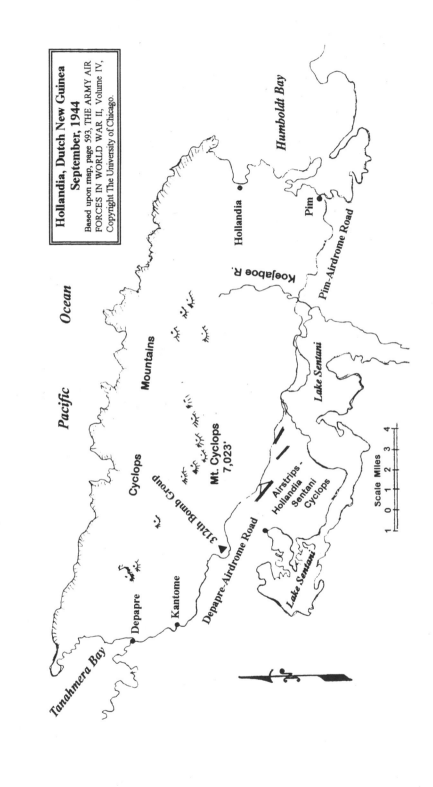

Hollandia, Dutch New Guinea
September, 1944
Based upon map, page 593, THE ARMY AIR
FORCES IN WORLD WAR II, Volume IV,
Copyright The University of Chicago.

Humboldt Bay

Hollandia

Pim

Koelaboe R.

Pim-Airdrome Road

Pacific   Ocean

Mountains

Cyclops

Mt. Cyclops
7,023'

312th Bomb Group

Lake Sentani

Airstrips -
Hollandia
Sentani
Cyclops

Lake Sentani

Depapre-Airdrome Road

Depapre

Kantome

Tanahmera Bay

Scale Miles

1 0 1 2 3 4

Chapter 5

AT HOME IN THE 389TH SQUADRON

THE 312TH BOMB GROUP CAMP was located about two miles from the Hollandia Airstrip along the road that eventually led to Tanahmerah Bay. The engineers were hard at work building a road out of what was not much more than a trail. The mud was deep, so deep that the jeep in which we were riding stalled a couple of times. The mountain range off to the right of this muddy track wore a halo of clouds with plumes of vapor moving off the peaks, evidence of some air movement. However, there was no breeze in the sweltering valley where we were and the temperature and humidity were both close to a hundred degrees. Rumbles of thunder up on the mountain indicated there would soon be some more rain, either on us or on the upper slopes.

The 312th, like most U.S. Army Air Forces medium bomber groups in World War II, had four combat squadrons. Our replacement crews were divided up to fill vacancies in these outfits as needed. Grant Peterson and I were assigned to the 389th Squadron, Cornelius and Montgomery went to the 386th, and Spencer and Irvin went to the 387th. On the same orders, but not in our shipment from the States, 1st Lt. James E. Strunck was assigned to the 388th. Another pilot, 2d Lt. Frank T. Happy, was transferred from the 22d Bomb Group, which flew B-24s, to the 386th Squadron.

Peterson and I, along with our gunners and baggage, were dropped off in front of the 389th's orderly room tent to make our introductions. We went inside and gave our orders to the squadron executive officer, Capt. Fred Wood. After taking care of the formalities, he led Peterson and me along a narrow path in the jungle surrounding the cleared camp area. The officers' tents for all squadrons were located beneath the shade of the tall trees, not far from a fast running stream that tumbled down a narrow valley from the nearby mountainside. The threatening clouds we had seen began to spill rain onto the thick foliage above us as Captain Wood stuck his head into a tent and said: "Here's two new boys. Give 'em a bed." He motioned us inside and then made a run for his own tent just as the rain started coming down in a sudden deluge.

The occupants of the tent, 1st Lts. Calvin B. Slade and Eliot "Babe" Young, looked up from a game of cribbage as we entered. As we exchanged introductions they looked a bit amused at our apparent bewilderment and pointed to two of the cots. "You guys can take those for the time being. Eddy is on leave in Sydney and the other sack is empty." Walter Van, we soon learned, had occupied the other cot until he failed to return from a mission to Babo in western New Guinea on July 9. The 389th Squadron had lost three planes on the Babo mission, hence the need for crew replacements.

We dumped our B-4 bags on the vacant cots and surveyed our temporary quarters, which were illuminated by a single bare light bulb. The sixteen-by-sixteen-foot pyramidal tent was raised on posts about two and one-half feet above the ground and had a wooden floor. A frame had been built to support the roof. Mosquito netting was tacked around the outside of the frame to obviate the need for mosquito bars over the cots and the canvas sides were raised outward to provide wide eaves.

The furnishings consisted of four folding cots, several homemade chairs, and a crude table. Flight suits and other clothing hung from nails driven into the center pole or the side framing. Our tent was typical of the quarters for officers in the 312th at Hollandia. The enlisted men were housed in similar tents located out in the cleared area.

Peterson and I tried to carry on a conversation with Slade and Young over the background roar of the deluge hitting the canvas roof. They told us we would have to set up our own tent and relocate before Lt. Albert Eddy returned from Sydney to reclaim his bed. It may have been that they expected another of the pilots on leave, Gordon Gerould, to occupy the fourth cot in the tent when he returned. Gerould had been on the disastrous Babo low-level mission (his thirty-sixth) on July 9. Afterward he had become depressed to the point of being sent on leave by the flight surgeon. The news that we could look forward to leaves in Australia every couple of months was an unexpected bright spot in the indoctrination we received on that dark, rainy afternoon.

Officers were responsible for locating and setting up their own quarters. The sixteen-by-sixteen-foot tents were available from the supply room and lumber for building a raised floor and frame came from an army sawmill located some distance away. The catch for us came when Slade suggested that a fifth of liquor would help encourage the sergeant running the mill to find available lumber. Without an offer of booze of some kind, the diligent sergeant invariably found that all of his lumber was needed elsewhere. Unfortunately, neither Pete nor I had thought to fill our B-4 bags with any of the heavy bottles before leaving San Francisco. Moreover, I was surprised to learn that the patriotic warriors out here in the war zone might practice bribery.

We spent the remainder of that rainy afternoon quizzing our hosts about the 312th Bomb Group. The group had been formed at Savannah, Georgia, in 1942 as a dive-bomber outfit. First equipped with the Vultee A-31 Vengeance and then the Douglas A-24 Dauntless dive-bombers, the 312th trained at Savannah and then moved to De Ridder, Louisiana. The A-31 looked like a great dive-bomber but proved to be difficult to maintain, whereas the A-24 was an obsolescent design. In any event, dive-bombing tactics, which had proven so successful in the early phases of the war in Europe, had changed. The result was that the 312th was reequipped with Curtiss P-40 Warhawk fighters and transferred to the California desert for additional training.

Shipped overseas to Australia in November, 1943, the 312th moved up to New Guinea in December to Gusap, the isolated airstrip near the Ramu River where we had stopped briefly earlier that afternoon. After flying a few missions in P-40s with limited success in late December and the first half of January, 1944, the 312th was withdrawn from combat and began retraining on the A-20 at Port Moresby.

The tactics developed in New Guinea by the 3rd Attack Group and the legendary Col. Pappy Gunn using A-20s and B-25s modified for ground strafing and low-level bombing (rather than medium altitude) had proved very successful. This caused the Fifth Air Force commander, Maj. Gen. George Kenny, to call for more ground-strafing attack groups and led to the 312th's conversion.

The transition to the larger twin-engine plane was a big step for most of the original 312th pilots, many of whom had flown only single-engine aircraft. Although they had many hours of flying experience, the A-20s and the tactics they would employ were new to them. By the middle of March, 1944, the entire group had been reequipped with A-20s and was operational back at Gusap in the low-level, light bombardment role.

Both Young and Slade had been replacement pilots assigned to the 312th after it arrived in New Guinea. They had gone through A-20 RTU training with the 46th Bomb Group at Will Rogers Field outside of Oklahoma City before that group moved to Charlotte. They both joined the 312th at Port Moresby, although Young had arrived in Australia in late 1943 and Slade a little later, in January, 1944. By the time we met them they had been flying missions since the group began its A-20 operations at Gusap.

In the summer of 1944 the 312th was operating all over the western end of Dutch New Guinea, mainly making low-level attacks on Japanese airfields. It also provided ground support for troops that had landed on the coast at Atape east of Hollandia and at Sarmi, about a hundred miles to the west, opposite the island of Wakde.

In general, the original members of an organization look upon later arrivals as green newcomers. It was true that we had less flying time and experience; we would be newcomers for some months to come. Although most of the replacement pilots probably had more twin-engine time than the original members of the 312th, we understood that this in no way offset our lack of combat experience. In time we replacements would become integrated into the club, but it would not happen overnight.

The rain slacked off toward evening on that first day and Babe and Cal escorted Pete and me to dinner. We were advised that khaki shirt and slacks were to be worn in the mess rather than flying suits or fatigue coveralls. The officers' mess in the 389th was a screened enclosure attached to the large enlisted mess hall. There was one long table with benches down both sides and a place for the commanding officer (CO) at one end. Two mess men served whatever was on the general mess menu, the only distinction being that we ate from enameled steel place settings rather than mess kits.

Already seated at the table were Maury Owen and Jim Rutledge, both of whom had joined the 389th a week earlier. Before Pete and I could be properly introduced to the others, one of the pilots chuckled and said, "Fresh meat!" Another announced that he thought we must be there to replace him and he wanted us treated kindly. Owen looked amused and commented, "Rut, you should have been here when it was rough." The head of the table was vacant as Major Wells, the squadron commander, was on leave.

The meal that evening—canned roast beef, dehydrated mashed potatoes, thick slabs of GI bread, canned peaches, and coffee—was a huge improvement over the replacement camp fare we had been enjoying. Not much later, the menu would be reduced to fried Spam, Spam in a loaf, or Spam salad, alternated with C-ration stew. Frequent repetition of those dishes eventually curbed my enthusiasm. The Australian bully beef that sometimes appeared turned out to be large blocks of pickled brisket or other poor cuts, an entirely different product from the small cans of corned beef used to make a favorite sandwich for lunches back home.

After supper, Captain Wood conducted Peterson and me to group headquarters, where all of the officers arriving that day were slated to meet Col. Robert Strauss, the group CO. Colonel Strauss was a 1935 West Point graduate and had been CO of the 312th since its formation in Savannah in September, 1942. Although I was, of course, unaware of the colonel's history and personality, I anticipated that this meeting would require observing the usual military customs. My hope was that I would remember the niceties of properly reporting to a superior.

We all trooped into the wooden-floored tent that served as the group orderly room and found Colonel Strauss standing by his desk. He was looking over some papers, perhaps the orders that had brought us here. He was thirty-two years old, tall, and ramrod erect. A rather thin face with a faint smile served to soften his very military bearing. We all came to the position of attention and Strauss just as quickly told us, "At ease." He then told us that he wanted to know each of his officers and that some of the formalities were more relaxed here than we may have found them to be stateside. After greeting each of us with a handshake instead of the anticipated salute and formal reporting, the colonel then talked informally about the situation in our sector of the Southwest Pacific and the 312th's role. The colonel's bearing and the eagles on his collar commanded respect, but his relaxed manner was welcome relief from the stiff demeanor of some of the West Pointers I had encountered. I would be very surprised if any in our group of newcomers that evening of July 29, 1944, was less than favorably impressed with Robert Strauss.

As we walked back to the 389th Squadron's area that evening I felt pleased with my assignment to the 312th. In the weeks and months that followed that meeting in Hollandia I never had reason to change my first impression of the colonel, even though my contacts with him were casual and few. As did each of the new pilots, Pete and I had to fly Colonel Strauss's wing a time or two. It was another example of his getting to know his pilots. I was to learn that the missions the colonel led seemed to run smoother than those led by some of the others. There is a wide gulf between a second lieutenant and a bird colonel, but Bob Strauss seemed to be a leader worth following, whatever the circumstances.

The following morning, Lt. Leonard Happ, the assistant operations officer, took Pete and me on a familiarization formation flight around the Hollandia area. He also checked us out on the procedures the group

The 312th Bomb Group moved to Hollandia in early July, 1944, and located its campsite about two miles from the Hollandia airstrip. The uneven terrain made an orderly tent layout difficult. The road in the middle-distance leads to Tanahmerah Bay, which was off to the right about fifteen to twenty miles.

followed relating to joining up, formation flying, and peeling off for landing. Hollandia, the westernmost of the three airfields, was close to the Cyclops mountain range on one side, while meandering Lake Sentani was under the downwind leg of our traffic pattern south of the landing strip. Except for the area around the three airfields (Cyclops, Sentani, and Hollandia) and the sizable lake, the countryside was covered with thick jungle that extended unbroken to the south, where mountains were visible in the humid haze.

We made a second formation flight on August 1, this one with the entire squadron, for further indoctrination. The planes sat on graded parking areas called hardstands located along taxiways that meandered around the north side of the airstrip. One had to be alert to move out onto the taxiway when the next plane ahead in the formation passed by. Large letters on the tails identified each plane, and a white spade (as in a suit of playing cards) painted on the rear fuselage under the horizontal stabilizer, identified the 389th Squadron. A club identified the 386th Squadron, a diamond the 387th, and a heart the 388th.

The engineers were still improving the airstrip, so visibility in the dust was a real problem after a plane or two had taxied by. The valley narrowed between rising hills toward Tanahmerah Bay. The traffic pattern at Hollandia was uniformly clockwise from west to east. The hour or so of squadron formation practice was helpful for getting acclimated to unit procedures and went off without any hitches on my part.

If my introduction to Colonel Strauss had left a positive impression about our associations in the group, reporting to the 389th Squadron's commanding officer proved to be an entirely different experience. Major Selmon Wells had commanded the squadron since the 312th's early days in Savannah. Our talks with Babe and Cal gave us the impression that the major was recognized as an excellent pilot and aggressive combat leader, but it was also hinted that he could be a bit autocratic. We should have been forewarned by Babe Young's smile and Slade's chuckle following their descriptions of our CO.

Several days after we joined the 389th, Major Wells returned from his leave in Sydney. Squadron Exec Wood officiously alerted Pete and me that we were expected to report to our CO without delay at the tent the major shared with the squadron flight surgeon, Doc Walsh, and Lieutenant Happ. As Pete and I started to leave, Babe Young suggested it might be well to wear our caps and button our shirt cuffs. Did Babe suppress a giggle?

We knocked on the screen door of the CO's tent and announced to Lieutenant Happ that we had come to report our presence in his squadron to Major Wells. It must have sounded by our tone that we were paying a social call, for Leonard Happ wore a serious expression as he invited us to enter. We stepped into the tent's dimly lit interior and saw Major Wells standing under the single naked light bulb hanging from the ceiling. Pete surprised me by immediately snapping to attention and saluting as he said, "Second Lieutenant Peterson reporting for duty, Sir."

Hadn't Pete gotten the message from our meeting with Colonel Strauss that things were more relaxed here in the war zone? I extended my hand and said, "I'm Lieutenant Rutter, Major." The look of distaste on Major Well's face immediately told me that I had made a serious mistake. The tent felt suddenly cool. My only avenue of recovery was to slowly withdraw my extended hand, assume the position of attention, and hope somebody would say something—maybe about the weather.

The major was all business as he inquired about our training, how much A-20 time we had, and the circumstances of our not being exposed

to the CRTC's training course while we were at the Port Moresby replacement camp. He lectured us on the necessity for sharp formation
flying, the maintenance of discipline when hitting a target, and so
forth—all without a smile. Lieutenant Happ seemed to save us from
more of the major's philosophy of command by saying he had already
checked us out on formation flying and the procedures followed at Hollandia. When he finally dismissed us, we were both happy to withdraw.
I was careful to exhibit a more military manner in departing, including
a crisp salute.

Babe Young was beaming with amused anticipation upon our return. When he saw the look on our faces he asked brightly, "Well,
what do think of the major?" Pete could laugh, but I groaned and
admitted to having made a serious faux pas. Major Wells would be
somewhat difficult for me to deal with in the months that followed,
try as I might to overcome that jaundiced first impression. Now, with
the perspective of the passing years, the major's reaction in the summer of 1944 to the too casual and very green replacement second lieutenant is understandable.

After living a few days with Slade and Young, and with Eddy scheduled to return from leave in another week, it was apparent that Pete and
I would have to start doing something about a place to live. The 389th
had lost four pilots during the month of July, so there were empty cots
around. However, we had received no invitations to move in with any-
body. We were unknown quantities and the old-timers were comfortably situated with their friends. Owen and Rutledge had faced the same
dilemma earlier, and Owen inferred from it that replacements were considered "Junior Birdmen" and would have an inferior status for the next
six months.

The Owen-Rutledge tent was a visual protest to all rules of military
camp planning. It was a sidewall latrine tent, smaller than the standard
pyramidal model, and they had pitched it out away from the trees on a
gravel bar at the edge of the mountain stream. No raised platform, just
a sand floor with most of the rocks removed and the canvas swooped low
over poles that were too short. The raised side flaps usually held deep
pockets of rainwater and emptied only when they threatened to collapse
the tent. Sagging mosquito bars were draped over the two cots. As we
stood there looking over their handiwork, Owen claimed that bribing a
sawmill sergeant was beneath his dignity! "Besides," Rutledge chimed in
brightly, "we decided to drink the whiskey."

Pete and I declined an invitation to move in with Owen and Rutledge,
thinking that we would like to be a little more comfortable and in a nicer

neighborhood. Squadron supply had no more pyramidal or even latrine tents, but we were offered a truck tarp of good size. Pete, who had grown up in the ranch country of western Colorado, said he had an idea for using the tarp to construct our house, so we accepted it.

After receiving instructions on the location of the sawmill we set out with a jeep and trailer to get the lumber for a floor and frame. The sergeant at the sawmill looked very serious when we inquired about some two-by-fours and floorboards. Just as we had been forewarned, he said he had orders to deliver lumber only to the quartermaster, "Sorry, I can't help you, Lieutenant," he added with a shrug. When he licked his lips and looked questioningly at the jeep, we could only shake our heads and gesture empty-handedly. We had no liquor to offer in exchange for a relaxation of the sergeant's scruples. We worked over the discard slab pile next to the sawmill and from it managed to cull out enough pieces, rough though they were, to serve our purposes.

Pete selected a location in the jungle between two trees as our site and we cleared out a twenty-by-twenty-foot square in the underbrush. A roof beam between the two trees supported the truck tarp with the sides stretched down over a rough frame made of trimmed saplings. The slab lumber was satisfactory for the floor, about eight by ten feet in size, which was supported on three or four logs we laid horizontally on the ground. The sides were screened with mosquito netting and Pete installed electric wiring complete with a switch at the door and a light bulb over each cot.

We obtained our electricity from the 386th Squadron's generator over a line leading to Capt. Pinky Wilson's nearby tent. Pinky was CO of the 386th and a nice guy. There was no need to excite Major Wells by drawing down the voltage on his line, which also passed nearby. Captain Wilson never did any more than grumble when his light bulb became a little dim or when my electric razor caused interference on his radio. I learned to shave when the radio was off and the squadron maintenance people never complained about our illegal tapping of their lines.

Grant Peterson was a good tent mate, although it was chance that threw us together in the 389th. He was from Delta, Colorado, near Grand Junction, and two or three years older than me. We had first become acquainted at Nadzab. Pete had done his training at Florence, South Carolina, and was engaged to a girl there. He had a muscular build and curly blond hair that topped a broad face. Pete was quiet, but he had a repertoire of cowboy songs he would occasionally sing for our amusement, including "Little Joe, the Wrangler" for my benefit. Little Joe died and would wrangle nevermore, said the song.

"Officers' country" at the 312th's camp was in a grove of trees near a fast-
running stream. Along with Lt. Grant Peterson, we built a house by placing a
truck tarp over a crude frame. Rutter stands by the door in the mosquito-
netting wall; the heavy foliage overhead minimized the effects of blowing rain.

A few days after our arrival in the squadron, Tom Jones and Don
Murison were assigned to the 389th. Tom and Don had completed the
training that Pete and I missed out on at the CRTC at Port Moresby.
Both had been my classmates at La Junta, and Don had also been at
Charlotte, but in another training squadron. Somehow, the Jones-
Murison team obtained a bottle of booze with which to buy lumber at
the sawmill. Within a few days they had carved out a tent site near ours
and erected a somewhat better looking house, raised floor and all, also
with a truck-tarp roof.

My first mission was on August 4. The assignment was to bomb and
strafe the supply dump at Sarmi on the mainland west of Wakde Island.
It would be a short trip, only a little over a hundred miles west of Hollandia.

After a briefing on the target by the group intelligence officer we were
loaded into trucks and jeeps for the ride over the rough and dusty road
down to the airstrip and the planes. The gunner checked the rear compartment and turret while the crew chief filled the pilot in on anything

about his ship that was not up to snuff. The practice usually followed in the States of the pilot doing a walk-around ground check of the plane before each flight was not necessary overseas in view of the dedication of the crew chiefs. They took great pride in their plane and felt responsible for its performance, so if a crew chief told a pilot that everything was okay, he was not going to find anything wrong by doing a casual walk-around.

The great majority of the 312th Bomb Group's missions were low-level bombing and strafing jobs. We usually flew to and from the target at low altitude—between one thousand and two thousand feet—unless adverse weather conditions dictated otherwise. Much of the flying was over water and jungle areas that posed no threat from enemy ground fire and our low altitude precluded enemy fighter attacks from below. For these reasons, the regular 312th crews consisted of just the pilot and top-turret gunner.

Instead of a .50-caliber machine gun in the bottom hatch, a rearward-facing four-by-five-inch aerial camera was mounted there to capture the effects of our bombing. The top-turret gunner activated it as soon as he saw the bombs falling to the rear and the camera would automatically take twenty-two to twenty-five frames. Although the oblique automatic camera was not used on the few medium altitude missions we conducted, there was not enough danger from enemy interception to warrant carrying the second gunner.

As the engine start-up time given to us at the mission briefing drew near, I settled into the cockpit with the crew chief assisting by first placing my chute in the seat and then helping me buckle the shoulder harness. When the flight leader began to start up, it was time for his wingmen to do likewise. The familiar routine needed no checklist: Master switch, "ON"; fuel boosters, "ON"; two shots of prime on the left engine; magneto switches, "ON"; throttles, cracked; mixtures, "RICH"; props, low pitch; brakes, set; left starter, "ON," and then "ENGAGE." The prop began to turn jerkily and then there was a loud bark and burst of blue smoke as the engine caught and roared to life, turning the propeller into a blurred disk. The same procedure was followed to start the right engine. The pilot always yelled "Clear!" out the open side windows before engaging the starters.

Once the engines were running it was time to check the oil, fuel, and hydraulic pressures and the fuel-level indicator was switched to each of the tanks in turn to ensure that they were full. Fuel booster pumps were turned off to assure that the engine-driven pumps were operating, after which the cowl flaps on the top and bottom of each engine were adjusted to keep the cylinder-head temperatures at the proper readings. The carburetor air intakes were always kept in the "FILTER" position while the plane was on the hardstand or taxiing out to the end of the runway to prevent the clouds of dust from damaging the engines. There would be time to check the intercom with the gunner and listen to the tower frequency to assure the radio was working before the flight leader moved out.

Missing your turn when it came time to roll onto the taxiway caused confusion in the takeoff sequence and was a sin not tolerated. On some days, when the dust had really been stirred up badly, the only thing visible was the tall rudder of the plane immediately ahead. Before pulling onto the end of the strip, most pilots paused to run up their engines. I was one of those who did. Some pilots figured there was no need to do so since the crew chief had run the engines up earlier, but I did not want to risk having a magneto or spark plug problem suddenly develop while I was trying to take off in a loaded plane. The final drill consisted of setting the flaps at twenty degrees, closing the top cowl flaps, opening the carburetor intakes for ram air, turning on the fuel booster pumps, and locking the shoulder harness.

As the plane ahead began to roll, the following plane moved to the end of the runway and waited until the preceding plane lifted off or the dust cleared sufficiently to permit a clear view. We were using 100/130 octane aviation fuel, which allowed us to run the engines up to forty-three inches of manifold pressure for takeoff compared to thirty-five inches with the ninety-one octane fuel used stateside. This resulted in a significant improvement in performance.

Each flight leader would climb straight ahead until his two wingmen were airborne and then begin a shallow right turn. This permitted the wingmen to cut across the inside of the turn with the second plane in the flight (the left wingman) sliding beneath and taking up his position on the outside of the leader. Should the pilot of the third plane in the flight judge the leader's turn more precisely and get into position first, it was logical for him to slide to the outside and leave a shorter distance for the other wingman to cover. Such preempting of wing position could be construed as indicating the other pilot was not particularly sharp that day, so it happened only occasionally.

The twenty-four A-20s (plus a spare) usually made only one circuit around the field for assembly before the formation set off for the target. After crossing the coast west of Tanahmerah Bay at about a thousand feet, the leader set course in the direction of Sarmi. I was too busy trying to maintain my place in formation to enjoy the view of the beach, the palm trees, and the changing colors of the sea, but on later trips I did my share of sightseeing. Ahead on this day, and before the landmark of Wakde Island was in full view, we could see a line of low clouds rolling out over the sea to block our path to Sarmi. The leader sized up the situation as we approached the cloudbank and, knowing the unpredictability of New Guinea's weather, made a sweeping turn seaward and headed for home. This was recorded as a "combat mission incomplete" (CMI) and thus did not count as a combat mission.

Although that aborted first mission was an easy dry run, it was not without excitement for me. When we arrived over Hollandia, the control tower called our leader's attention to an A-20 sitting directly across the approach end of the runway. A truck-mounted crane sitting beside it was being rigged to support the plane so that a maintenance crew could replace a blown tire on one of its main landing gear. The squadron's final approach had become stretched out that day and, as the last plane in the 389th's flights, I was encountering prop wash from the planes up ahead as they stayed high to clear the obstruction at the end of the runway. When I saw the men atop the stationary plane rigging the crane begin jumping to the ground, I realized I was getting too low and immediately added power. This made my approach flatter than desirable. Just as we cleared the obstruction with little room to spare we hit the disturbed air.

The plane bucked and wallowed and the nose dropped abruptly with the control yoke fully back. Even with a burst of the throttles to get the nose up it looked as if we were going to hit squarely on the nosewheel and pancake into the runway. The plane must have just started to respond to the full-up elevators when the nosewheel made contact with the ground because although the strut compressed all the way to the stop, it did not collapse. As the nose continued to rise, the main gear hit hard, fully compressing the struts, and the plane bounced high into the air and stayed there as I added full power to go around again. The A-20 staggered to regain flying speed as we roared along just above the runway past gaping spectators in front of the control tower. I was without an explanation as to how we managed to escape disaster, but we somehow had. I retracted the gear to gain speed and altitude and prepared to go around again.

Pity the poor man riding in the back and wondering what was causing all the commotion. I called back to the gunner to assure him that all seemed to be okay in my end of the plane as I headed out over Lake Sentani to see if the five-hundred-pound bombs we were carrying were still securely shackled. I alerted the gunner to watch, but nothing fell out when I opened the bomb-bay doors. The landing gear lights on the control panel showed green when I dropped the gear, so we circled around and landed behind the rest of the group. Others had also experienced the severe prop wash that day, compounded by the obstruction on the end of the runway, but no one had come as close to a pileup as I had.

I told the crew chief about the hard landing and asked him to give the aircraft a thorough going over. Much to my surprise, he later reported finding no cracks, buckled bulkheads, or other damage. At lunch, Major Wells asked only why I had chosen to abort the landing. "I didn't want to try making a good landing out of a bad one," I replied, quoting the sage advice repeated by most instructors. On August 6 we reran the mission to bomb the supply dump at Sarmi and experienced no problems with the weather.

On August 9 we were sent out to bomb and strafe a village complex just thirty miles south of Hollandia where the Japanese were reported to be gathering. The village was called Ampus and there were a number of new thatched buildings on a hillside within a bowl of higher hills. Because of the target's small size, the squadron leader put us in a line-astern (trail) formation and instructed us to make individual passes on the visible buildings and surrounding jungle. The attack soon became a rat race with A-20s crisscrossing the valley in several directions as each pilot tried to line up on a thatched roof. It was easy to misjudge the height of the hills while flying a loaded plane, and sometimes my airspeed got uncomfortably low before we skimmed over the trees on the ridge tops. Finally, the leader called for us to reform and return to base. I made one last run to dump my remaining bombs and then strained to catch up. I felt lonely straggling behind the formation, even on a short mission such as this.

On August 16 and 18, my fourth and fifth missions, we went back to the area on the coast near Wakde Island and strafed troops on a piece of high ground called Mount Hakko. These were short runs and were usually completed in two hours or so, but on the second of the two there was a serious complication. The formation was just off the coast west of Hollandia when, forty-five minutes after takeoff, my gunner, Leon Schnell, called to report that there was some kind of red fluid all over his rear compartment. A quick glance at the hydraulic pressure gauge showed that the normal four hundred pounds per square inch had dropped to zero.

A hydraulic line had broken somewhere in the bomb bay and sprayed the fluid around, finally to be blown back into Leon's compartment. Without system pressure, the only way to open the bomb-bay doors was by hand pumping, so we would have to take the bombs back home. However, we were within half an hour of the target, so I decided we might as well get credit for another mission. After I advised Corporal Schnell of my decision, we continued on. By running my engines at a higher rpm setting and staying a little above the flight leader I had no difficulty maintaining position on our strafing runs. The other planes toggled their bombs on two successive runs, but there was no reason for the flight leader to notice that my bomb-bay doors stayed closed.

As we turned back toward Hollandia I reviewed the handbook instructions on hydraulic system emergency operations in my mind. There was a reserve supply of hydraulic fluid in the unpressurized reservoir that could be used by opening a bypass valve and operating an emergency hand pump located to the left of the pilot's seat. After operating each hydraulic device (cowl flaps, landing gear, wing flaps, brakes, and such) the particular selecting lever should be returned to neutral to isolate that system. The reserve supply was good for about seventy-five strokes on the pump handle—enough, I thought, to at least get the gear down and operate the brakes. There was no way to tell which of the hydraulic lines had broken, but I hoped that it was not one of those supplying a system critical for landing.

When the formation came over the airstrip at a thousand feet to peel off to land I continued straight ahead, probably to the consternation of the leader of the flight behind us. After I contacted the tower to advise them of my problem I was instructed to circle until the entire formation was on the ground. Once the pattern was clear I slowed the plane down to about 150 miles per hour and pulled the emergency landing gear release. Ideally, the gear should drop on its own and lock in place, but in this instance the right main gear and the nosewheel dangled without locking. Their indicator lights on the panel glowed red. I pulled the control yoke back sharply several times and the right gear finally swung down and locked. The nose gear was still dangling, however, so I squandered some precious hydraulic fluid pumping it down by hand. All of the lights were green; apparently the break was not in the landing gear operating system.

The slow flying had caused the engine temperatures to climb so, acting more confidently this time, I pumped the lower cowl flaps open a bit—again with no indication of a line leak. Figuring that trying to operate the wing flaps just might squander all of the remaining hydraulic fluid, I elected to land without flaps. While we circled I could see more and more men gathering around the airfield, waiting to see how this would work out. The crash crew was standing by in its truck, ready to go.

If I depressed the brake pedals after landing and used the hand pump, the brakes should work—provided the line break was not in the braking system. If all else failed, there was an emergency air bottle on the braking system that could be opened for a one-shot actuation. I cut the safety wire on the hand valve, just to be ready in the event I needed it. Using the air bottle was a last resort, for it would lock both brakes leaving no means of controlling the plane—and we still had those bombs on board. I called the tower to confirm that the landing gear appeared to be down and locked. The tower operator responded in the affirmative and cleared me to land.

In view of the weight of the bomb load and the fact that I had no flaps it was prudent to make the approach at 135 miles per hour rather than the 120 that I usually employed. The wheels touched down not too far past the end of the runway and, after holding the nose off just long enough to kill off some speed, I let the nosewheel touch down, depressed the brake pedals, and began vigorously working the emergency hand pump. There seemed at first to be no effect, but then I could feel the plane begin to slow. Elated, I released the brakes and continued the landing roll.

What a mistake! The brake pressure I had built up was instantly released when I let up on the pedals and the end of the runway was now coming up at about fifty miles per hour. Again I depressed the brake pedals and pumped like mad. Just before it was necessary to resort to the air bottle, we began to slow. I applied a little power to the right engine and the plane swung off onto a taxiway. However, it was impossible to taxi without the brakes. Several crew chiefs appeared in a jeep and blocked the wheels with chocks while I kept the engines running to hold the plane on the slight incline where we sat.

When the chocks were in place I snapped off the switches and the sound of the engines died out. A wave of relief washed over me as I suddenly realized how happy I was that this adventure was over. Leon Schnell dropped out of the rear hatch and gave me a broad smile of approval, as relieved as I that the landing had been successful. I used the hand pump to open the bomb-bay doors and one of the ordnance men put safety wires back in the bomb fuses.

Major Wells, of course, had observed the entire exercise, which in my mind had been a stellar performance. He now drove up in his jeep and offered Schnell and me a lift to camp. His only comment was, "Come on, Rutter, you've made us late for lunch," but he did manage a little half-smile. The break in the hydraulic system, which had occurred in the fitting on the hydraulic pressure accumulator located in the front of the bomb bay, was easily fixed.

In the A-20 armament lectures back at Charlotte we had been cautioned about prolonged firing of the .50-caliber nose guns. The gun barrels were air cooled, so we were instructed to make short bursts of twenty-five to fifty rounds per burst to prevent overheating them. Seventy-five rounds in a single burst was the absolute maximum. "The barrels will lose their grooves if you clamp down on the trigger," one of the instructors sternly observed. It was easy enough to follow this advice when shooting at practice targets, but on one of my early missions, with live enemy troops clearly in view and shooting back, I forgot all of the cautions. As I held down the trigger, the concentrated stream of tracers pouring out of the nose began to wander in spirals as first one of my guns and then another lost its rifling.

On our second pass at the target one or more of the nose guns did not fire at all when I depressed the trigger. Several more stopped until only a single .50 caliber was left firing. The A-20 I was flying, an early model, was equipped with a row of handles at the bottom of the instrument panel for hand charging the guns. This seemed like a good idea, but pulling the handles in an attempt to clear the jams in the overheated guns resulted in a tangle of T-handles and cables on the cockpit floor. All six barrels had to be changed after the mission—a costly reminder to fire in short bursts.

From time to time, perhaps because so many new crews had been added to the squadron, we flew practice formation flights on days when missions were not scheduled. Often, after spending an hour or so trying such maneuvers as echelon by flights or line abreast or with flights stepped up rather than down, the leader would put us into trail for a rat race or follow-the-leader drill before landing. These rat races required some skill and judgment to keep up with the plane ahead and duplicate his maneuvers. By and large they were fun for the pilots. On one such exercise I could have sworn that the leader took us through a loop, but probably not. Keeping alert to the moves of the plane ahead left little opportunity to watch the gyrations of the horizon. The crew chiefs, I should add, did not like rat racing at all. They were the ones who had to check the planes out and repair any popped rivets they found. They also had to stow away loose equipment that we had dislodged.

One day we were practicing low-level formation flying with Capt. Ken Hedges, our operations officer, in the lead. He was an excellent if somewhat exuberant pilot. Hedges took us down the coast east of Hollandia with the flights stepped up above the leader even though we never flew such a formation on missions. At one point he was so low over the water that his props were kicking up spray like a pair of speedboats. It was an impressive sight. A moment later somebody spotted a school of porpoises and one of the other flights strafed it. It was an act that seemed exceedingly stupid to me, but it was all in the name of training, I guess.

Nabire, a Japanese airstrip on the south end of Geelvink Bay, appeared to be inactive but was not. It was a small base with one runway carved from the jungle and ending on the shore. A few buildings were visible in the jungle here and there, but no serviceable planes were visible when we went over a time or two. Evidence pointed to Nabire being used to stage planes for raids on Biak and Owi Islands 225 miles to the north, where we now had several operational bases. The Japanese would fly planes into Nabire and other small bases late in the afternoon, refuel, and dispatch them to a target after dark to return to their home bases far to the west.

A mission to Nabire was my seventh, and especially instructive of Colonel Strauss's handling of a formation. Leaving Hollandia, the course was roughly parallel with the north coast for more than a hundred miles before angling inland to the southwest. Some mountains with peaks ranging from five thousand to nine thousand feet appeared through the haze to the south, but the area was marked "Unexplored" on our maps. We flew down valleys covered with a mat of dense jungle, past ridges so similar as to be indistinguishable (at least to me), and then, after about two hours of flying at not over a thousand feet, the squadron ahead began a turn to the right. We had entered a valley that looked like all the rest, but the bomb-bay doors on the planes ahead were opening so I knew we were close to the target.

The formation began descending and picking up speed. As we made the usual preparations—props to twenty-one hundred rpm; booster pumps; gun switches; mixtures; bomb-bay doors; bombs armed—the end of the Nabire airstrip appeared straight ahead. We swept the length of the runway three abreast at about 275 miles per hour, strafing the jungle and toggling 250-pound bombs. Out over Geelvink Bay the squadrons reformed as Colonel Strauss made a wide circle before setting course toward the northeast and home. How had Strauss led us over all that expanse of jungle and then chosen the right valley leading to Nabire? Not all mission leaders were as accomplished as the colonel when it came to navigation.

The formation relaxed a bit on the way home, which permitted some sightseeing as we passed over the tropical world of New Guinea. The isolated villages along the shoreline were built on pilings above the surrounding swamp, the beaches were narrow strips with a few palm trees, and then there would be a waterway or swamp before there was solid ground. Occasionally, we would see a native boat of strange design with its sail raised. It all looked to me like a peaceful scene in *National Geographic* magazine.

After more than a month in the 389th Squadron I was becoming comfortable flying missions. Although there had been no more landing problems or emergencies, I still had a lot to learn.

Chapter 6

Just About Enough Excitement

Trouble is said to come in threes and my third landing mishap occurred on September 7. We had been out practicing formation flying when, after a brief rat race that seemed intended more to entertain the spectators on the ground than benefit the pilot, our leader put us into an echelon formation and led us back to the field for landing. The plane I was flying was one that had recently been assigned to Cal Slade to replace his rather tired "Ravin' Rachael."

My landing was no grease job, but it was not particularly rough either. The plane bounced lightly only once before settling onto the runway. All seemed normal until, about midway along the runway, I tapped the brakes lightly to ensure they had hydraulic pressure. There was a loud bang and the plane's right wing dropped sharply, followed by the squeal of rubber on metal as the ship veered to the right. By applying the left brake I was able to hold a straight course down the runway. Perplexed at what had happened and still rolling along at a good clip, I took a quick look at the right landing gear and saw the bottom of the engine nacelle resting on top of the tire. The friction was producing a cloud of smoke and rubber dust with an accompanying loud, screeching howl.

My speed rapidly dropped off, but before stopping completely I released some pressure on the left brake and allowed the plane to swing to the right onto the grass so it would be clear of the runway. The plane came to rest facing in the opposite direction, the right prop barely clearing the ground as the engine idled. I quickly cut the switches. The right landing gear had somehow managed to rotate forward, allowing the tire to come into contact with the nacelle. Landing gear can collapse when the mechanism that locks them down does not properly engage, but this results in the wheel folding to the rear and up into the nacelle. That in turn drops the wing tip onto the runway, causing the prop blades to dig into the ground. The result could have been disastrous had that occurred. Luck had prevailed again.

With my plane clear of the runway, the rest of the squadron continued to land. I climbed out of the cockpit and sat on the wing to watch. There had been nobody riding in the back of the plane during this episode. As Owen rolled by he waved and shook his head in disbelief at my predicament. A big grin split his face.

In due time two corporals from the Corps of Engineers detachment drove up in a six-by-six truck equipped with a mobile crane. The engineers were responsible for airfield construction and maintenance and the corporals were intent on clearing the obstruction of my plane. "Okay, Lieutenant, we'll take over," one of them said. "We'll drag that son of a bitch out of there in no time flat." As they proceeded to attach cables to the plane it quickly became apparent that *drag* was the operative word. My protests that the plane was not damaged enough to justify such draconian measures seemed to have little weight. They had a job to do and they were intent on doing it quickly their way. As far as they were concerned, it was just another wreck. Fortunately, the 389th's engineering officers, Capt. Dick Powers and Lt. Leo Brashier, arrived on the scene and stopped the wrecking crew. The corporals, looking a bit disappointed, stood back to watch as a crew from the service squadron arrived.

When the maintenance crew lifted the plane, the right gear dropped back into normal position against the down lock. Mechanics then clamped it in place for towing to the service squadron's area for repairs. There they discovered that the retraction strut had broken, permitting the gear to rotate forward rather than to the rear, as was usually the case. The crack where the retraction strut had failed showed that it had started sometime earlier and finally snapped when I applied and then released the brakes. Replacing the strut and tire and repairing the damaged skin and frames on the bottom of the engine nacelle kept Slade's A-20 out of service for a few weeks.

Major Wells had observed the practice flight's return and watched our landings, as was often his custom. When I arrived back at the squadron he fixed me with a look of distinct displeasure and snapped, "Rutter, you're grounded." He turned and walked away before I could reply.

My confrontations with the major were beginning to give me a martyr complex. It seemed to me that the admittedly less than smooth landing had little to do with the accident. My tapping the brakes, which was customary, was simply the final jolt that broke the already weakened retraction strut. Grounding seemed like pretty harsh punishment—especially considering the way I had kept the plane under control, avoided hitting anything, and then neatly parked it clear of the runway. Not even a prop had been nicked (albeit more a matter of luck than skill). The whole event could have turned out much worse for the plane and others, including me.

My pride as a pilot was injured by the grounding order. He had said nothing about the length of my punishment; for all I knew, the grounding might be permanent. I prepared the required written accident report after viewing the plane at the service squadron and getting an explanation from the mechanics about the failure of the strut, an obviously important part not usually given to failure. The squadron continued to fly missions while I stayed on the ground and spent my time improving our tent by weaving palm-leaf mats for the floor, building a couple of chairs, and clearing away underbrush. After a couple of days, Leonard Happ, who recently had become the squadron operations officer, suggested that I talk to the major and ask to be put back on flying status. My reply was youthful and stiff-necked: "The major grounded me, let him decide when to unground me." In the meantime, there was no sign that he was about to relent.

Happ apparently took it upon himself to untangle the impasse created by my bullheadedness. At supper that evening he announced that he would check me out for flying the following morning. The three days of uncertainty I had endured seemed like three weeks and I welcomed Len's intercession on my behalf. On September 10 we went down to the strip and Happ made a circuit of the field with me lying on the deck behind him observing. Then we traded places and I took his plane around the pattern one time while he observed. In the smooth morning air I had no problem demonstrating that I did not always bounce my landings. Happ did notice that my 120 mile per hour approach speed was slower than he used and suggested that 130 might be better. The higher speed on the final did provide better control, a logical suggestion that I should have adopted on my own since the planes were somewhat heavier than those we had flown at Charlotte. Although the incident was over, I suspected that Major Wells would not soon forget.

The loss of three ships at Babo in July was still fresh in the minds of the 389th Squadron's crews when I joined the outfit. Two of the group's other squadrons were surprised at Utarom in August. Utarom was located on the shore of Kamrau Bay on the south coast in western New Guinea and was active as a staging field for raids by Japanese planes against Biak and other U.S. bases. On August 11, 1944, the 386th and 387th Squadrons lost three planes and five crewmembers on a low-level bombing and strafing mission there. Years later, Capt. Jack Klein recalled the events: "Lieutenant Colonel Pagh was leading and there must have been two squadrons (386th and 387th), twelve ships altogether. Pagh went in first and we (387th) circled over the water waiting to follow in single file. We were waiting out there over the water and it was just like a shooting gallery: We watched Pagh and Wells (1st. Lt. Frank Wells) go in—*boom, boom*—just like that."

After watching Bill Pagh and Frank Wells go down, Klein—leading the 387th's second flight behind Major Horton—led his trio of planes in single-ship passes over the length of the airstrip. "Yes, we just went on in," he said. "Give them credit: there wasn't a man in that outfit that didn't follow right on through. Those guys were marvelous. Looking back on that, they were amazing. It sounded like some guy took two handfuls of gravel and threw it on a tin roof. Then the plane started bucking and wanted to go nose up. I think the trim tab must have been jammed and was forcing the elevator up."

The tail of Klein's plane was seriously damaged and he was unable to contact his gunner after they were hit. Even at reduced speed it was difficult for Klein to maintain level flight, but he was able to get back to Geelvink Bay, about fifty miles to the north, and finally ditched near Roon Island when he thought he could control the plane no longer. The gunner, who most likely was killed during the attack or died shortly afterward, went down with the plane. A PBY—brought to the scene by Capt. Ed Pool, who was also flying on the mission—rescued Klein.

Low-level sweeps were not worth the price at such places as Babo and Utarom when there was little likelihood of finding aircraft so tactics were changed to bombing the runways from five thousand to six thousand feet. I recall being on two medium-level missions to Utarom when there was some cause for amusement. On the first, a number of black puffs of 75-mm flak suddenly burst at our altitude just ahead of the lead flight, which was being led by a B-25. This was followed by the sudden appearance of an even closer barrage of flak that spooked Chris Parsons, who instinctively took evasive action. He peeled up and away from his leader and left for parts unknown. Chris, who had joined the 389th in February and flown a number of missions, was razzed appropriately when we got back on the ground.

On the second occasion we were at about five thousand feet, flying above broken clouds, as the lead bombardier took the formation this way and that trying to line up on the Utarom airstrip through the clouds. Radio silence was suddenly broken when an excited pilot shouted, "I've lost an engine!" Colonel Strauss was a stickler for radio silence on the way to a target, so no one responded to the cry for help. After about half a minute the pilot who was in trouble made another now frantic call: "Red Leader! Red Leader! I've lost an engine!" This time someone in the formation answered with a calm, sardonic, "Tough fucking luck!" The leader, whoever he was, responded with the brusque command, "Get off the air! Someone go home with that single engine." The plane that was in trouble made a safe landing at Biak, about 225 miles north, but the dry, unsympathetic remark gave us a chuckle.

On low-level runs you seldom noticed the guns firing at you whereas at medium altitude the puffs from the guns below and the appearance of black balls with angry, red centers were all too evident. The thud and crack of antiaircraft bursts, whether near or not, was always disconcerting. It was consoling to remember the adage that the burst you saw could not hurt you. I do not recall us losing any planes to medium-altitude flak, but holes in the aircraft were not uncommon and sometimes there was more serious damage. The intelligence briefers frequently reported that Japanese gunners were inaccurate and that we could anticipate encountering only light antiaircraft fire. However, that did not always prove to be the case. Medium altitude or not, Babo's reputation was such that I stayed awake for a long time the night before making my first trip there.

By mid-September, 1944, Allied forces were operating from not only Biak and Owi Islands, but also farther west from Noemfoor Island and Sansapor on New Guinea's west end. Because the persistent Japanese continued to raid our western bases by staging for refueling through Babo, Utarom, and Nabire, these fields continued to be frequent 312th targets. It took about four hours to fly to Nabire, and five and one-half to six hours to reach Utarom or Babo. That is a long time to sit on a one-man life raft and fly in formation. The A-20 did not have an autopilot.

After hitting a target and getting away again, we were more or less relaxed on the return trip. As was his custom, Owen, who was flying across from me on the left wing of our flight when we hit Babo on September 12, loosened his parachute straps and lit a cigarette before pouring a cup of coffee from his thermos. Occasionally he would motion for me to loosen the formation and threaten the flight leader with his fist to indicate displeasure at any jockeying of the throttles that caused us work. For my part, I stayed strapped in the chute, no matter how uncomfortable it might be, and also put up with sitting on a rock-hard life raft rather than discarding it for a seat cushion, which is what most of the pilots did. Why wear a chute if it was not instantly available? Similarly, the raft would be a real comfort if I ever went down in the water. I wondered how quickly the relaxed Owen would move if he suddenly had to use that parachute. Fortunately for him, he never did. Owen was often a showman—a self-styled maverick at times—a good pilot, and basically conservative, notwithstanding the fact that he enjoyed bending the rules.

The trip home usually permitted some sightseeing unless the weather caused problems or the flight leader was an erratic type who required close attention. Several small islands off New Guinea's north coast west of Hollandia had been laid out as coconut plantations, with the trees standing in straight rows stretching from shore to shore. The colors of the tropical ocean varied from deep blue to light green depending upon the depth over the sand or coral. I never tired of taking in all that tropical scenery and wondering what life was like in the remote native villages we passed. Some of the trading settlements along the coast had small white churches as evidence that missionaries had been there before the war. We were warned not to trust the missionary natives if we had to walk out of the jungle, but just contemplating existing down there in that forbidding green tangle was bad enough.

We customarily flew at about a thousand feet and kept the sliding side windows in the cockpit open for ventilation. The engines roaring just outside for four or five hours at a stretch would cause deafness for two days afterward should a pilot neglect to stuff his ears with cotton before takeoff. A green sliding curtain under the cockpit canopy provided protection from the sun, but using this sunshade on the way to the target was not a good idea because there might be enemy fighters out hunting.

The flight coveralls I usually wore on missions were always soaked with sweat after each flight, but it was easy enough to wash out. Many pilots wore their regular khaki uniforms, which would probably be more practical than a flight suit if you ever had to walk home through the jungle. The mess hall packed lunches for us to take on long flights. These usually consisted of a fried-egg sandwich on thick GI bread with either coffee or synthetic lemonade in the thermos bottle clipped onto the shelf behind the pilot's seat. A real fried egg, rather than a dehydrated one, was a treat.

Using the pilot's relief tube in the A-20 was sometimes necessary and entailed some complicated contortions. First, undoing your fly usually required unfastening the seatbelt and loosening the between-the-leg straps on the Mae West life vest and the parachute. The relief tube, which was stowed beneath the seat, was held in proper position by the left hand while the pilot kept an eye on the flight leader as he relieved himself. Fortunately, the A-20 could be flown hands-off when properly trimmed in smooth air. However, the procedure could become quite messy if you ran into turbulence. It was bad form not to enter "Relief tube used" on the pilot's Form 1A after the flight so the tube could be washed out with bicarbonate of soda. The smell of stale urine in a confined cockpit in the New Guinea heat was not at all pleasant.

Around September 20 my tent-mate, Grant Peterson, was chosen to go on detached service to the Replacement Combat Training Center at Nadzab. Pete was to act as an instructor for approximately two months and upon his return would be named a flight leader. With the position came the likelihood of promotion to first lieutenant. Pete's quiet way of doing things and his avoidance of any flying problems such as mine had attracted the major's favorable notice. I did not particularly want to be sent to Nadzab, but the prospect of a quick promotion admittedly left me feeling a bit envious. Pete and I had become good friends while living in our little house in the jungle and we agreed that I would hold the quarters open pending his return.

Living conditions at the Hollandia camp were comfortable enough in the jungle shade with the nearby stream for bathing and washing clothes. An enlisted man assigned to the motor pool operated a laundry service that many of the officers and enlisted men patronized, although I preferred doing my own washing in the creek. Several washing machines had been brought up from Australia and the laundryman had no other duty than running his business. His fees were modest enough, but he reportedly was able to send sizable sums of money home. The laundry enterprise was operated with the blessing of Lt. Porky Jones, the motor pool officer.

An important everyday event was the arrival of mail. A letter from family or friend brought a welcome break in the routine and we experienced serious disappointment when no mail arrived. Harriett and I wrote at least weekly, and I carried on a lively correspondence with Nancy in Charlotte and my parents. Several of the girls in the Pittsburgh FBI office were good correspondents who wrote to me from time to time as well as to other ex-clerks and kept us all up to date. Fred Way's younger sister was a senior in high school and supplied news about her brother and others.

Letters sent via airmail required six cents postage and there was also a free military V-Mail service by air. V-Mail used a letter-size form that was copied onto microfilm and then reprinted, reduced to four inches by

V-mail was a free armed services letter system that used microfilm to transmit the original letters. V-mail was limited by the size of the form and microfilm processing was not always prompt. This sample was sent by Lt. J. R. McMaster from England. The censor deleted references to crossing the Atlantic aboard the Queen Mary.

five inches, for delivery. There was some delay in handling the microfilm on our end, however, so I seldom used V-Mail. Receiving a package in the mail, no matter how damaged or damp, was always a big event. Packages came by ship and took four or five weeks on average; the contents had to be well packed to survive.

When we were not flying, our time was pretty much our own. For many, taking a nap ("catching some sack time") directly after lunch was a habit. We often walked up the creek to where there was a pool that had some sand and spent several hours sunbathing and talking. We infrequently received a beer ration and the creek offered a means of cooling it.

Sometimes Major Wells announced that there would be an afternoon volleyball game. It was a game I enjoyed, although I lacked much skill at it. Owen, had worked at a YMCA gym during college, was a good volleyball player. He seemed to take perverse pleasure in confounding the major, at least some of the time. Whether chosen for the major's side or playing against him, Owen could make almost impossible saves or fall flat on his back, depending upon the score at the moment and his mood that day. It was good fun and exercise, but some days the heat and humidity was just too high for gamboling around the volleyball net.

A movie was shown for entertainment almost every evening on a screen out in the open. Sometimes a showing had to be called off on account of rain. Watching for shooting stars was almost as enjoyable as anticipating the evening's feature. I never saw stars that shone brighter than they did at Hollandia, and it seemed like shooting stars could be observed almost every night. Sometimes three or four could be seen dropping simultaneously toward the northern horizon and I wondered if our location, just south of the equator, had something to do with the very regular display.

Before the movie each evening, Capt. Nate Rothstein, the assistant group intelligence officer, would give a daily news report over the public address system. To spice up the dry military news bulletins, Nate took to throwing in some humor—usually the crude GI type—into his reports. On at least one occasion these added Rothstein remarks were more humorous than he anticipated. The news one day concerned the Allies being about to take the Italian city of Florence. Nate enlivened the report with allusions to the female anatomy. For starters, he made references to the main target being protected by mounded hills to the north, enveloping curves, and narrowing valleys. "Our troops are approaching from the south," said Nate, imitating the sonorous tones and serious delivery of radio newscasters of the time.

The audience was laughing louder than usual that night, which encouraged comedian Rothstein to render even more outrageous reports. However, Nate had failed to notice that several chaplains from Fifth Air Force headquarters and other units, guests of the 312th's chaplain, Father Clatus Snyder, occupied the front-row seats. The chaplains were understandably discomforted and Father Snyder let it be known that he

Tent-mate Grant Peterson was from western Colorado near Grand Junction. Pete was killed at Wewak, Papua New Guinea, on November 10, 1944, while assigned to the Combat Training Center at Nadzab.

was extremely unhappy with Nate's performance. Captain Rothstein's news reports were observed to be more factual, and correspondingly less interesting, for a few weeks afterward.

Many of the pilots and crew chiefs undertook to decorate their planes with paintings of cartoon characters or sexy females from *Esquire* magazine accompanied by snappy names or slogans. A sergeant in the 312th was a talented artist and for a bottle of whiskey or gin could be persuaded to paint a professional likeness of a chosen subject on the side of the fuselage below the cockpit. Some of the names I recall include "Queen of Spades," "Mischievous Mary II," "California Sunshine," "My Akin Back," "Windy City Kitty," "Hellzapoppin," "Shu-Shu Baby," "Virgin on the Verge," and "Hot Box." Most captions referred to well-endowed, scantily clad females. One of the more amusing pieces of artwork (not on a 312th plane) was a painting of the Disney cartoon dog Pluto with a leg raised beside a fire hydrant adorned with the head of Japanese premier Hideki Tojo. The title read simply, "Pysonia!" A few of the artworks were a little too graphic, so the CO directed the owners to add some tasteful, strategic covering in deference to the army nurses and Red Cross girls who occasionally wandered down to the flight line.

These artistic decorations were innocent enough fun and denoted no great moral breakdown by the valiant troops, but Chaplain Snyder deplored the practice. Father Snyder mentioned his disfavor at several Sunday services for his Catholic flock and finally wrote a strong editorial against the art form in his "Chaplain Chatter" newsletter. He argued that our heathen enemy did not decorate his planes in such a manner and said he feared some of us might go to our deaths with these obscene paintings and worse slogans as our epitaph. The chaplain inadvertently used "Hot Box" as an example of the nose art to which he objected, only to learn that the plane and its crew had been lost, causing him some remorse and embarrassment. The good father's views may have been sincere, but most of us failed to see the connection between mildly risqué cartoons or slogans and damnation. We called such artistic efforts "chaplain shockers."

September was the first month that the 312th did not lose any personnel, but it was a very near thing on September 28 when Lt. Ken Dufour of the 388th Squadron went into the woods near the Hollandia strip. The 388th had been on a mission to Utarom but aborted because of weather. Meanwhile, the 389th went out that morning to practice formation flying. The 388th's formation arrived back at the field shortly after we landed and the word soon got around that one of the returning planes was coming in on a single engine. Dufour had lost an engine near Wakde Island and experienced fuel starvation on the good engine over Tanahmerah Bay. His gunner, Sgt. Thomas Smith, elected to bail out and find his own way home.

The good engine restarted as soon as Dufour switched tanks and we watched as the crippled A-20 came down the valley just over the treetops toward the end of the airstrip. It appeared that Dufour would make it to the field okay. However, he was off to the right of the runway and the plane's landing gear failed to lock down, so the tower fired a red flare to warn him off. We watched the A-20 turn toward Lake Sentani as he attempted to go around again on one engine, but it failed to gain any altitude. Suddenly it disappeared into the trees. A rising column of black smoke marked the spot.

It appeared that Ken Dufour was surely a goner, but a jeep dispatched to locate the crash site between the airstrip and the lake met the pilot walking dazedly out of the jungle. Later, in the hospital, Dufour related to Don Dyer that he went straight into the trees and was uninjured by the crash. However, he had neglected to jettison the cockpit hatch. The plane immediately burst into flame, trapping Dufour in the cockpit until the hatch warped sufficiently for him to kick it open. He was badly burned and had a gash in one leg made by a round in his .45-caliber automatic that cooked off from the heat. Although he survived the crash, he never again flew with the 312th.

On September 30, two days after Ken Dufour's crash, we witnessed another crash at Hollandia. This time it was an A-20 from the 3d Attack Group, which was also based there. We were getting ready to start our engines for a mission to Utarom as the planes of the 3d Attack were taking off and forming up for a mission of their own. My crew chief was standing with me on the wing helping with the parachute when we both heard a break in the thundering drone coming from the planes circling in formation overhead. We glanced upward and quickly picked out the plane that was in trouble: a trail of smoke was streaming back from one of its engines. The crippled A-20 began to drop back as we watched the pilot continue in the same direction for a time before starting a turn to the right.

The pilot could have dropped his landing gear and landed at either Sentani or Cyclops, both of which lay almost directly ahead. Instead, he chose to make a normal right-hand pattern that would bring him back onto the Hollandia strip. The plane, which was full of fuel and carried a bomb load, was losing altitude as it circled out over Lake Sentani. Rather than salvo his bombs as expected, the pilot continued to lose

Lieutenant Maurice Owen, frequently mentioned in this chronicle, poses here by an A-20's rear turret in a photo taken for his wife Rosalie. Note the gunner's escape hatch beneath the twin .50-caliber machine guns. Designated P in the squadron, it carried the name "Flossie III" and was assigned to Capt. Mack Austin, 389th Squadron.

Maury Owen, seated in an A-20 cockpit, demonstrates the close quarters. The top hatch was twenty-two inches wide by ninety-four inches long. The armor plate behind the pilot's head was hinged and folded down; a five-man raft was carried on the deck behind the cockpit.

altitude as his sweeping turn carried him onto the final approach. Unfortunately he was too low and too far out. The A-20 plunged into the trees on the west end of the runway while we stood there watching. There was a loud *crump* followed by a cloud of black smoke billowing into the sky. Meanwhile, the 3d Attack Group's formation headed northwest on its mission, a spare plane taking the place of the one that was now burning in the jungle.

We had watched the tragedy unfold from the first break in the sound of the engines until the end and I wondered how it could have happened. Our mission leader was starting his engines, so we spectators dropped into our cockpits. When we returned some five hours later the first question I asked the crew chief concerned the crash. The pilot who died that morning was 2d Lt. Glen Mellgren. We had trained together at Charlotte and been in the same shipment to California. His gunner was thrown through the top of the Plexiglas turret when the plane hit the ground but miraculously survived.

In October, some of the replacement crews began to come up on the leave roster for ten days of rest and relaxation (R&R) in Sydney. Supposedly, those who were flying the missions came up in rotation about every two months and the orderly room, under the direction of Capt. Fred Wood, the squadron exec, was in charge of the roster. Although Maury Owen and Jim Rutledge had joined the 389th a week or so ahead of me, the first replacements to go on leave were Don Murison and Tom Jones, who had arrived during the first week in August. No one questioned the apparent discrepancy in the roster order, particularly since it appeared that all of us were now eligible and would be coming up for R&R in a week or so. Murison and Jones, surprised at their good fortune, skipped off to Sydney.

The old-timers told tall stories about the wonderful Aussie beer, the multitude of friendly girls, the attractions of the racetrack and all the thick steaks and other delights available. Don and Tom returned in two weeks, rested and relaxed to confirm most of what we had heard from the veterans of Sydney. The only difference was that they preferred milk shakes to beer (!) and added ice-skating and family dinners to the list of attractions. Theirs had been a nontraditional leave. Tom Jones, who had fallen instantly in love with a girl he met at an ice rink, announced that he was now engaged to Miss Patricia Kenny, age seventeen.

After hearing Jones's enthusiastic descriptions of milk bars and ice-skating, Owen and Rutledge were the next to depart for Sydney, the former muttering, "Who the hell's going to drink milk?" The Owen-

Rutledge team returned two weeks later (travel time included) after having spent a more traditional time in the big city. They showed signs of wear from the daily grind of making pub calls at the Royal Australian Hotel and other watering holes.

My name should have been next on the list, at least I thought so, but two of the old-timers were tapped for R&R ahead of me. I protested to Executive Officer Wood, who managed to look uncomfortable when he offered the excuse that I did not have enough missions. "So, what about Jones and Murison?" No answer. It appeared to me that Major Wells's hand must be on the leave roster, so I added another thorn or two to my martyr's crown. Passing the matter off as nothing at all, I vowed to remind Wood that I was still around each time another group of officers went to Sydney—I wanted to be sure he stayed uncomfortable—but nothing changed.

Early in October, three replacements crews came into the 389th as more of the original contingent of pilots rotated home. All three of the pilots had been instructors at the Florence, South Carolina, Replacement Training Unit. Two of them in particular gave an impression of superiority by virtue of their experience. Those of us who had been at Charlotte tired of hearing how things were done at Florence, but after they were exposed to a few missions, the ex-instructors became somewhat subdued and dropped the air of condescension when dealing with those who had been their students. The newcomers soon found favor with the major by participating in evening bridge games with him.

The morning of October 11 was overcast at Hollandia and it threatened to be a day of steady rain. We were eating breakfast in the 389th mess when Len Happ, the operations officer, asked Lt. Albert Eddy if he was going to take the squadron's B-25 to Nadzab that morning. There were a number of gunners and pilots in the 312th Group who had completed their missions and were going to Nadzab to await transportation back to the States. Having looked at the lead-colored sky with low, smoky scud and a gusty wind from the southwest portending changing weather, I was surprised when Eddy said, "Oh sure, we can get down there okay."

Happ also seemed a little surprised by Eddy's offhanded reply, but he looked around the table for a copilot to go with Eddy. Having judged by the weather that it was no morning to go anywhere, I concentrated on my dehydrated eggs and fried Spam. For reasons now lost in time, probably from flying his wing on a mission or two, I was not impressed by Eddy's style or his competence in a B-25. I hoped that Happ would not notice me and felt a wave of relief when he assigned Flt. Off. Ralph Preston, a new man, to go along as copilot.

A 388th Squadron B-25 was also taking some passengers to Nadzab that morning, and Lieutenant Happ, with Don Dyer as copilot, was flying the group's C-47 to the same destination with some additional passengers and to pick up cargo. The passengers were divided up, with the pilots traveling in the B-25 nicknamed "Eager Beaver" being flown by Walt Hill, and the gunners going with Eddy in "Five Minutes to Midnite." The weather front was moving in fast and soon after taking off, all three of the planes headed for Nadzab were on instruments.

After first trying to get through the bad weather on instruments and then going beneath it on the deck, Len Happ elected to return home. "Eager Beaver" also attempted to get through the bad weather but eventually, with the strong encouragement of his pilot passengers, Hill turned around. Hollandia was closed in by then, so both the C-47 and "Eager Beaver" continued west along the coast and eventually landed on Biak Island.

Nothing was ever heard from Lieutenant Eddy and Flight Officer Preston in "Five Minutes to Midnite." In all likelihood, the plane had gone down in the ocean when Eddy attempted to fly on instruments in the turbulent air and pouring, blowing rain. The loss of twelve men in this incident was doubly regrettable since the passengers were all on their way home after having completed their tours. New Guinea's weather was an unpredictable factor and many planes were lost during the war because of it, either over the sea or over those parts of the map marked "Unexplored."

The 386th Squadron flew a low-level mission to Sarmi on October 12. This target had become routine—considered a milk run by most—since the Japanese there were isolated and it was only a matter of time before our infantry obliterated them. Milk run or not, however, the enemy was still dangerous. Ground gunners hit the plane piloted by 1st Lt. William Cornelius and it crashed into the sea off the Sarmi Peninsula. Cornelius was one of the replacement pilots who joined the group when I did. We had also trained together at Charlotte.

The 389th lost another plane on October 17, this one piloted by one of the former instructor pilots. The squadron set off that morning for another medium-altitude run over Babo. We cleared the coast at Tanahmerah Bay and the formation took up a westerly heading just off the shore. It was a bright, clear morning and we settled down for the two-hour-plus flight to Babo, cruising along at our usual altitude of one thousand feet. We were flying in two sections with two three-ship flights in each section. Along the shore, a rather narrow strand of beach with palm trees was separated from the main shore and jungle by a lagoon perhaps as much as five hundred feet wide.

Parallel on the left and a little lower than our section, the other section was passing over the lagoon a little higher than the palm trees. The trim A-20s flying in close formation were a pretty sight with palm trees in the foreground and the dark green wall of jungle behind. Then, as I was admiring the picture, I saw the propeller on the right engine of the closest plane across the way slow down to windmill speed, evidently losing power. The thought crossed my mind that at least the pilot would not have to sweat out Babo that morning, that he had only a short distance to go to get back to Hollandia.

My mind went over the drill the pilot in the other cockpit would be following when the engine quit: Throttle, "CLOSED"; mixture to idle-cutoff; feather right propeller; right ignition switch, "OFF"; right gas, "OFF." The plane momentarily held its position in the formation with the prop still windmilling, then slowly began to drop back.

A voice in my head repeated, "Open the bomb bay! Dump the bombs!" However, the pilot made no attempt to get rid of the load. Perhaps he was busy trying to restart the dead engine. The plane still flew straight ahead, but it was steadily losing altitude. I wanted to yell, "Feather the prop! Salvo the bombs! Turn for the beach, for Christ's sake!" Soon the plane would be below the level of the palms and unable to reach the beach to belly in if he must. As our formation pulled ahead another plane joined the one in trouble and the radio crackled with directions to feather the prop, drop the bomb load, and so forth. I figured the pilot of the crippled plane would be all right now that he had someone to prompt him and lead him back to Hollandia.

We continued on toward Babo as the spare plane eased into the vacant spot. However, in another hour the clouds were building up and the weather front was solid on the west side of Geelvink Bay. The mission was aborted when our leader could find no way to penetrate the weather to reach Babo and we returned to Hollandia in about three and a half hours. We were stunned to learn that the plane with the windmilling prop had crashed in the jungle, killing the pilot, 2d Lt. Thomas Harkey, and his gunner, Cpl. Herbert Hampton.

The pilot who had attempted to shepherd Harkey home reported that the prop was never feathered nor the bomb load dropped. The plane could not maintain altitude on a single engine and went into the jungle less than thirty miles from Hollandia. The crewmen's bodies were recovered a day or so later. Harkey was the least pretentious of the three ex-instructors who had joined us and was on his second mission. He had reportedly taken a course in A-20 single-engine operation at Wright-Patterson Field, which made his actions all the more difficult to explain.

How did we react to such losses as these? It may have been a little quieter at the first meal or two after Eddy and Preston disappeared, and Harkey's two friends from Florence undoubtedly were shocked. Nevertheless, little was said. We sometimes dated events from "the day so-and-so went in," but it was an unusually close relationship that found any of us still outwardly affected a week or so after a crash. Inwardly, each of us was touched in his own way by such events and our confidence jolted to a greater or lesser extent. It was just part of the game. I, and probably most of the others, continued to reject morbid thoughts about the obviously dangerous circumstances we sometimes faced—just as I knew the next accident would also happen to someone else. When a man lost confidence that he would somehow make it safely through his tour, it seemed to bring on trouble for that individual.

The gunners who had come over as part of the three-man crews were often uncomfortable when they found they had to fly with another pilot than the one to which they had originally been assigned. However, with two gunners in each crew and only one gunner flying on a mission, there was a surplus, so they were assigned to fly in rotation. In any event, a gunner sitting back in the A-20's turret wondering what was coming up ahead, sometimes with a pilot of unknown quality, could understandably develop apprehensions.

George Millson and Leon Schnell came around to the tent one evening, accompanied by Cpl. James Trumpey from Peterson's crew. They wanted to tell me that they were of a mind to request relief from flying status. They said they did not mind flying with me, but they were distrustful of pilots they did not know. We discussed the risks involved weighed against the opportunity to go home within a year, but I was unable to urge them to stick it out. I thought none the less of them for their decisions. Jim Trumpey may have gone back to flying a little later, the draw of going home to his wife in Evansville, Indiana, outweighing his qualms. One of these fellows would often be at my hardstand after a mission, just to find out how things had gone and offer to help service the plane if needed.

The group or squadron soon became your family, and activities outside that sphere were of secondary concern. The 3d Attack Group was also based at Hollandia while we were there. Its A-20s were parked on the opposite side of the runway from ours and their tent area was located beyond the east end of the strip, off toward Lake Sentani. Although it was not far away, I can recall going over there to visit my friends Bob Mosley and Bill Morgan on only two or three occasions. We had been in the same family back at Charlotte, the 53d Squadron, but now our paths seldom crossed.

On my first visit to Mosley and Morgan after we had been in New Guinea for six weeks or so I was struck by the change in their appearance. They seemed older and quieter. It was not just the noticeable yellow tint of our skins caused by Atabrine. The more serious aspects of life were changing us all, even if it was not noticeable on a day-to-day basis. During my second visit, Mosley and Morgan reported that Capt. Bill Neel from Charlotte was back with the 3d Attack Group for a second combat tour. Mosley observed that Neel did not seem to be the same fellow we had known in the 53d Squadron. None of the pilots he had known in 1942–43 were still in the group.

Bill Neel had gone to Nadzab that day, so we did not meet. Nevertheless, I could not help recalling his premonition about a second tour. When I went back a couple of weeks later to look up Neel, Morgan and Mosley told me that Bill's plane and another A-20 were missing on a later flight to Nadzab. It was thought that they had run into bad weather. Bill Neel's premonition had proven to be all too true. Planes that disappeared into the New Guinea jungle during the war are still turning up more than fifty years later. However, I have never been able to confirm that Bill Neel's was ever located.

Chapter 7

MARKING TIME

DAY AFTER DAY IN EARLY OCTOBER, 1944, navy vessels and transport ships gathered in the Hollandia anchorage until they filled most of Humboldt Bay. The invasion of the Philippines was MacArthur's next step up the island ladder toward Japan. It was an indication to us that the time was getting close for the 312th to begin moving north. On some of our practice flights we came across the harbor at low altitude to show the navy how good we looked. The word came down to cease and desist after Major Wells led us across on a particularly realistic run, weaving in and around the ships and then pulling up at the last minute as we crossed the shore.

As we watched the growing exhibition of naval power I wondered where all the ships were coming from. The Seventh Fleet had been supporting MacArthur's campaign in New Guinea since 1943, but until now it had been small, consisting mainly of submarines, troop transports, and destroyers to protect them. The Philippine invasion demanded most of the naval power in the Pacific, so ships from the Third Fleet based at Pearl Harbor were transferred to the Seventh for the planned landings on Leyte. Part of the invasion force had at first gathered at the naval base at Manus in the Admiralty Islands, then the two fleets joined up at Hollandia to sail north. General MacArthur, quite understandably, chose not to share his invasion plans with us at this time.

The 389th was flying the day the main force set off toward the northwest for Leyte and it was a sight to behold. There were more carriers in evidence than I had imagined existed, plus numerous cruisers, destroyers, and several battleships. The convoy, which included countless transport ships and specially designed Landing Ship Tanks (LSTs), stretched to the northern horizon and for miles to the east and west as it moved off. Within two days, the Humboldt Bay anchorage was empty.

The news of the successful invasion of Leyte in the central Philippines on October 20 was well covered by Capt. Nate Rothstein's newscast at the evening movie. I do not recall Nate attempting anything but straight reporting of the story for, after viewing the gathering invasion force, it was a serious business—even for Nate. Within a day or so, Tokyo Rose, the Japanese propagandist whose voice we sometimes heard, was on the air making pronouncements about the defeat of our troops. She was able to identify many units and where they were located with remarkable accuracy. If she ever identified the 312th Bomb Group, however, I missed it.

The landings on Leyte raised speculation as to which of the light bomb groups would move up first. Rumor had it that since the 417th had gone into Noemfoor Island west of Biak and the 3rd Attack had preceded us to Hollandia, then the 312th would be the first into Leyte. Unlike most rumors, this one proved to be reasonably correct, although our move north would be much farther off than we anticipated. In the meantime, we waited and wondered.

About mid-October there was a shuffle of commanding officers for the 389th. Major Wells was promoted to lieutenant colonel and moved up to group headquarters as deputy group commander under Colonel Strauss. Wells's place was taken by Capt. Clifton Graber, one of the original 312th members who had been in the group operations section before coming to the 389th. Those who knew Clif Graber liked him and he was welcomed as the new CO. However, he caused a stir when he proposed bringing a new squadron intelligence officer with him.

The 389th's intelligence officer was Capt. Leonard Dulac. He would be sent to an opening at Fifth Air Force headquarters in order to open the squadron position for Graber's new man. Dulac had been with the 389th since the beginning and seemed to most of us to have done a conscientious job as intelligence officer. Although moving to Fifth Air Force headquarters might have sounded impressive, Dulac did not look upon leaving the 312th as a step up. Len expressed his objections to Captain Graber to no avail. The 389th's old-timers, who knew him best, had some fun kidding Dulac about his "prestigious promotion" to headquarters, but Leonard was not amused.

At some point, before the transfer could take place, Colonel Strauss gave Dulac an opportunity to express his view that the move to a higher echelon was neither his idea nor desired. Suddenly, the officer who was to replace Dulac was himself on the way to Fifth Air Force headquarters.

At lunch a few days after the dustup over the intelligence officer position there were a few comments about so-and-so taking the Fifth Air Force job, which was a *big* promotion. Len Dulac smiled but kept eating his Spam without comment. Quiet and scholarly John Edmunds, the squadron communications officer, had not taken part in needling Len, but now he looked carefully around the table to attract our attention before speaking with solemnity and seriousness. "There's a lesson here for all of us," he said. We waited as John paused theatrically before delivering his wisdom: "Don't fuck with Dulac!" Leonard looked pleased as we roared at John's incongruous and unexpected comment.

Later, in appropriate situations when he was the subject of kidding, Len would smile and say, "Remember what Edmunds told you!"

October ended with a pleasant surprise for Maury Owen and me: we were assigned our own planes on the thirtieth. They were new A-20G-45DO models with only eight hours of ferry time on them and bore the serial numbers 43–21957 and 43–21958. It was like taking delivery of a new car, untouched by others and with the distinctive smell of fresh paint and insulation. For the majority of my future flights in the 389th, my call sign would be "Sugar 958."

The crew chief assigned to my plane was Sgt. Ernest Koch of West Hazleton, Pennsylvania, who took much pride in having the new ship. It was not until years later that Ernie admitted to experiencing some disquietude when he learned that "Rough Landing" Rutter would be his pilot. Owen and I put five or six hours of slow-time flying on the engines in the next few days and found only a few bugs that needed minor correction.

To me, "Sugar 958" would always seem just a bit superior in feel and performance to most ships, probably due in large part to Ernie's meticulous attention. Ernie was so particular about *our* plane that he once complained about other pilots who occasionally flew it smoking and throwing their cigarette butts on the cockpit floor. "How about telling your buddies to knock off throwing the butts around, Lieutenant?" Ernie growled. It would have been amusing to post a "No Smoking" sign in the cockpit, for nonsmokers were a rarity in the armed forces during the war.

A large *C* was painted on the vertical stabilizer and rudder, a white spade under the horizontal stabilizer to identify the ship as being in the 389th Squadron, and our names were lettered just below the cockpit window on the left side. There was no personal decoration on 958 since neither Ernie nor I thought up an appropriate name or artwork, at least none that was entertaining enough to be worth a bottle of whiskey to have it painted on the aircraft. It was one of only a few A-20s in the 389th without at least a pet name painted on the fuselage. Owen's was another, although his crew chief did decorate the wheel covers with the squadron spade on a white background. Ernie's response when I asked if he was going to do the same was, "To hell with it!"

My sixteenth and seventeenth missions were short ones to the Sarmi Peninsula near Wakde Island flown on November 5 and 6. The Japanese were still resisting as they had been since my first mission on August 4. Our ground forces had only one objective: prevent interference with the airstrip on Wakde by keeping the enemy away from the shore opposite the island. An occasional bombing and strafing run on the Japanese lines served as support for the troops holding our perimeter line. There was little danger that the enemy would be reinforced.

Both the rainy season and the determined Japanese resistance slowed the conquest of Leyte, located at about the midpoint on the eastern side of the Philippines chain. The main enemy forces were on the larger islands of Luzon and Mindanao, but reinforcements were quickly moved to Leyte. The 312th's ground echelon, which included most of our equipment and men other than those directly needed to maintain and fly the planes, was scheduled to depart for Leyte on November 12. When our support facilities departed we would not be able to fly any more combat missions. We would then be limited to practice flying until the planes and crews could be moved north when an airfield became available.

Early in November, the 312th struck camp. All of the individual tents, including truck tarps such as mine, were packed up for the trip to Leyte. Two large hospital tents were provided for the 389th's pilots and the remaining enlisted men, mostly gunners and crew chiefs. The tent for the officers had been the enlisted men's club. It boasted such amenities as a cement floor and parachutes lining the ceiling. A small generator with a single-cylinder engine provided enough power for a few light bulbs. One mess hall was left intact to feed the men remaining behind in all four squadrons and everyone shared the common chow line with mess kit service. The 389th's latrine was a four-holer left out in the open with nothing, not even a truck tarp, for shade or rain protection. We hoped our stay would be short.

One thing could be said for everybody living together: we got to know each other better, whether we wanted to or not. The living really was not that much more primitive than when we were in the pyramidal tents, although we now had to use mosquito bars over our cots. The small generator permitted me to continue to use my Remington electric razor, although the electrical interference it caused was a source of annoyance for those trying to listen to Armed Forces Radio or Tokyo Rose. The generator eventually broke down and we were all reduced to using safety razors and lantern light.

One of the newer pilots in the 389th was 2d Lt. John P. Downey, a Wisconsin native who had joined us sometime in October. Downey was a quiet fellow who seemed to wear every bit of equipment he had ever been issued, including a helmet and large plastic goggles with an orange-tinted face piece, when flying. Most of us found the full-face piece to be too hot and tossed it away. At about this time, Owen received a box of books from his wife, Rosalie, and shared them around. Downey, who borrowed one titled *Laughing Boy*, would sit outside of the tent in the afternoon reading his new favorite literature and giggle or roar with laughter as he turned the pages. Thereafter, his name was "Laughing Boy" as far as Owen was concerned. Downey did not seem to mind the handle, but not everyone Owen nicknamed was so accepting.

The plan had called for the new airfields on Leyte to become operational reasonably quickly. It supposedly was just a matter of upgrading the enemy airstrips on the island's eastern side, but as it turned out, the selected ground near Dulag proved unsuitable for the large airfield complex planned for us and the monsoon rains slowed construction efforts. We had figured on moving the planes up to the Philippines two or three weeks after our ground contingent landed, but it wound up being six weeks.

Grant Peterson, my tent mate, was still at Nadzab instructing at the Combat Replacement Training Center as we anticipated the move to Leyte. He was expected to return to the 389th by the end of November, but it did not work out that way. Pete was shot down on November 10 while leading a group of A-20 trainees over the airstrip at Wewak. Wewak had once been a very hot target and there were still thousands of Japanese Eighteenth Army troops in the area. The airstrips had been more or less neutralized in the spring, before the Hollandia landings, so the CRTC used Wewak as a target for realistic training missions. The danger from ground fire was considered minimal, but on more than one occasion the dormant guns came to life and surprised the attackers.

Later, one of the trainees who had been with Pete the day he went down told us the story of his fatal flight. After making a low-level sweep over one of the airstrips, Pete was not satisfied with his students' performance. He instructed them to watch while he made a second run to demonstrate how it should be done. The Japanese antiaircraft gunners were waiting: a 75-mm gun at the end of the airstrip barked once and Pete crashed. It was a rash demonstration: a single plane making a run after the ground gunners had been alerted was a sitting duck. I suppose Pete had led so many missions there that it seemed safe enough. His body was reportedly found at Wewak after the war.

Our new squadron CO, Captain Graber, was as friendly and approachable as Major, now Lieutenant Colonel, Wells had been distant and aloof. He was a ruggedly handsome rascal and usually wore a pleasant smile on his face. After a few days of observation, the inimitable Owen dubbed Graber "Smilin' Jack," after the main character in the popular comic strip drawn by Zack Mosley. Soon, whenever he was beyond earshot, several of us would refer to Graber by his new nickname.

On the day before the LSTs carrying the 312th Group's troops to the Philippines set sail, Graber led the squadron across the harbor at Hollandia in one last low-level pass to inspire the boys. The sight from the LSTs must have been extremely impressive: Smilin' Jack was so low that he knocked the radio antenna off one of the ships, putting a neat slice in the skin of his wing. Later, somewhat embarrassed, Graber said, "I didn't know they had those damn antennas on those tubs."

The 312th Bomb Group's ground echelon sailed in convoy for Leyte as scheduled on Sunday, November 12, and landed near Dulag a week later. Those in the ground party found little more than confusion and mud even though it had been a month since the initial landings. Moreover, it continued to rain almost daily, adding to their misery. The plan to base our planes on an airstrip near Dulag was not feasible because of the ground conditions, so the engineers hurriedly built a new airstrip along the beach north of the village of Tanauan. These delays and other changes in plans meant that the crews back at Hollandia would have to live in the large hospital tents until the end of December.

Even before we moved into the communal tents to await the flight to the Philippines, the quality of our food had been declining. Our fare had seemed good to me back in August and September, mainly because the 389th's cooks were inventive in their preparation of the GI staples of dehydrated potatoes, desiccated vegetables, corned (bully) beef, and dried fruits. Breakfasts typically consisted of dehydrated eggs, dehydrated potatoes (fried as hashed browns and a little greasy), dried prunes or apricots, and coffee. Strangely, there was never any juice with the stewed prunes or apricots and we wondered

In November, 1944—while the flight crews were waiting to move to the Philippines—the 389th Squadron CO called for a formal inspection. Here, Lieutenants Rutter and Rutledge try to make a good impression; the helmets made good washbasins and were seldom worn except on special occasions.

why. The juice, we learned much later, went to an outlying antiaircraft battery in exchange for homemade liquor with a fruity flavor which the cooks enjoyed.

The cooks were innovative with the ubiquitous canned meat product called Spam. They would serve fried Spam for breakfast, Spam salad at lunch, and Spam meat loaf with mashed potatoes for supper. It tasted good the first ten times or so, but then one's palate became jaded. C-ration stew became a welcome change. The disruptions caused by the wholesale move of the Fifth Air Force's units to the Philippines were probably responsible for the monotonous diet. The vitamin pills that Doc Walsh mandated we take daily probably saved us from having any serious health problems.

One night, some men from the quartermaster depot came through our area with a jeep and trailer loaded with cases of frozen pork chops. The price was $20 per fifty-four-pound case, so we bought several cases of the obviously purloined pork. Soon, everyone in the tent with a gasoline stove was busy frying pork chops in mess kits greased with tropical butter, a concoction that was almost impossible to melt.

Our Jewish pilot, Melvin Kapson, was bent over his stove when I reminded him that he was cooking *pork* chops. With hardly a pause, Mel made a sign over the skillet and intoned, "Hocus, Pocus! You're beef!" We ate pork chops for several days—until they became a little gamy because of the lack of refrigeration. There was another pork chop feed a week or so later when our enlisted men hijacked the jeep as the enterprising quartermaster merchants again drove through the area.

Occasionally someone in the tent would offer a bottle of gin or two if a volunteer would drive down to the navy galley for ice cream. The naval headquarters was in the village of Hollandia, a trip of about twenty miles each way over a gravel road in the dark. The thought of ice cream was usually enough to ensure at least one volunteer driver would speak up. The U.S. Navy was programmed to construct elaborate galleys with concrete floors, screened walls, and an ice cream machine before any other buildings were built at a base. As with the sergeant at the sawmill, liquor was required to coax the petty officer in charge of the galley to find some surplus ice cream for us.

The planes traveling between Australia and Hollandia provided us a steady supply of booze, and the navy was always thirsty. The rate of exchange was fifteen to twenty-five gallons of ice cream per quart of gin, but the transaction had to be made in the dark of night after regular mess hours. The ice cream was carefully packed in a large lard can and the split when the jeep returned to the 389th's area was ten gallons for the officers and fifteen gallons for the enlisted men. Ice cream, no matter what flavor the navy supplied, never tasted better.

A radio beacon was installed at Hollandia in November to serve as a navigation aid. Each pilot flew a practice homing problem using the new beacon. The drill consisted of going north over the sea about one hundred to 150 miles. Using the radio compass tuned to the beacon, we would find our approximate location by taking several bearings and then return home on the beacon's beam.

My plane was out of service when I was scheduled for a training flight on November 21, so I took the plane assigned to Don Murison. Don's plane was an older one that he had inherited from Ken Hedges in October when Ken went back to the States. It bore a large *H* on the tail and the name "Queen of Spades" on the nose. Don commented from time to time that his plane did not feel right in the air, that the control column had a somewhat loose feeling when moved fore and aft, but the crew chief was unable to figure out the cause.

Don asked to go along with me on the homing beacon flight to see what I thought of the plane's responses, especially the sloppy feel of the elevators. We took out the five-man life raft and Don lay on the shelf behind me while we flew the navigation problem. Looking back, it is indicative of the attitudes of youth that we discarded the life raft even though we were going to spend upward of two hours flying over water in a plane that seemed to have some quirks.

The radio compass had no trouble homing in on the beacon a hundred or more miles from Hollandia and we successfully ran the problem.

The feel of the control column, which Don had correctly described, was similar to what I had experienced with one or two other A-20s. It was annoying, but not particularly alarming. When leveling out after climbing or making a shallow dive, the control column moved back and forth or "hunted" and the plane would bob a bit in pitch before settling down to level flight. The control column did not move very far either way, but it was still quite noticeable. Could it have been worn pulleys or slack cables somewhere in the elevator control system, or perhaps worn hinges or loose fabric on the elevators? Don's crew chief reportedly had replaced the hinges and otherwise checked around and found nothing amiss. Whatever the cause, I did not think the condition was anything dangerous, although it was obviously not right, and I told Don so.

Back at the tent we all talked about the peculiarity, which other pilots had noticed when flying Don's plane. It was suggested that on the next flight he try a not too severe pullout at a little higher speed to see how the plane reacted. Maybe something would show up. None of us were engineers, but we thought that if the hunting was more severe at higher speeds the cause might be pinpointed. Don was considerably more concerned about the plane's condition than I might have been, but he was the one who had to fly it on every mission.

The next day, November 22, Don was back in the air with *H* trying to solve the mystery. Several crew chiefs on the flight line saw him diving steeply down through a scattered cloud layer to the west of the field when the plane failed to pull out. The observers saw something come off the descending A-20, but whether it was a structural piece or just the canopy being released as Don tried to leave the plane was uncertain. Was he too low to pull out at the speed he was diving, or had something failed at a higher altitude? In any event, the plane, as verified when it was later located, had hit the ground hard on the edge of Lake Sentani a few miles southwest of the Hollandia airstrip.

After lunch, a group of pilots and a couple of crew chiefs made an effort to reach the crash site, which from the air seemed to be close and accessible. The plan was to get to the top of a steep, conical hill from which we might see the wreckage and get a line to hike through the *kunai* grass to the edge of the lake. The hill was so steep that Cal Slade alone drove the jeep up while we passengers pushed. Then, after getting a visual line on the crash site, we hiked down the other side toward the lake.

The crash site was perhaps a half-mile away across a patch of *kunai* grass and we anticipated an easy jaunt. The *kunai* grass was seven or more feet high and had tough, sharp blades. The ground turned out to be spongy under foot when not just plain swampy. The *kunai* did not bend easily, and hacking at it with machetes was hard work in the heat and humidity out of reach of any breeze. The expected short hike soon became intolerable. We finally gave up in defeat and retreated to the hilltop and the jeep.

An amusing incident on this otherwise sad mission occurred as we were crossing a wide, but shallow stream before getting to the hill. A group of natives had been watching our expedition earlier and they were watching again as we approached the stream on the return trip. We started across but did not get far before the jeep bogged down in about two feet of water. As we pulled off our shoes in preparation for getting out to push, five or six natives started out toward us. They were rather rough looking customers with their loincloths, fuzzy hair, and betel-nut-stained teeth. We wondered about their intent. They approached the jeep very deliberately and then stood around eyeing us in a noncommittal manner. Finally, the tallest native, who apparently was the leader, put his hands on the back of the jeep and looked up at us with a wide, red-stained, gapped-tooth grin and shouted the universal GI cry, "Hubba! Hubba!" Both sides burst into laughter and the natives shoved the jeep onto firm gravel in nothing flat.

The following day, Thanksgiving, Mel Kapson, using a sack of rice as payment, went across the lake with some natives in canoes and retrieved Don Murison's body. Kapson had been in at least two other 312th squadrons before being shuffled into the 389th from the 387th. He was something of an unknown quantity to us and the word was he had been traded around because he had problems getting along. Mel earned our respect for what he did that Thanksgiving Day.

Twenty-year-old Don Murison was buried in the military cemetery at Hollandia the day after Thanksgiving, 1944. Most of the 389th's pilots attended. The cemetery was located on a small hill, a natural clearing where the earth had been scraped bare in preparation for the graves. The GI casket rested on trestles in a tent. After brief instructions from a Graves Registration Unit officer regarding the formalities of a military funeral, we picked up the casket and slowly carried it out into the sunshine and down a row of graves heaped with bare red soil to the open hole. The chaplain said a short prayer, there was the plaintive call of taps, and the service was over. If there was any more to the ceremony I cannot recall it. Yet, for most of us, it seemed entirely befitting.

I never heard anyone knowledgeable say exactly what had caused Don's plane to go in, nor was a specific cause identified for the control column's annoying "hunting"—in other planes as well as Don's. Don, a native of Albany, California, had been well liked by members of the squadron. He was one of the happy-go-lucky characters when we were flying cadets together and at Charlotte, however, after flying a few missions, Don changed noticeably. He took a sincere interest in religion and became a Roman Catholic while with the 389th, as was his tent mate, Tom Jones. The change in Murison's outlook surprised me. I had known him rather well at Charlotte, and he was very serious about his conversion.

The group had two B-25s that were used as utility transports when not needed as lead ships on medium-altitude bombing missions. A B-25 went down to Cairns, Queensland, on the northeast coast of Australia about every two weeks to pick up fresh vegetables, aircraft parts, and other supplies. Captain Graber surprised me one evening by asking how much B-25 time I had. He said he needed a copilot for the trip south to

Cairns. Faced with the prospect of a trip to the land of milk and honey, not to mention beer, bathtubs, and clean sheets, I did not hide my B-25 experience. What an unexpected surprise!

We flew down the north coast of New Guinea the morning of December 6 with pleasant weather and Graber doing the flying. I could pick out such places as Atape, Wewak, and Lae on the coast and saw distant mountains, some with snow showing, to the south. We climbed steadily as we passed over Nadzab and then crossed over the Owen Stanley Mountains before stopping at Port Moresby for fuel and lunch. The flight thus far had been a pleasant sightseeing trip for me, while landmarks familiar to Graber all along the way made for easy visual navigation. We had not bothered with courses marked on the chart because of the clear conditions and the fact that we were over familiar territory. It was my job as copilot to plot the courses, but I was taking my lead from Smilin' Jack.

After we finished refueling and were about ready to get into the plane to fly the leg to Australia, the captain surprised me by asking if I had a course laid out for Cairns. He was visibly irked when I answered, "No! We can't miss if we just fly south, can we?" My attitude was a bit too nonchalant for a jump of about five hundred miles over water, no matter how favorable the weather might appear and how many times Graber had been over the route. I at once realized that it was poor form for the copilot to assume that the pilot had the route charted. At the least, I should have asked if he wanted a course laid out.

Graber took the chart, pinched it at Port Moresby and Cairns and made a crease so I could measure the course heading. It was not south, 180 degrees, but rather 192 degrees, and we would not have made landfall until far south of Cairns. It took us about two and one-half hours to fly over the Coral Sea and, to my surprise, Captain Graber was able to sleep most of the way with his careless copilot at the controls. The weather held fair for the entire distance and there were several reefs for checkpoints along our roughly plotted route. On the return trip I would plot my course legs and headings with fifty-mile checkpoints marked all the way to Hollandia.

The officer who had the job at Cairns—living in a house on the beach and buying supplies to fill the food orders—must have been a great politician in civilian life. This duty could hardly have been called work and Cairns was not very dangerous. Being diligent about his responsibilities, the Cairns trooper was at the airfield shortly after we landed. We turned over the food requisition and funds and the Cairns huckster gave us his jeep. He suggested that we might enjoy spending a few days in the village of Innisfail, about forty miles south of Cairns, while he got our food ready to go.

The road to Innisfail was paved, but was mostly a single lane with turnouts here and there in case you encountered oncoming traffic. Graber took the wheel, the B-25 crew chief and radio operator hopped in back, and we headed for Innisfail at high speed. Fortunately, there was little traffic, so we had only two or three close shaves on that narrow, winding road.

Innisfail's main street looked like a stage set for a Hollywood western with wooden false-fronted stores, wooden awnings extending over the sidewalks, and here and there a second-story gallery. The Exchange Hotel was in keeping with the rest of the town: a frame two- or three-story building on the main street. We checked into rooms that had plain wooden walls without plaster, no upholstered furniture, narrow single beds with a mosquito bar above, and a washbasin with running water. Other facilities were down the hall.

We all made a beeline for the showers, after which the crew chief, who had been to Innisfail on other trips, went out and rounded up a case with twenty-four quart-sized bottles of cold beer. The four of us relaxed on the second-story gallery overlooking the main street and enjoyed the scene. We had come a long way in a day and the civilized surroundings were most welcome compared to New Guinea. Innisfail was not entirely a rough country town, however. There was a bowling green, and bowlers dressed in their whites would gather in the evening for a few games.

We stayed at the Exchange Hotel for three nights, each of us relaxing in our own way. We had steak and eggs for breakfast and steak each evening for supper. The Australian liquor laws limited the number of hours a licensed establishment could remain open each day, but not all pubs kept the same hours. By inquiring around we were able to determine that a little driving about the countryside would ensure beer was available from noon onward. It also gave us an incentive for exploring the local scenery. The most notable sight in the region was an attractive waterfall not far from Innisfail with a pub adjacent to it. I was learning to like the mild Australian beer, but there was also an ice cream parlor in Innisfail. An American-sized cone could be built up for a tuppence per dip and I stopped there several times.

One strange character at the Exchange Hotel was a U.S. Navy seaman we noticed in the dining room the first evening. He was obviously on good terms with one of the waitresses. After waving to us at our table, he kept his distance the rest of the night. At breakfast the second morning, the sailor came over, introduced himself, and pulled up a chair at our invitation. He knew quite a lot about the community, which we found interesting. After considerable general discussion he said, "You fellows might as well know that I'm AWOL [absent without leave]. I've been living here for six weeks and I don't intend to go back until they come and get me. You won't turn me in will you?" We assured him we had no interest in telling the navy where to find their errant seaman. I have often wondered how long he was able to sit out the war in peaceful Innisfail.

We went back to Cairns on December 9 with the expectation that our grocery order would probably be ready for loading. Perhaps because he knew how enjoyable a visit to Australia was for his compatriots living in New Guinea, the supply officer reported there had been a delay in filling our order. We also had some parts to pick up at the air depot in Townsville, about 175 miles farther down the coast, so we spent the afternoon flying down there and back. We stayed at the 312th's rented house in Cairns that night and, after loading the food aboard the following morning, took off for the north.

The trip back to Hollandia was uneventful. We had good weather all the way and I kept the map with my plotted courses on my knee. The operator of a restaurant in Cairns, a Chinese woman who was well acquainted with the supply trips made by the 312th Group, had given us a basket of fried chicken to eat for lunch when we landed at Port Moresby. After eating and refueling we hopped over the Owen Stanleys and set down at Nadzab to pick up some more parts. The heat and humidity there were stifling. We quickly agreed, at the prompting of the crew chief, that the fresh milk we had on board would probably go sour before we got to Hollandia, so we all drank our fill. The crew chief and radio operator smiled when I said, "I thought we were supposed to be taking the milk to Hollandia." We each took another swig, our consciences clear. Sour milk would hardly be worthwhile, would it?

The usual method of transporting the fresh food back from Australia was to cruise at about ten thousand feet where the temperature was cool and make only one short stop for fuel. However, on this trip we had to make another stop at Gusap where there were still some 312th men packing equipment to ship north. At Gusap I recall someone congratulating Graber upon his just-announced promotion to major. It was the first time he had heard the good news. We finally arrived at Hollandia just before supper and, as might be anticipated, our three extended stops had not been good for the perishables. The milk was sour, the lettuce had spoiled, and the tomatoes and cabbage looked doubtful. At least the onions would help improve the C-ration stew, and the radishes would also be welcome.

While we were marking time in the big tent at Hollandia there were some additions to the 389th's roster: William C. Clark, a young second lieutenant, and Maj. Theodore A. Suiter, a veteran pilot who had been assigned to the training command, were both fresh from the States. They were followed by a second lieutenant named Osborn, who came to us from a fighter group elsewhere in the SWPA. He was an experienced pilot who had been flying P-40s most recently. Major Suiter appeared to be well into his thirties (or more) and had been a BT-13 instructor pilot at a basic flying school for some time. Although he lacked experience in both the A-20 and combat flying, he was slated by rank to become our squadron commander. These three will appear later in this chronicle in roles that are tragic, sad, and amusing.

A few days after the supply flight to Cairns, Major Graber approached me and said: "Rutter, I've been looking over the files and it looks like you've never gone on leave. Why is that?"

"I don't know, Major," I replied. "Maybe you should ask Colonel Wells."

"Well, we'll see that you get down on the next leave trip." He was as good as his word; Mel Kapson and I were both on the December 15 leave roster.

Delighted at the prospect of seeing Sydney, I began to pack at once. I celebrated the occasion by opening the bottle of combat whiskey I had accumulated. Rather than downing the two ounces of liquor that we were given after each mission, I had followed the example of several others and saved my ration in a quart bottle. Without hesitating, I took two big swigs from the bottle and let out a war whoop. Owen and Don Dyer watched this performance with some amusement, knowing that my drinking of anything stronger than beer was unusual.

Owen smiled and licked his lips when I proffered the bottle. He took a modest gulp and then shouted, "Goddam!" As Owen shook his head in puzzlement, Don accepted my invitation and then, after a good swig, cried out, "Jeez-us! What the hell is that?"

"It's just regular combat whiskey," I said and then downed another sip. "Doc Walsh changed brands a couple of months back, so it's about two-thirds Ancient Age bourbon and one-third scotch."

Major Graber confirmed that the combination made for a bad drink, but took another sip anyhow. Owen and Dyer refused any more of the concoction, which was a notable event. The bourbon-scotch mixture did not seem to bother me, pleasant or otherwise.

The morning of December 16 was dark and gloomy. Rain was falling steadily when Kapson and I were dropped off at the Air Transport Command (ATC) operations office on the Cyclops strip. There would be no flights leaving until the weather improved, so we sat down with our bags to wait. After an hour or so the ATC clerk said that the weather reports were no better and there would probably be no flights going out that day. Kapson, who had been to Sydney on other leaves, was not about to delay our departure if there was any way to get out of Hollandia. We got a ride over to the Sentani strip, from which the troop carrier planes operated, in the hope that they had less stringent weather standards than the ATC.

The rain was still falling steadily and even the reputedly irresponsible troop carrier folks were not flying. It looked as if we would be delayed at least a day. There was, however, some activity out on the ramp around a bare-metal C-47 with "Australian Airlines" painted on the fuselage. Cargo was being loaded despite the pouring rain, so we ran out and talked to the crew chief, who was directing the loading. Yes, he told us, they proposed to take off for Brisbane as soon as the cargo was aboard. He said there were two or three other passengers (Australians) waiting inside out of the rain and suggested we join them. We raced back to the operations office for our bags and called ATC operations to let them know we were flying out with the Aussies.

The aircraft clearly had seen better days. It was a civilian DC-3 that had been stripped when the war began and outfitted similar to the military C-47. A nameplate on the right side of the cockpit read, "Douglas Aircraft Company, April 6, 1937." In response to an inquiry about the patched holes decorating the cabin and one wing, the crew chief said that the ship had been caught on the ground at Port Moresby during an air raid early in the war. However, C-47s (or DC-3s) had a wonderful reputation for reliability and the age and condition were of little concern to us. The plane was going south, that was all we cared about.

The pilots, one a weather-beaten fellow of indeterminate age and the other very young, were the last to board. Their blue Australian uniforms were soaked through from the rain still beating down. The pilots spoke to us as they came walking up the cabin aisle pulling off their wet tunics. The crew chief pulled the door shut and gave the cargo lashed in the rear of the cabin one final check before he went forward to the cockpit. The rain continued to beat down on the uninsulated cabin.

The wind was blowing the low-hanging scud across the field and there was no sign of any flying activity on the Sentani strip. Kapson and I exchanged glances, resigned to further delay. However, the left prop soon began to turn and the engine burst into life. The right engine also turned over and settled into a steady roar after some initial sputtering.

Streamers of condensation and water blew back from the props as the plane began to move toward the end of the runway. Flying in such conditions was a new experience for me. I walked up and stood in the cockpit doorway to watch how they managed the takeoff.

The Australians had a reputation for having a devil-may-care attitude, being less restricted by regulations than we were, and perhaps a bit reckless but good at what they did. In the pouring rain and low, blowing clouds on that dark morning, the only reason for confidence that we would make a successful takeoff rested with the age and relaxed assurance of the man in the left seat. According to the crew chief, our pilot had been flying in New Guinea since before the war and such weather was neither unusual nor a reason for delaying the trip.

The following radio exchange is verbatim, to the best of my recollection:

"Tower from Aussie Airlines, ready to take the runway. Over."

"Aussie Airlines, this field is closed. Hold your position."

The tower operator had followed protocol. The decision was up to our pilot, who responded, "Tower, our position is on the end of the strip. Believe we shall go, old boy. Please improve the weather next trip."

I could see about two runway lights ahead as the pilot advanced the throttles and the DC-3/C-47 began to roll. The tail came up as we bored into the smoky downpour. Neither of the pilots showed any concern. The pilot fiddled with the trim and glanced across the instrument panel in a relaxed fashion before gently pulling back on the wheel. The ground was instantly gone as we went into the cloud. In all of my attempts at simulated instrument takeoffs, despite intense concentration on holding the heading on the directional gyro, I still had drifted to the edge of the runway. This demonstration made it all look so easy.

The gear came up and the compass showed we were in a gentle turn to the right, away from the Cyclops Mountains, as the plane rocked and bucked in the turbulence and slowly gained altitude. At times the plane seemed to wallow in bands of air currents and sheets of rain, vapor streaming back from the prop and wing tips. As we climbed in and out of patches of darker cloud, the ease with which the Australian pilot flew in that downpour was fascinating to watch. The sound of the engines was a bit ragged from all the moisture and the young copilot turned to look out the side window when the engine on that side gave an unusual cough of the exhaust. They kept running, however, and we continued to climb.

All U.S. planes making the run from Hollandia to Australia at the time were instructed to fly parallel to New Guinea's north coast to the vicinity of Nadzab and then cross over the Owen Stanleys to Port

Moresby and continue on south. The maps of central New Guinea were largely marked "Unexplored," although there were known to be peaks of twelve thousand feet or higher in the mountain range that formed the center spine of the island. The direct route south from Hollandia was much shorter, but there would be a huge area to search in the unexplored zone should a plane go down.

Kapson looked rather doubtful about the wisdom of taking this flight when I reported that we were on a heading of about 170 degrees. We continued to climb and in an hour or so the weather became less severe and the rain slackened, although we never did climb out on top. When the clouds finally cleared in another two hours or so there was nothing but endless jungle visible below and we were well down from the altitude that took us over whatever was sticking up from those unexplored mountains.

We left the seemingly endless swamps of New Guinea's south coast at about noon and crossed the narrow Torres Strait before landing on a rough, unpaved airstrip in the dry country of Cape York on the northeast tip of Australia. We were about six hundred miles from Hollandia, and now that we were safely on the ground it seemed to be the only logical route to follow—given that we had the Australian pilots, of course.

There was a Royal Australian Air Force (RAAF) canteen of sorts at the airstrip where we ate lunch. The fare consisted of thick bread, bully beef, and water. "Tea is later, mate," said the Australian KP dishing out the limited menu when we asked for something better than the warm, chemical-flavored water.

The crew chief and pilot were now looking closely at the right engine. They wiggled some wires and checked several spark plugs at random, but eventually decided that nothing was seriously wrong. Soon we were back in the air, roaring along at low altitude over the scrub trees and giant anthills that cover much of this section of northern Queensland. The sky was cloudless and Brisbane about twelve hundred miles ahead, but it was obvious that all was not well with the right engine. After a couple of hours the crew chief let us know that it would be necessary to stop at Townsville to take another look at the engine. He did not expect the delay to be too great—a set of spark plugs should fix things. Kapson and I were still smiling. By all rights we should still be back cooling our heels at Hollandia with the rain coming down in buckets.

Unfortunately, the new set of plugs the mechanics at Townsville installed did not cure whatever it was that ailed the tired right engine. It was late in the afternoon and the Australians decided they would have to stay over. The aircrew had already put in a long day. We bid the nonchalant pilots and crew chief "Good-bye," along with our sincere thanks for the lift.

Kapson, who knew his way around, soon found a troop carrier plane bound for Brisbane and after a hurried supper we were on our way south again. It was almost midnight by the time we landed at a field outside of Brisbane, too late to hope for a ride to Sydney. A call to a motor pool brought a car and driver to take us to a field near Ipswich where we could sleep and find an ATC flight headed south in the morning.

We arrived at Mascot Field, Sydney, at noon the next day aboard a plush C-47 with an airliner interior that was assigned to some general. Mel had wangled us seats and we feigned an air of nonchalance amidst the other passengers of higher rank and pressed uniforms.

Kapson's idea of a leave was the traditional beer and babes in an apartment. I was just glad to get away from New Guinea and, this being my first visit to Sydney, more interested in the quieter attractions. We parted at the Hotel Australia and I did not sense any disappointment when I declined Mel's offer of sharing an apartment. I took a cab to Cheverill's Red Cross Hotel located not far from King's Cross, which even in wartime was a lively part of the city. The Red Cross maintained several hotels for officers and enlisted men on leave and Cheverill's with its soft, clean beds and steak and eggs for breakfast suited me just fine.

It was wonderful to get away from New Guinea's stifling climate and primitive army life, although I could not claim that we had recently been exposed to dangerous duty. Aside from enjoying the civilian surroundings, with plentiful food and the sights and sounds of a big city, I also had some serious business: I needed to buy some photographic supplies for developing and printing pictures and visit a dentist. The last objective was to have some teeth filled and thus avoid the hand-cranked drill and outdoor clinic run by the group's dentist, Dr. Lawrence Heiman—good as he may have been. The Sydney clinic gave me pause when I first entered, however, as the sign over the doorway proclaimed the dentist to be "The Mad Doctor." Fortunately, he proved to be quite efficient, if not completely painless.

Tom Jones had insisted that I look up his young fiancée, Pat Kenny, and after a few days I did so. Pat and her family were very hospitable toward a friend of Tom's and quickly adopted me. Pat's older sister, Joyce, was getting married over the Christmas holidays and I was included in the celebrations. The wedding was held in an Anglican Church with a good turnout. I was placed in the care of one of Pat's uncles, who explained the daily racing form to me during the marriage ceremony.

Later, there was a reception with a band and dancing where I was treated like a visiting relative.

Pat, who was out of high school and doing some entertaining by playing an accordion at parties, had time to take me to the beaches at Bondi and Manley, ice-skating, and to visit the zoo, among other local sights. Mrs. Kenny invited me to Christmas dinner, which featured roast duck and the traditional plum pudding. Threepence coins had been baked inside the plum pudding for good luck and just happened to be in the piece I was served. It was an interesting, enjoyable, and relaxing week for me primarily because of the hospitality of the Kenny family at 132A Blues Point Road, North Sydney. It perfectly suited my needs.

Mel Kapson and I met at the Mascot Field terminal on the morning of December 29 for the flight back north. Mel had little to say about how he had spent his time and seemed a little under the weather, the residual effects of quarts of Aussie beer. We were again assigned transportation on an ATC C-47 with airline seats. A brigadier general was one of the passengers on this flight. The distinctive arch of the Sydney Harbor Bridge (known as the "Coat Hanger") passed below as we headed north. We spent that night at Nadzab after a long day of flying.

During that flight I read in the Sydney papers of the German offensive then taking place in the Ardennes. The attack had begun on December 16. The reports of what came to be called the "Battle of the Bulge" seemed surprisingly gloomy considering my general impression that the Germans were being steadily pushed back in Europe. For us in New Guinea, the European war was far, far away.

Mel and I arrived back at Hollandia early in the afternoon on December 30 and found the big tent abuzz with talk of moving to the Philippines within a few days. After that single leave to Sydney my name never again came up on the 389th's leave roster.

20° N

Cape Bojeador
South China Sea
Laoag

Cape Engano

Luzon

Lingayen Gulf
San Fernando
Baguio

Cape Bolinao
Lingayen

Clark Field

-15° N

Manila
Subic Bay
Manila Bay
Laguna de Bay

Lubang Is.

Legaspi

Philippine Sea

San Bernardino Strait

Mindoro
San Jose
Sibuyan Sea

Moro Strait

Samar

Visayan Sea
Panay

Tanauan
Leyte Gulf

Panay Gulf
Cebu
Leyte

-10° N

Puerto Princesa

Negros
Bohol

Mindanao Sea

Palawan

Sulu Sea

Mindanao

Statute Miles
0   100   200
0   100   200   300
Kilometers
Zamboanga

⟨N⟩

120° E

⟿**Philippines**

125° E

Chapter 8

THE PHILIPPINES AND SERIOUS BUSINESS

THE SQUADRON FLEW its last combat mission from Hollandia on November 6, 1944, and we awaited developments from the Philippines. The 312th Bomb Group's ground echelon had landed on November 19, but it was having a difficult time organizing our camp area because of the terrain selected, the heavy rainfall, and the general confusion that follows any major landing. The engineers were also struggling to complete an airstrip for us.

It was the wet season on the east side of the Philippines and rain fell at some time practically every day. Thirty-five inches of rain fell in the Dulag area during the first forty days following the invasion. The engineers, stymied by the mud, finally gave up building a field for us at Dulag. Although the Japanese had built an airstrip there, inspiring our higher-ups to plan extensive development in the area, they had reached that conclusion before ground conditions were properly assessed. More suitable ground was found along the ocean shore farther north toward Tacloban at the village of Tanauan. An emergency airstrip with a steel mat surface was completed at the new location by December 16. In early January, the strip was extended to a reported length of six thousand feet and the necessary parking areas were built on a filled-in swamp, clearing the way for the 312th's planes to be moved to Leyte to join the ground echelon.

The 389th was selected to begin the move north on the morning of January 3, 1945, with the remaining three squadrons to follow starting the next day. As we drove down the now graveled and relatively smooth road from our camp area to the Hollandia strip for the last time, the day promised to do justice to the South Seas travel brochures I had seen so long ago in Pittsburgh. Fluffy clouds drifted up from the southwest against a backdrop of clear, blue sky. Even the top of Mount Cyclops, which normally was shrouded in mist, was in the clear that morning.

Each plane carried a gunner and the crew chief riding in the rear compartment while our cots, duffle bags, and a large tool box were loaded into the bomb bay with any other belongings or spare parts that the crew chief saw fit to take along. Ernie Koch had never expressed much enthusiasm for flying and even on this ideal day the prospect of a lovely sightseeing trip failed to brighten his outlook. The gunner kidded Ernie about his obvious reluctance as we loaded up. When I inquired if there might be something he had forgotten to check, Ernie was not amused. To my innocently phrased question, "Is this plane safe to fly, Sergeant Koch?" he growled and said, "Watch those landings, Lieutenant." We were ready to go.

Colonel Strauss had earlier made an inspection flight to Leyte to check the Tanauan airstrip and the group's bivouac area so he was well acquainted with our route and the local weather conditions. After leading the squadron off from Hollandia, Strauss made a couple of extra swings around the field and Lake Sentani as a farewell salute to our base for the past six months. One of the 389th Squadron's planes, piloted by 2d Lt. Bill Clark, failed to get off the ground that morning because of a sick engine. Bill had joined the 389th only a short time earlier and so had not flown any missions. I had gotten to know him somewhat and found him to be a friendly, likable fellow. Clark coasted to the end of the airstrip as we circled above and then the formation headed out over Tanahmerah Bay and set a northwest course along the coast.

Flying at about two thousand feet, we settled into a loose, comfortable formation as Colonel Strauss led us toward our first stop at Biak, about two hours flying time away. I enjoyed this still-interesting landscape with its varied blues and greens of the sea, the orderly rows of coconut palms on the plantation islands a short distance offshore, and the dark green carpet of the jungle stretching off to the southern horizon. On the beach halfway to Wakde Island were the remains of a Japanese Dinah reconnaissance plane, which had become a landmark for me. Small villages dotted the shore as we moved along and I idly wondered if any enemy troops were living down there. I checked the instrument panel and the position of the wingman on the opposite side of our flight leader before going back to sightseeing. It was a pleasure trip that morning.

We landed at Biak for fuel and ate lunch in a temporary mess hall set up on the field. The heat seemed more oppressive than at Hollandia and clouds of dust were blowing across the airstrip. Some fighting was still going on in the hills. Although our troops had occupied Biak since the previous summer, there was still an air of raw frontier activity about the place. Even Ernie Koch seemed to welcome climbing back into the plane to get away from Biak's dust, heat, and flies.

It was a three-hour flight on to Morotai in the Molucca Islands, where we would spend the night. Along our route we saw several sizable native sailing vessels and an outrigger canoe or two. I wondered where those boats were headed and speculated that perhaps the larger ones might in fact be carrying Japanese. Who would know? The weather remained generally clear, with only some puffy fair-weather cumulus clouds. However, thunderheads were building up as we circled before landing on Morotai late that afternoon.

To those of us who had joined the 312th Group at Hollandia, Morotai seemed like the front lines, even though it had been invaded the middle of September. Morotai was two degrees above the equator and Hollandia about two degrees below. It was just north of the Japanese-held island of Halmahera, where some of the night raids against Wakde, Biak, and Owi Islands were thought to originate.

The truck hauling us from the flight line to the tent area had to stop and wait at the end of the airstrip while a flight of Australian Beaufighters took off on a dusk raid against the Halmahera airfields. The purr of the Bristol Hercules sleeve-valve engines was distinctive as the three-ship flight flashed by, the stubby Beaufighters looking all business. Halmahera was almost within sight across the channel to the south and in my mind's eye was crawling with enemy troops.

Colonel Strauss called the pilots together that evening and reminded us that the flight north to Leyte the following day was a combat mission both in name and in truth. He said there were lots of serviceable Japanese aircraft on the large southern Philippine island of Mindanao, which lay just to the west of our route, so we should anticipate being jumped by fighters. I suspect that most of us lay awake a little while that night, thinking about the Philippines—where a war was being actively fought—and what lay ahead. Strauss also mentioned that the weather in the area was questionable at that time of year and warned us that Leyte's east coast was often closed in by early afternoon. It was imperative that we get off early. Secure in the thought that the colonel would be leading and that his navigation had never failed, I drifted off to sleep.

The trip north the next day proved to be almost routine. The weather was clear and bright when we took off from Morotai and we formed up without a hitch. The flight leaders did not have to motion the wingmen in closer as we took up our northerly heading. Heads swiveled as we nervously scanned the sky for any sign of approaching black dots. Colonel Strauss positioned us well off the coast of Mindanao and by the time we were opposite the island the clouds had begun to pile up to the west. We were able to catch only a few glimpses of the distant coast through the rainsqualls. The overcast became solid as we continued north. By the time the colonel began a wide, sweeping turn to the left into Leyte Gulf, the ceiling was lowering rapidly.

We ran into gray sheets of scattered rain as we approached Leyte's coast and then the island's green hills appeared ahead through the columns of mist and rain. Samar Island was close by on the right. Ships, both navy and merchant, seemed to fill the anchorage, just as they had six weeks earlier at Hollandia.

The airstrip at Tanauan had been constructed on a low, narrow peninsula—really little more than a sandbar—along the shore of Leyte Gulf. The main airfield on Leyte at this time was farther north along the coast at Tacloban, the provincial capital. Between the two airstrips was the small village of Palo. As the formation circled in preparation for landing, I looked down on the glistening steel matting that extended from the water's edge on the north end of the runway toward a three-hundred-foot conical hill on the south end. The traffic pattern had to be toward the hill for landings and away from it for takeoffs no matter what direction the wind might be blowing. Wrecked planes were visible on the beach near the runway, pushed there earlier after emergency landings made before the strip was completed. A number of fighters were parked on a wide metal apron at the south end, but it was impossible to tell where our A-20s would park.

Although the official reports stated that the Tanauan strip was between five thousand and six thousand feet long, they must have been counting the overrun to the waterline and the parking area. As I turned onto the final approach, the runway looked short to me. Furthermore, it was raining again, making the steel matting slicker than slick. We all managed to get down safely, but there was considerable sliding whenever the brakes were gingerly applied. I was pleasantly surprised at being able to get 958 slowed down sufficiently to make a sharp turn to the right at the end of the runway onto a very soft taxiway.

It took almost full power to taxi through the mud as the ground crews waved frantically at us to keep going so as not to bog down. Go too slow or stop and the ten tons of A-20 would sink into the soft muck and could only be extracted with a tractor. Some of the hardstands could not be used because of the still-soft soil. I felt a great sense of relief after getting 958 into its designated space and then turned around.

The 312th's ground personnel, after working and living in the mud and rain for six weeks, were obviously pleased to see the arrival of the first planes. When we expressed dismay at the amount of mud and the crude conditions, the ground pounders responded, "You should have been here when it was rough!"

The group's bivouac area was established in a palm grove west of the beach road near the village of Toloso. Tents had been set up for us, the mess hall was completed—including a cement floor—and work was progressing on the shower building. But there was black, sticky mud everywhere and the jeeps bringing us from the airstrip bogged down in the main roadway as the rain fell in a steady downpour. It was a dreary introduction to the Philippines. Jim Rutledge and I, who had agreed to share a tent with Maury Owen, immediately vowed to find materials for more comfortable quarters. The sagging tent to which we had been assigned had a dirt floor rapidly being covered with water. It was a powerful incentive to build something better.

Bill Clark's aborted takeoff at Hollandia on January 3 was to have tragic consequences. After the bad engine was changed, it was decided to send Clark and his plane to the navy's maintenance facility in the Admiralty Islands for some modifications. The navy had experienced considerable success with rockets mounted under the wings of their planes and it was thought rockets might be equally useful on A-20s. An armament man from the 388th, Sgt. Joe Nondahl, who had been schooled on the new rockets, was assigned to go with Clark. The two flew across to Los Negros Island in the Admiralties, some six hundred miles east of Hollandia, on the morning of January 28.

Upon landing, Clark ran into an old friend. Before taking the plane over to another field where the modification facility was located, he offered his buddy a demonstration ride—probably hoping to impress the watching navy personnel, too. Sergeant Nondahl ordered a milkshake at the navy canteen on the field and sat down to await Clark's return. Nondahl had a front-row seat to the events that followed.

With his buddy riding on the shelf behind the pilot's seat, Clark buzzed the field before coming in to land and got just a bit too low. The A-20 clipped some trees and exploded as it crashed into a housing area nearby. Lieutenant Clark and his passenger, along with a number of navy personnel, were killed. Commander Morton Woodason, the family friend who had entertained me at Squantum NAS while on leave a year earlier, was then stationed at Momote Airfield with the navy's Aviation Repair and Overhaul Unit 1. He, too, had been watching Clark's last flight. He later wrote to me about seeing it. I met Joe Nondahl years later at a 312th Bomb Group reunion and he recounted the details leading up to the loss of the 389th pilot so few of us had gotten to know.

We flew our first Philippines mission on January 6, after taking a day off to get settled in the muddy bivouac area at Leyte and to allow some more work on the taxiways and hardstands. It was a short hop over to the island's west coast and then south along the west coast of the neighboring island of Cebu. Cebu is narrow and runs generally north and south with a spine of mountains up to twenty-eight hundred feet high down the middle. Our target was the Japanese airfield at Opon or Lahug village on the north end of Mactan Island in the harbor at Cebu City.

Fighting was still taking place in Leyte's interior and we all did some rubbernecking as our formation crossed over the central ridge of this new territory. The town of Ormoc, where the Japanese had landed reinforcements, was almost completely destroyed. It had been burned out, and the nearby beach and shallow water were littered with wrecked barges and several large ships. After a short flight down Cebu's west coast we made a turn to cross the mountain spine that brought us within sight of Cebu City. It was a large, modern-looking place; a worthwhile target compared to New Guinea's jungles and grass houses. There were paved streets, substantial white buildings that stood several stories high, and the airfield on the island was more than just a strip carved out of the lush green jungle.

We made a single low pass across the airfield. It felt good to be flying with a purpose again after almost two months of marking time. There did not seem to be much opposition but there was no doubt the Japanese were there, albeit unseen: 958 picked up six holes at Lahug.

As soon as we landed back at Tanauan and shut the engines down, we heard that a big mission was on for the next day. The flight crews met in the mess hall after supper that evening for a briefing by Colonel Strauss, who told us we were going to Clark Field on the northern island of Luzon. It was the largest Japanese base in the Philippines. Our troops were scheduled to make an assault landing at Lingayen on January 9 and begin the drive south to retake Manila, so the remaining Japanese airpower had to be eliminated. Clark Field was a large complex with a number of airstrips scattered around the prewar U.S. air base and neighboring army camp, Fort Stotsenburg. The plan was to cover all of the dozen or more airfields with a low-level sweep by A-20s and B-25s immediately after a medium-altitude bombing run by B-24s.

The planning for the mission had been cooked up by the 310th Bomb Wing and called for two closely timed line-abreast formations to cross the Clark Field complex on different headings. A formation composed of the 312th's A-20s and the 345th Bomb Group's B-25s would hit the target coming down from the northwest, to be followed within minutes by A-20s from the 417th Group making a sweep from the northeast to southwest. The 312th's A-20s would be to the right of the 345th's B-25s, making a line of some sixty to seventy planes. It was an impressive concept on paper, but not very practical. (The account of the raid in volume 5 of *The Army Air Forces in World War II* states that some 312th planes were attached to the 417th's formation, which is a surprise to me if correct.)

Just the number of planes involved would make it difficult to maintain our alignment. Even under perfect conditions it is doubtful we could have properly executed the plan. The first formation, approaching from the northwest, had to make a forty-degree-plus turn, from east to southeast, in order to make its attack, which was sure to disrupt a line-abreast formation. Factors such as the strange terrain, low-level flying, and concentrating on targets up ahead—not to mention enemy action—all added to the difficulties of trying to hold position. The A-20s were faster than the B-25s. Who, amidst all that excitement, would be looking to the left to make sure they stayed lined up? Some of the pilots expressed dismay at the plan during the evening briefing—trying to stay in line with so many planes and the impact of the required turn—but that was the plan. We would just have to do our best, good or bad.

We got off from Tanauan without difficulty on the morning of January 7 and formed into the group formation before heading west to the island of Mindoro. Major Clif Graber was back leading the 389th Squadron, although he was then the group operations officer. The 345th, based at Tacloban up the coast, was in formation heading west on schedule off to our right. I was leading the last flight in the 389th, making us the tail end of the 312th's formation. Tom Jones, flying "Little Joe" (a plane originally assigned to Len Happ, who had gone home), was on my right wing. On my left was a new man from another squadron whose name I cannot now recall.

January 7, 1945, was an anniversary day for me. It had been one year since Class 44-A graduated at La Junta, Colorado. We certainly had come a long way from those cold, bleak prairies. It was my first mission as a flight leader and I hoped to handle the job with some degree of competence. The wingmen had an easy job as long as the leader maintained position without fiddling with the throttles too much. A position guide

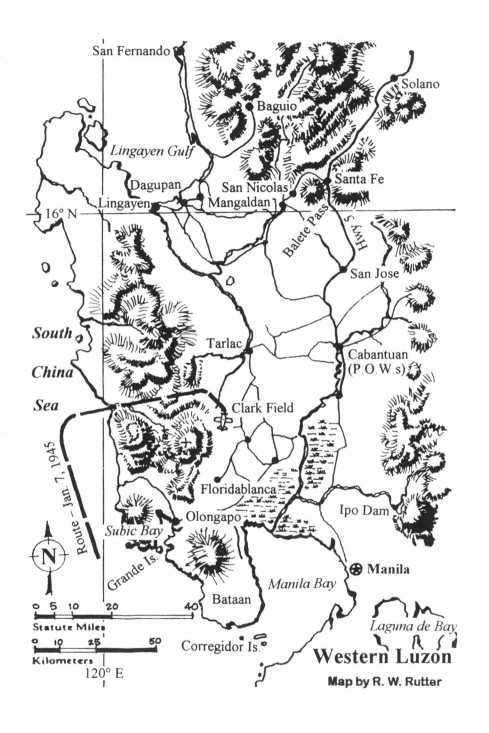

San Fernando

Solano

Baguio

Lingayen Gulf

Dagupan

San Nicolas

Santa Fe

Lingayen

Mangaldan

16° N

Balete Pass

Hwy 5

San Jose

South

China

Tarlac

Sea

Cabantuan
(P.O.W.s)

Route — Jan. 7, 1945

Clark Field

Floridablanca

Ipo Dam

Subic Bay

Olongapo

⊕ **Manila**

Grande Is.

Manila Bay

Laguna de Bay

N

Bataan

0   5   10   20   40

Statute Miles

0   10   25   50

Corregidor Is.

Western Luzon

Kilometers

120° E

Map by R. W. Rutter

for the leader of the second flight in a box was to keep the lead ship of the flight above framed in the triangular window over the windscreen.

The prospect of going against the largest airfield complex in the Philippines was very much on my mind that morning, as it must have been for the other pilots and gunners, too. It would do no good to ponder the possibilities. It was to our benefit that we did not know for sure what to expect when we hit Clark Field. *Yank*, a weekly army news magazine, had recently published a paraphrasing of the "Lord's Prayer" that began, "The Lord is my pilot, I shall not falter." It may sound trite today, but it offered a little comfort. Colonel Strauss was leading the group and I placed some faith in him as well as the good Lord as we headed west over Leyte's dripping green hills that morning. I felt certain we would be all right with the colonel in charge.

After meeting the 417th Group's formation over Mindoro we headed north toward Luzon, staying west of the coast and well clear of the Lingayen invasion fleet—which soon came into view, plowing its way along two or three miles west of our course. It was a clear morning and the sight of the fleet spread out over the smooth blue sea was an impressive picture. The sky was full of the planes of our three groups and we could see fighters flying much higher above, providing air cover over the fleet.

As we slid past the ships to our left, two planes suddenly appeared out of the haze up ahead. They crossed low over our formation and headed toward the lines of ships that made up the invasion fleet. A distinctive twin-engine P-38 was in hot pursuit of a single-engine Japanese fighter of some sort. Both pilots ignored us as they continued their deadly race. Ahead of them an intense flak barrage arose as the two planes neared the convoy. This performance confirmed the warning we had received in our briefing to stay well away from the convoy as it was perhaps more dangerous than the enemy. The convoy received several attacks during its run to Lingayen Gulf, but the kamikazes would be all but eliminated after our raid on Clark Field. I wonder if the P-38 pilot got his man?

Manila Bay was visible through the haze to the east as we passed by and continued north along the coast past the mouth of Subic Bay. When we reached a point opposite a wide gap in the hills that rose several miles back from the shore, we were to turn east, form up line abreast, and follow the 345th on the same heading ahead of us. Beyond the hills lay Clark Field and its complex of a dozen or more airstrips spread over the west side of Luzon's central valley. There the two groups were to join up in a sixty-ship front on a generally southeast heading.

Both groups made sweeping right turns over the sea and headed toward the coast as we changed from flights of three into a line-abreast formation. Colonel Strauss did his usual smooth job of leading to place us in the proper position behind the 345th. Once we were through the pass, each group would turn from an east to a southeast heading and, according to the planners, end up in a single beautiful line before sweeping across the airstrips. It was a neat plan on paper, but there were simply too many ships involved.

My flight, after making the turn toward land, was on the extreme right of the 312th's line and the formation appeared to be in good order as we crossed over the coast. Shortly afterward, however, I saw an A-20 some distance to our left start to lag behind with light smoke streaming back from its right engine. I watched as he continued to fall farther behind and thought it was better to lose an engine here than over the target. He should have been able to salvo his bombs and turn back to Mindoro without too much difficulty. Whoever he was, he did not break radio silence. I turned back to the problem of holding formation and the gap in the hills up ahead.

A decision was fast approaching: it had remained generally clear over the sea, but there was a layer of clouds on the inland hilltops, typical of the island weather in the tropics. The gap in the hills toward which the formation was aiming was not wide enough below the cloud layer to hold all of us. My flight had been squeezed south of the gap and our choices were to drop behind and follow the formation into the pass or climb up through the clouds to clear the hills and then drop into position on the other side through the hopefully thinning clouds over the valley. Slowing and tucking in behind that formation at low altitude was not an attractive option, so I used hand signals to tell my wingmen that we would go up and over. They nodded in agreement and we began climbing while holding steady on the same compass heading.

The clouds were only a few hundred feet thick and as soon as we broke through we continued on an easterly heading for perhaps three or four minutes before, as expected, the clouds thinned out and we dropped down toward the visible valley floor.

We were about three hundred feet above ground level and I slowed down to 160 miles per hour in an attempt to keep from overrunning the formation that should by then have started turning toward the southeast. I looked ahead and then to the left but there were no planes in sight. Even though we had lost a few minutes climbing up and letting down, it was inconceivable that the massive formation of A-20s and B-25s was nowhere to be seen. Perhaps, I thought, it was still swinging around in a big arc (and undoubtedly it was), but I could not or did not spot a single plane where dozens should have been. Where the hell did they go? I wondered. To lose such a large group was unbelievable to me—a mystery.

The sweeping forty-five-degree turn to the southeast in line-abreast formation was a serious flaw in the plan of attack. It would require those on the inside of the turn to almost stall out trying to hold position while the planes on the left of the line lagged behind, even with their throttles wide open. Although unplanned, our climb up over the hills had been a good way to lose some time and then be in our approximate proper position with the formation while still maintaining a safe airspeed. My fear now, however, was of overshooting and winding up in the middle of the formation if we continued flying east.

Responding to this analysis I started to circle to the right to stay on the west side of the valley where we belonged when a new doubt crossed my mind: had we killed so much time that we were now behind the formation? Tom Jones and my other wingman had by then apparently spotted the line of 312th planes some distance to the north and still in the process of making the sweeping turn and lining up with the 345th. But I did not see them, and several heavy machine-gun emplacements almost directly below were now firing on our three-ship flight.

The circle to the right was taking us away from the buildings of Fort Stotsenburg visible in the distance and the airstrips and wrecked hangars spread out to the east. We were about where we should have been in relation to the main body of the formation, but I had no idea where it was. The snap judgment that I made at that point is still clear to me after all these years: We've somehow missed the formation but there's the target. We've come this far—let's hit it. Prompted by the machine-gun fire coming from below, I abruptly stopped the turn to the right without much thought about surprising my wingmen, banked steeply back to the left, dropped the nose, and added power for a run at those intact planes and the buildings beyond. It was a reflex action taken without pause to consider alternatives—or even to alert my wingmen of my intentions.

I was now aiming at a Tony fighter parked in a revetment straight ahead. I could make out some other planes partly hidden. Master Sergeant Wilfred Boyd was the gunner that day. It was the first time we had flown together, and he was probably as startled as my two wingmen by the sudden change of direction. I called on the intercom as we started the strafing run, "Okay, Boyd, we're going in. Keep your eyes open." Sergeant Boyd was new to the 389th and, as the senior-ranking gunner, it was his job to make the mission assignments. We had just met that morning.

Picking up speed to something over 250 miles per hour and leveling off at about fifty or a hundred feet, we headed somewhat south of east across a revetment area and toward some trees and buildings. Several fighters were parked around in sight and I spotted a Betty bomber in a revetment off to one side, although it was difficult to pick out the good targets at that speed and altitude. Behind a row of taller trees coming up I saw a large frame barracks, which I judged to be part of Fort Stotsenburg, and beyond that the airstrips and the frames of several wrecked hangars.

The bomb load consisted of parachute fragmentation bombs (parafrags). After opening the bomb-bay doors, I tripped the automatic racks and started spewing bombs out over the first of the parked planes. As was customary, Sergeant Boyd started the automatic camera mounted in the lower hatch as soon as he saw the first parachutes begin to blossom behind us. As we ran toward the trees and the ruined hangars beyond I worked the rudder pedals and strafed every likely target. There was no shortage of planes, trucks, or buildings. I could see planes everywhere I looked—fat Bettys, hump-backed Tonys, delicate Oscars, twin-engine and single-engine, some in the open and others in revetments, most with camouflage netting over them. It was beautiful! What a field day!

The strafing run probably took no more than three or four minutes. Despite the excitement, I still had a nagging thought: Where did that damn formation go? Are we ahead of it, or what? Just before we reached the wrecked hangars, Sergeant Boyd urgently warned on the intercom: "B-25s on the left!" At the same time I heard a rattling sound like a wash pan half-full of gravel hitting our tail. It could mean only one thing: I had flown past the distant 312th and was now crossing at an angle in front of the fast-overtaking 345th Group's B-25s. The ricocheting .50-caliber slugs coming from their nose guns were skipping around and hitting us.

It was time to get out of the way. The instant Boyd gave his warning I instinctively pulled the A-20 up steeply out of the way and made a climbing turn to the right under full power. Without me ever seeing them, the B-25s passed safely underneath our tail as I headed back to where the 312th's formation should have been.

We had been very lucky thus far: 958 was still running smoothly and making fast time toward the southwest. Below us, the ragged line of planes—some very low and on a straight course, some jinking in wild evasive action, and others much too high and sitting ducks for any gun within reach—was racing off to the southeast. To the north columns of black smoke were starting to rise and the area that had been so full of planes suddenly was empty.

I made my way back to the west side of the valley and spotted four A-20s several miles ahead on a southerly heading at about five hundred feet. After a bit of a chase we caught up with this group and, as if nothing had gone wrong, I slid up under Cal Slade's lead plane. Cal was taking us along the west side of the valley with the intention of crossing lower Manila Bay and then making for Leyte. A short time later, Tom Jones caught up with us and resumed his position on my right wing.

Jones looked across from his cockpit, shaking his head and laughing. My wingmen, who had seen the 312th's formation when I did not, had not followed my mad dash. They wisely continued to circle and tacked onto the right end of the big formation. The pilot on my left wing disappeared during the confused attack and returned to Leyte with the main body of the group, probably wondering what kind of flight leaders they had in the 389th Squadron.

Before long, Slade's wingmen called to report that they were low on fuel. Cal opted to head for Mindoro rather than continue on to Leyte. I still had plenty of fuel, as did Jones, but we stayed with the formation since the rest of the group was by then well on its way home. Instead of crossing over Manila Bay, our course was taking us along the coast of the Bataan Peninsula toward the mouth of the bay. Cal gave Corregidor a wide berth and took us over the South Channel, close to Fort Drum. Fort Drum had been built on El Fraile Island before World War I and was aptly called the "Concrete Battleship," for that is what it resembled with its two turrets holding fourteen-inch naval guns. Some members of the Japanese garrison could be seen standing on top of Fort Drum as we passed by that morning. I wondered what they were thinking. If there were any antiaircraft batteries, they did not bother to fire at us. The enemy seemed to be watching us with the same curiosity with which we watched them.

Our small formation encountered heavy traffic at San Jose on Mindoro as the 417th's planes were returning from the Clark Field mission and a handful of 345th planes with damage or wounded aboard had also been diverted there. The 417th, which arrived over the target after we had stirred up the hornet's nest, had encountered considerable opposition. Its planes with serious damage or wounded aboard were trying to get on the ground fast. We circled until the 417th's A-20s were on the ground and then were cleared to land.

The 312th's planes were not expected and ours, along with one or two other strays, only added to the overall confusion in the 417th's parking area. The 417th's planes were being serviced while we waited our turn; aviation fuel was in short supply. Our plane had received relatively little damage considering that it had stirred up the Japanese machine-gun positions and then gone through the 345th's shooting gallery. Several slugs dropped to the ground when the bomb-bay doors were opened and the vertical stabilizer and rudder looked a bit ragged.

An enemy incendiary round had angled up into the radio compass set and burned it out. Another slug had put a hole neatly through the VHF radio box, but the set was still working. The radios in an A-20 were mounted on the deck at the top of the fuselage between the cockpit hatch and the gunner's turret. We had been moving at just the right speed that morning: a fraction slower and the cockpit would have been the recipient; a bit faster and it would have been the turret. A dozen or so additional holes would show up when 958 was examined more closely.

After his planes had been refueled, the 417th's engineering officer allotted two hundred gallons apiece for the 312th ships so we could make the trip back to Tanauan. It was almost 6 P.M. when we were finally cleared for takeoff, but Boyd and I did not get off that evening. The nosewheel snubber (a small shock absorber that dampens out the vibrations of the swiveling nosewheel) on 958 failed as we started to take off. When the wheel began to shimmy violently at sixty miles per hour, I pulled back on the throttles and coasted to the end of the runway. Meanwhile, Cal Slade's flight, which included Tom Jones and one or two other strays from the 312th who had landed at Mindoro, headed for home. We limped slowly back along the runway (there was no taxiway at that time) with the nosewheel wiggling all the way and again parked in the 417th's area.

The engineering officer eyed my return with distaste. There was no interest in our problem, though: the 417th people were busy enough with their own. One of their crew chiefs finally stopped long enough to listen to my description of what seemed to be wrong and agreed. "Yes," he said, "it's the snubber all right. We'll have to get a new one from maintenance, but we're busy right now, Lieutenant." I pointed to a nearby A-20 with a rather large hole in the vertical stabilizer and other obvious damage and asked, "How about taking the snubber off of that one? It looks like Class Twenty-six [junk]." The crew chief nodded, pulled a crescent wrench from the pocket of his coveralls, and went to work. The job took only a few minutes. My thanks were sincere as the crew chief disappeared in the direction of planes with more serious problems. The plane was flyable again, but it was too late to get back to Leyte before dark. Boyd and I hunted around and found cots for the night with the 417th.

January 8, 1945, was to be another eventful day, although the prospect of an early morning flight across to Leyte under the clear, blue sky gave no hint of it. I filed the mandatory flight plan with base operations at the San Jose airstrip and took a look at the charts for the approximate course to Leyte and Tanauan. On each mission we were given charts prepared by the intelligence section and squadron operations with the course to and from the target marked on the clear plastic folder. The course heading shown for the previous day on our route to Clark Field was from Tacloban to the north tip of Mindoro and, of course, the return route from Luzon to Leyte was entirely different. Two charts were needed to cover the territory but it made no difference: a little Kentucky windage from the reciprocal heading should take care of the seventy-five miles between San Jose and the northern tip of Mindoro. With the mostly clear sky and good visibility it would be an hour and a half pleasure flight, a piece of cake.

The sea was calm and the clouds had not begun to form over the islands as we took off to the west and made a climbing turn to the left around the southern tip of Mindoro. A tanker, one of two sunk on Christmas Day, was still burning offshore just south of San Jose and sending up a tall column of black smoke into the still morning air. The direct distance from San Jose to Tanauan was about three hundred miles, maybe a little more, and our economical cruising speed was around two hundred miles per hour.

From a thousand feet over the water, the several small islands in view looked lush and peaceful that morning. There were even a few fishing boats out. The war seemed not to be in evidence, although there was the nagging possibility that a Japanese fighter or two from a field on one of the larger islands along the way might also be out doing some sightseeing that morning. At the time, Mindoro was the only island we held west of Leyte. Major Thomas B. McGuire, one of the leading aces in the Pacific, had been lost the day before after encountering a lone Japanese fighter over Negros Island, fifty-five miles south of our intended route.

About half an hour into the flight I saw a large island off to the south up ahead and after forty-five minutes I could make out a sizable town and harbor breakwater. From a distance, it looked a little bit like the harbor of Carigara on the north side of Leyte, which I had noticed briefly the previous day. Could the wind from the west be stronger than given at San Jose? Could that possibly be Leyte? I wondered. It was not a rational hypothesis, but I was feeling pretty relaxed that morning. After the single westbound flight I had made the day before I was not at all familiar with the landmarks. Nor could I immediately identify the large island from the map. We had a good supply of fuel in the tanks, so I decided to take a closer look at the north shore of the island and see if I could identify it.

Although there was a passing similarity to what I had seen of Carigara from a distance, it was quickly obvious that the town and walled harbor below were not that place. In any event, Samar Island would have been in view to the east if it had been Leyte. So, turning back toward the east, I made another estimate of the proper heading after my southward diversion and continued on. A few clouds were starting to build up over some of the islands scattered around the Visayan Sea, but it would be another two hours or so before the weather could be expected to start to close in on Leyte's east coast.

When an island resembling what I supposed should be Leyte did not show up as soon as expected I began to doubt my heading. I also regretted straying from my planned course to look at the unknown island. Islands that were visible in the increasing haze were of no help—they were all unfamiliar, of course. A sinking feeling was beginning in my stomach as I recognized that wandering off to the south had only wasted time and fuel. The only course left seemed to be to return to the unknown large island, take the time to identify it properly, and then plot a correct course.

A short distance inland from the northeastern point of my unknown island was an airstrip with a concrete runway of good length and in apparent good condition. From a thousand feet there were no signs of life or aircraft, so it could not have been in our hands. Any temptation to land on that attractive real estate was quickly put out of mind. After wasting fifteen minutes or more scanning the outline of the coast, the map, and even talking to an unseen B-25 nearby, I admitted defeat. My navigation had been too nonchalant and curiosity had led me farther astray.

"Sergeant Boyd," I announced on the intercom, "it looks like my navigation is off somewhere. We'll go back to Mindoro for some more gas and try again." I did know enough not to press on, but I am sure Wilfred Boyd was having serious doubts about his pilot at this point.

After holding a westerly heading for about forty minutes, and just when it seemed we might have gone too far, I saw a column of black smoke from the burning tanker showing off to the north marking Mindoro. It was much farther north than I had anticipated, an indication of just how far south of my intended course I had strayed. It was a welcome sight, nonetheless. I had wasted two and one-half hours flying to nowhere.

The 417th's line crew was not at all happy to see us return. It took some talking with one of the engineering officers to get another two hundred gallons of precious fuel, but eventually we were accommodated with the admonition, "Now, Lieutenant, this is *it*, understand?" I replied very meekly, "Yes, Sir."

The VHF radio set had stopped receiving or transmitting just as we touched down on the San Jose runway. I asked for a radioman to look into the matter, but the 417th crews were still busy patching up their own planes and it took a while before someone was free. The bullet that had gone through the set had nicked two wires and they had evidently broken with the vibration of the landing; a little soldering restored the set. The radioman warned that there appeared to be other damage inside the case, so the VHF set might not work for long. However, there was a command set with lower frequencies that could be used if necessary. I was again ready to try to find Leyte Island, chastened by my sloppy procedures that had caused failure the first time.

I went back to base operations and closed the original flight plan before being reported overdue at Tanauan and filed a new one. Then I took a closer look at the navigation charts. The two charts did not match up as I had assumed they did, so trying to guess the interception heading from San Jose to the reciprocal of the course I had flown the day before was an error that had taken me too far south to start. The misalignment of the charts, undiscovered because I had not taken the opportunity to plot a new course line, had led me off. The lure of that distant coast had done the rest. We had been over Panay, the harbor and town was Capiz, and the beautiful concrete airstrip I had circled near the northeastern tip was Pilar—and still very much in Japanese hands. Lucky again!

After the fiasco of the morning flight, I carefully laid out the charts on the proper match line, drew the course, and then marked the checkpoints every fifty miles or about fifteen minutes' flying time. The calculation of the heading included the proper adjustments for magnetic variation and compass deviation—check and double check. Master Sergeant Boyd took great interest in the procedure and asked me to explain what I was doing. Hopefully I was able to allay his apprehensions. At least he did not decline to go with me.

The weather report was the expected, "Deteriorating on the east coast of Leyte by afternoon." We started back to the 417th flight line to get into 958 and try again. However, before starting the engines the sergeant line chief had one last admonishment for me: "No more goddam gas!" It made no difference; we were ready to go. It was Leyte or bust!

This time, paying attention to very basic navigation procedures, I had no difficulty checking off the islands as they came along. All were just where they should have been and I could see the coast of Panay far off to the south, almost obscured by a rainsquall. The question now was what the weather in the vicinity of Leyte would be like. Ahead of us, rain had begun to fall in isolated patches. If the clouds were already down on Leyte's hilltops I was not about to climb up through them hoping to find some space under the ceiling over Leyte Gulf. There was not enough fuel for much messing around, so if we could not cross the island in the clear we would have to stay under the clouds over the water and go around the north end to the eastern side.

In due time Leyte's west coast was coming up ahead. Our course would make landfall about twenty-five to thirty miles north of Ormoc Bay. It was obvious we had no chance of getting over the hills, which disappeared into the clouds and rain, without going on instruments and letting down blind on the other side. I wanted none of that. The clouds were lowering as we approached the coast and rain was coming down steadily. I dropped down to about three hundred feet over the sea in the rain and scud. My only choice was to bank left onto a north heading and stay close enough to the coast to keep it in sight. If the ceiling held and I could follow the shoreline, we should be able to sneak around the north end of the island and reach Tanauan. I kept Sergeant Boyd posted on the plan.

Biliran Island lay off Leyte's northwestern tip and, in the interest of conserving fuel, I did not want to go around it. The ceiling had lowered to about two hundred feet and it was becoming more difficult to see ahead through the sheets of rain as we approached the strait between Biliran and Leyte. The passage is fairly wide at the beginning and goes in a southeast direction. However, it makes a sharp turn back to the east and narrows abruptly about two-thirds of the way along before opening out into Carigara Bay. A dead-end bay continues to the southeast for several miles from the narrow exit channel, so it was imperative to identify the exit and avoid the dead end.

From the entrance to the strait the view was not very appealing: a slate-gray wall with black columns of rain falling and no light spots showing. It was worth a try, though, so I turned into the narrowing channel to take the shortcut. The A-20's responsiveness was cause for some confidence that it could be done. The passage was only about twenty miles long and by following the north (Biliran) shore closely and ignoring the swirling mist and rain directly ahead I hoped to find the exit channel. The key was keeping Biliran's shore in sight while avoiding any random outcroppings from the rather rocky-looking coast. It was a long seven or eight minutes but at least there were no power lines to worry about. We scooted through on the deck and out over the water of Carigara Bay, then I managed to switch my focus and started following Leyte's north shore.

We were now down to about one hundred to two hundred feet in order to keep the water in sight, but it did not look any worse up ahead, and Leyte's coastline was just visible on the right. A straight course over the bay would have saved time but there was also the chance of missing the channel between Samar and Leyte, not to mention losing the horizon and winding up in the water. The shoreline curved gradually around to the northeast and I saw the stone breakwater of the harbor at Carigara flash by, which gave me some hope.

The rain came down in sheets and the ceiling at times pressed lower as we roared along at not much less than two hundred miles per hour. For another ten minutes or so I concentrated on the shore just in sight and then land started to show occasionally through the mists on our left side. We had to be in the channel leading to the narrow San Juanico Strait. The rain and mist blended with the gray water, but there was just enough difference to serve as a horizon. There was no turning back. If the narrowing channel was blocked by weather or proved to be a false lead, the possibility of having to ditch crossed my mind.

Suddenly, masts were whizzing by on either side, almost at our level. I glanced quickly down and caught glimpses of ships just below. We obviously were going through the cargo ship anchorage in the narrow strait just north of Tacloban. Again we were in luck: the navy gunners must have decided that the birds were all walking that day. We had made it!

"Sergeant Boyd, we're home!" I announced on the intercom.

"Hot damn, Lieutenant!" Boyd replied, equally elated.

Still flying just offshore, the town of Tacloban was almost hidden. Then Tanauan airstrip became visible ahead as a rainsquall moved out into Leyte Gulf.

"Tanauan Tower, Sugar Nine-Five-Eight approaching from the north for landing. Field in sight. Over."

"Sugar Nine-Five-Eight, the field is closed but if you can see it you're clear to land."

The ceiling had lifted to between three hundred and five hundred feet as the curtain of rain moved to the east. With a wide circle for a pattern we touched down on the wet steel mat. The on-the-water detour around the island's north end had cost about thirty minutes, but it seemed much longer to me. The one-hour-and-fifty-minute trip left us with precious little of the two hundred gallons of gas we had been reluctantly given at Mindoro, but it had not been wasted this time.

Ernie Koch was there at our parking spot with his wide, crooked grin. How he knew we would be in that afternoon I can no longer recall. Someone in base operations at the tower probably had passed along word of the flight plan I had filed at Mindoro. Sergeant Boyd and I were patting ourselves on the back as we related some of our adventures to Ernie when Len Dulac drove up, jumped out of the jeep, and grabbed my hand. "Jesus Christ, Rutter!" he shouted. "We heard you crashed at Mindoro and had given you up." It was an unexpected welcome home and I probably looked a little sheepish, but there was no use going into the circumstances of our delayed arrival just then.

I wrote up the Form 1A, noted the repairs made at Mindoro, and listed the other damage to the plane that needed tending to by the boys in the sheet metal and radio shops. The compass did not seem to be just on the mark, so I asked that it be "swung"—although I was sure that any deviation they might find had not contributed to my navigation problems that morning.

Finally, as we were walking to Dulac's jeep, Wilfred Boyd said: "I guess I'll fly with you regular, Lieutenant. After Clark Field and the ride home, what else could happen?" Boyd and I flew as a team on most of my missions thereafter.

Although the low-level sweep over Clark Field the previous morning was a poorly planned operation, it did achieve its purpose of destroying a lot of Japanese planes. The kamikaze attacks dropped noticeably after January 7 and the air force was able to point to this fact to refute the navy's claims that its carrier fighters had earlier eliminated this new Japanese weapon. Volume 5 of *The Army Air Forces in World War II* credits our wing with sending 132 planes on the Clark Field raid with a loss of four A-20s and one B-25.

Second Lieutenant Harry Lillard flew the plane with the smoking engine seen after we crossed the Luzon coast before reaching Clark Field. "Sleepy Time Gal" had been assigned to Babe Young. We never learned what happened to Lillard. He was a new pilot in the squadron and Boyd and I seemed to have been the only ones in the formation who noticed him drop back. Heeding radio silence, Harry Lillard had made no call and was on his own after he encountered the engine problem. In all, the 312th lost three planes and seven men that day.

Several pilots in the 312th's other squadrons had noted my solo run across the front of the formation that morning and were free with their kidding. The B-25s of the 345th Bomb Group whose path I crossed even closer were more than a little discomforted by the performance. We had been overtaken by the 499th Squadron, led by Capt. Floyd Fox, and in 1987 Fox, of Shelby, Michigan, wrote:

> As I recall the briefing, 39 B-25s would be in a line on my left and 32 A-20s would extend the line on my right. The A-20 I remember so well was the one that angled across my flight path dropping parafrags. Fortunately, he ran out of bombs just in time to save us from bomb blast damage. I had made up my mind that I was not going to pull up and be exposed to antiaircraft fire.
>
> In retrospect, that mission assignment was impossible to carry out as planned, especially considering the A-20's greater speed. We had found it difficult to keep six B-25s in line let alone 72. But, it was considered a successful mission and that was most important to the people who planned it and didn't participate in it.

First Lieutenant Isaac H. McKinney of the 345th Bomb Group's 488th Squadron had also watched with some consternation as the lone A-20 crossed his path. McKinney was to the left of Captain Fox and also headed for the wrecked hangars that served as my guide. He passed directly under my tail as I pulled up after becoming aware that the B-25s were on us. McKinney also mentioned the phosphorus bombs that blossom in several of the frames of film taken by the camera in Sugar 958 that morning. Dropping air-to-air phosphorus bombs from fighters about a thousand feet above the intended victim was a technique the Japanese developed. It was an intimidating but not very effective weapon. Thank goodness Fox and McKinney were experienced and had not been spooked.

The experience of those two days did wake me up to the fact that my performance had been anything but professional as a flight leader—neither in terms of holding my assigned position or being considerate of my wingmen. It also was a lesson in the necessity of paying attention to elementary navigation and following headings and checkpoints with some discipline. The fiasco of my first attempt at flying to Leyte from Mindoro was humbling all the way around.

The photos taken by 958's automatic camera were posted on the wall of the 389th's intelligence tent. Len Dulac pronounced them the best taken on the mission. They should have been good. Boyd and I had a grandstand seat out there in front of the parade.

The 312th Bomb Group arrived at Tanauan, Leyte Island, Philippines, from Hollandia, Dutch New Guinea, on January 4, 1945. On January 7 it joined with the A-20s of the 417th Group and the B-25s of the 345th Group in a low-level sweep of the large Japanese base at Clark Field on Luzon. This photo, taken from the rear-facing automatic camera mounted in the lower hatch of Sugar 958, shows parafrag bombs trailing behind.

Sugar 958 missed joining up with other 312th A-20s and then ran diagonally across the planned line of the attack marked by the scattered A-20s in the distance. The line of trees marks the location of Fort Stotsenburg. Strafing B-25s approaching from the right are kicking up the dust; the plane in the center remains low and on course as Sugar 958 climbs out of the way.

Safely above the strafing 345th Bomb Group planes, Sugar 958 begins a steep turn as two B-25s in a line-abreast formation pass beneath. The white mushroom in the middle-distance is a phosphorus aerial bomb dropped by a Japanese fighter. Its target is the upper B-25 passing over the wrecked hangar.

A B-25 sticks to business (upper left) while Sugar 958 makes a steep climbing turn over the wrecked Clark Field hangars. The Japanese bomb spreads phosphorus streamers harmlessly over the string of parafrags dropped from the departed B-25. The black top border is the bottom of the fuselage; the protrusion is the protective bumper.

Chapter 9

Leyte Is Wet in January

THERE WAS NO QUESTION that January was the rainy season on Leyte. It often was raining when we got up for breakfast, and it would sprinkle, drip, or pour for the rest of the day. The ceiling varied from zero in low fog to a solid layer resting on the ridges in the center of the island with lower clouds scudding across the bay toward Samar. When the ceiling lifted and missions could get off, the weather would usually remain decent until ten o'clock or so and then marginal for flying thereafter. The weather briefing regularly included a warning that the field would be closed for varying periods after 1 P.M. The few days when no rain fell and clouds remained fluffy and high were exceptional. My memory, however, has perhaps accentuated Tanauan's wet weather, for we flew missions practically every day.

Ernie Koch and the people from the sheet metal and radio shops had 958 back in service for the mission on January 9, the day following my return from Mindoro. Colonel Wells may have been aware of my questionable performance at Clark Field, for on this day I was assigned to fly on his right wing while Danny Whalen, one of the old-timers, was on the left. The twelve ships assigned to fly this strafing and bombing mission were to destroy rolling stock and warehouses on the railroad leading south from Manila to Legaspi, which was at Luzon's southeastern tip.

The plan was to pick up the railroad near San Pablo, south of a big lake named Laguna de Bay, and follow it to Legaspi. The distance was well over two hundred miles, but it was difficult to estimate exactly how much what with all the twists and turns. The intelligence briefing warned us that the people around Laguna de Bay were reported to be pro-Japanese and we probably would not last long if forced down in that area. The warning not to trust the natives defined Laguna de Bay for me thereafter. Four days later, Francis Vedo—another member of La Junta Class 44-A—and his gunner were forced to ditch in the lake. They were seen in the water but then disappeared. Later reports confirmed that the crew had ditched successfully only to be machine-gunned by Japanese in a patrol boat.

The 389th provided five planes and crews for the first section, with Colonel Wells flying the sixth. The second six-plane section came from another squadron. The weather was marginal when we left Tanauan and, as usual, the group meteorologist predicted the field would be closed-in by early afternoon. We knew that it would be a long mission, so as soon as we were en route I adjusted the cowl flaps to hold the optimum head temperature of 205 degrees Celsius, pulled the throttles back until the engines were running at sixteen hundred rpm, and set the mixture controls to auto-lean. Flying on Colonel Wells's wing was easy and I aimed to save as much fuel as possible until more lively performance was needed at the railroad. Dan Whalen flashed a big grin as he noticed my props slow and motioned that we should open up the formation a bit and relax.

Colonel Wells picked up the railroad within sight of Laguna de Bay and the formation then broke down into three-ship flights. The colonel, who was an aggressive pilot, took us down on the deck to make several passes at the first group of boxcars he saw as if there would be no more targets. We made firing passes in formation whenever our leader saw anything that looked worthwhile. Our targets included a convoy of trucks sheltering in a grove of trees, boxcars on sidings, some bridges, and a country station. Most bridges had a pillbox protecting them and we sprayed these with .50-caliber fire if we had enough time to line up on them. There was little chance of knocking out a bridge itself with the 250-pound demolition bombs we carried.

The A-20's engines backfired whenever the manifold pressure got too high in the auto-lean setting, so I had to raise the rpm to two thousand and go back to auto-rich on the mixtures in order to stay with the leader. I usually ran at twenty-one hundred rpm when making a low-level pass over airfields, but this railroad was going to be a long target and there was no need to maintain close formation. Roaring down the twisting narrow-gauge railroad with trees on either side, strafing and occasionally dropping a bomb when there was something worthwhile was exhilarating. Employing this low-level, follow-the-leader style also burned fuel at a rapid rate, so I checked my gauges frequently.

Several objects caused Colonel Wells to wheel around and make another pass, somewhat to the consternation of the six-ship section behind us. Whalen and I would fall in single file behind the colonel whenever he pulled these didoes.

At some point along the way, about four hours into the mission, the leader of the second section called and said he was running low on fuel. He was also worried about the weather and wanted to pull out and return to Leyte. Wells released him without comment. Within another fifteen minutes the leader of our section's second flight called and said that he also needed to return because of low fuel. Wells looked over at me and I gave him the okay sign with thumb and forefinger; Danny Whalen shook his head negatively and left to join the returning flight.

Now it was just the two of us. Mindful of being on one of Colonel Wells's infamous lists but also enjoying the challenge of flying his wing, I was determined to hang with him, no matter what. By trailing the colonel and keeping my rpm somewhat reduced I could save a little fuel. There was no doubt in my mind that Wells would get us back safely. However, it was up to me to have enough gas to stick with him. He showed no sign of cutting the mission short. We continued following the rails as they twisted around the hills and through the villages along the rugged peninsula. I was a little disappointed that we found no trains operating or locomotives with steam up.

The clouds were down on the ridge tops when we finally roared low over the end of the railroad line, out over the Legaspi harbor, and continued to the gulf beyond. We encountered rainsqualls here and there over the water as the colonel led around the tip of Luzon and through the San Bernardino Strait. We still had 150 miles to go to reach our base.

When we reached the beginning of the narrow strait between Leyte and Samar the red lights on my fuel gauges still had not lit up. Soon the ship anchorage I had seen close-up the previous day came into view. Our two A-20s zipped by the ships, knowing they carried a number of trigger-happy navy gunners, but were not fired upon. We landed at Tanauan without incident shortly afterward. It had been an even six hours in the air, much of the time having been spent in an extended, low-level rat race. I landed with very little fuel showing on the gauges, but the needles still wiggled a bit on the inboard wing tanks and the engines had not quit, so there obviously was something left.

It was then that I lost my chance to redeem my standing somewhat with the colonel. He came by the hardstand in his jeep, a big smile on his face, and greeted me with, "Well Rutter, that wasn't so bad was it? I have about fifty gallons left, how about you?"

"I'm not sure, Colonel," I answered. "About seventy-five gallons." It was probably a truthful reply, but it was clear I had made a mistake by coming up with a number that topped my leader.

"Get in Rutter," he said curtly. The smile vanished. I should have known better, been a little more diplomatic, but such is youth.

We were back strafing railroads and roads on the following day, January 10. The landings at Lingayen on the ninth had been successful and our troops would soon be pushing south, so the enemy's transportation facilities had to be restricted as much as possible. The plan again called for two sections of six ships each to sweep along the railroad but this time we would come from north of Manila and work our way back toward the city. Another squadron led this mission and I was flying as a wingman in the second section, which was made up of 389th Squadron aircraft.

As we traveled along at about a thousand feet over the central plain north of Manila toward the designated starting point for our sweep, someone spotted an unfortunate 1939 Plymouth sedan coming along the highway toward us. Any vehicle seen moving in the area was assumed to be Japanese, although there were reports that some of the guerrillas also had cars. Whoever was leading the mission immediately decided to attack this important rolling target with his flight while the remaining three flights circled overhead and observed.

The Plymouth was making good speed as it headed south, but the driver went even faster as the three A-20s peeled off and went after him. We spectators continued to circle as the strafers made pass after pass at that lone car until it finally went off the road into a rice paddy. Did the ferocious attacks with .50-caliber machine-gun fire from the air cause the driver to leave the road, or was it just the distraction of watching the air show? It seemed to me a waste of taxpayers' money to run a single 1939 Plymouth off of the Manila highway when we had a more important target to hit.

We eventually reached the place near Tarlac where our low-level work was supposed to begin and started back south along the railroad. However, there was less rail traffic in evidence on this line compared to what we had found on the Legaspi line. Moreover, the challenge of staying with Colonel Wells was lacking. I suppose the effort was worthwhile, but to me it was just another six-hour mission.

The look of our camp area near Tanauan improved slowly, but the road into it from the coast highway remained a muddy bog. The day that the shower building was completed and we could give up washing from a helmet was also noteworthy. Everybody planned improvements for their tents to get them out of the mud, with most opting to build raised floors made from fragmentation bomb boxes or other scrap lumber. Owen, Rutledge, and I had agreed to share a tent at Leyte, but then Owen had conveniently gone on leave to Sydney just before we left Hollandia. Since he would not be present to enjoy the satisfaction of contributing physical labor toward improving the tent setup, Owen offered to pro-vide the wherewithal (booze from Sydney) for the materials. Liquor had even more value as trading material in the Philippines than it had in New Guinea, so when Owen ordered, "Build us a goddam good house!" Rut-ledge and I attempted to comply.

With the blank check from Owen, Rutledge and I thought big. We envisioned a concrete floor, screened walls, and the space divided up for a sitting room, a bedroom, and a darkroom in one corner so Rutledge and I could pursue our hobby of photography. One of my purchases in Sydney had been photographic chemicals, printing paper, and several printing frames to process the rolls of exposed but undeveloped film I was accumulating, stored in condoms. We ventured forth in search of materials with several bottles of gin and whiskey in hand, borrowed against Owen's return. At that time whiskey was valued at $35 a bottle while gin brought $20 and only booze would get us the scarce materials we needed.

Rutledge acquired ten bags of cement for two bottles of gin from some navy Seabees who were working on the Seventh Fleet headquar-ters. Neither of us knew much about mixing cement, but several sages who claimed to have construction experience assured us that one part cement to six of sand was a plenty strong mix for a tent floor. It sounded like a lopsided proportion to me, remembering a few concrete projects I had witnessed back on the farm, but we built a mixing box and got to work. According to the information on the bags, the cement was a couple of years old and had been made near Manila during the Japanese occupation. Either this cement did not conform to the stateside product familiar to our advisers or our experts were not the experts they had led us to believe they were. In any event, after hauling sand from the beach, water from a nearby creek, and mixing by hand enough concrete to form a sixteen-by-sixteen-foot square slab four inches thick, we had only a semicoagulated layer of sand that crumbled when touched.

Was it the saltwater entrapped in the damp sand, or were our advisers misleading us? Whatever the case, it had been a lot of hard work for nothing. We started over. We took out another loan of two bottles of gin (I have long since forgotten who our banker was and the interest rate he charged) and acquired ten more bags of cement from the willing Seabees. This time we used a mixture of one part cement to two of sand and threw in a goodly amount of gravel and rocks to boot. The resulting floor met our expectations: it was hard and smooth and well above the surrounding mud. Those who had scoffed or laughed as we sweated over the mixing box came to admire the result and inquire about the source of the cement.

Getting the wood with which to frame the tent was our next challenge. Lumber was hard to come by since there were a number of outfits in the vicinity and all were trying to improve their facilities. Walking by one of the group headquarters tents one day, Rutledge and I noticed a flooring project under way and an attractive pile of boards nearby. With a great amount of cunning and luck we were able to liberate some of the boards by picking them up in broad daylight and carrying them home as if we had been ordered to do so. We made two or three trips to that pile and were never challenged. The noise of sawing and hammering coming from under the limp canvas of our tent was followed by the sudden development of straight eaves and square corners, but somehow this transformation occasioned no questions.

We knocked together a few chairs, a table, and stacked ammunition cases beside the three cots to use for chests. The work had taken us most of two weeks in between flying missions about every other day. Owen, meanwhile, enjoyed an extended leave in Sydney because there was a shortage of planes coming north.

The Japanese army resisted strongly on Luzon and Leyte was not yet completely secure. Meanwhile, the heavy rain continued to upset the planners' schedules. At Tanauan, the 389th Squadron officially received Maj. Theodore Suiter as its new commanding officer and Major Graber moved back to group headquarters as operations officer. Major Suiter, you will recall, had come overseas directly from Training Command. He had no background in combat aircraft and joined us at Hollandia just before the move north. After checking out in the A-20 at Hollandia he had flown some missions, but we pilots looked upon his assumption of command with some skepticism. We judged Major Suiter to be an old man—perhaps as old as forty, we supposed—and with his recent background of instructing cadets, he did not seem to be the type to quickly win our trust as a leader.

Suiter was pleasant enough and approachable, but his bearing was that of an instructor and he frequently lectured us about our nonconforming flying procedures. There was almost universal doubt about how this old instructor would perform in our world. Major Graber had led the squadron on the Clark Field raid, but afterward Major Suiter started to lead us on missions despite not getting much time flying as a wingman or even leading a flight. He thus had not become entirely familiar with our proven procedures before taking over. I suppose that Suiter's long flying experience and instructor background gave him a degree of self-assurance that we could not appreciate. Two things were obvious: he could fly an A-20 and he never shrank from flying missions.

One event over Tanauan airstrip gained my respect for the major's dedication. Just after we had formed up to go on a mission, as the formation circled over the field, gas could be seen streaming from the right wing tank on Suiter's plane. One of his wingmen called the loose fuel cap to his attention. The major ordered us to continue circling as he requested clearance to land. He stopped at the far end of the airstrip after landing, jumped out on the wing without shutting down the engines, secured the gas cap, and immediately took off to rejoin and lead the squadron. Whether it was good judgment or not to delay the departure of the mission for perhaps ten or fifteen minutes is hard to say, but it was a unique performance and clearly demonstrated his resourcefulness and sense of duty.

Major Suiter attempted to initiate some changes in the way formation flying and landing procedures were conducted, but achieved only limited success. His signals for preparing to land or echeloning to the left or right involved exaggerated dives and pull-ups or dropping a wing as if beginning a barrel roll rather than a barely noticeable dip by the flight leader. When first demonstrated, these unexpected gyrations caused his wingmen to decamp for safer territory, which displeased our leader even more. Anyone who had flown in formation for even a mission or two needed no more than a subtle dip of the nose or wing—perhaps only a hand signal—to indicate what the leader intended. The major, however, did not approve of our practical methods and instead sought to reeducate us with lectures.

The weather was fair for a change on the morning of January 15 when the squadron dispatched a six-ship formation to attack the airfield at Puerto Princesa on the island of Palawan. The mission leader was Colonel Strauss, with either Slade or Valentine leading the second flight in which I was flying right wing. Palawan is a long, narrow island on the far west side of the Philippines, southwest of Mindoro, and our target was about one-third of the way down from Palawan's northern tip.

As had become my habit after my earlier experience with sloppy navigating, the chart folder was open on my lap and I closely watched our course and checkpoints as the flight progressed. After settling down on the course to the west there was time to enjoy the calm beauty of the islands spread out below, the changing colors of the sea, and the white cumulus clouds floating here and there in the deep blue sky. Probably because I had never experienced an actual interception by enemy fighters, the possibility of attack from the air was not of great concern to me as I watched the unfolding panorama. The gunner was, hopefully, alert and watching the sky behind while we cruised along at the customary one thousand feet to minimize the possibility of a fighter sneaking up underneath where there was no protection. What could be better than flying an A-20 on such a perfect day with the confidence that Colonel Strauss was handling the navigation?

We crossed the Visayan Sea and stayed north of Panay, which had been my Lorelei on January 8. Our westerly heading would take us over the north end of Palawan and then we would turn to the southwest along the western side of the island. The mountain range that formed Palawan's spine had peaks of up to five thousand feet elevation. Colonel Strauss's navigation was right on the money as he swung to the east and headed toward land after passing a distinctive mountain. We began to climb to cross over the ridge behind what had to be Puerto Princesa.

Our two flights were each to make three-ship passes flying line abreast across the airfield close to the town and then make our getaway out over the open water of the Sulu Sea. Preparations for low-level attacks involved the following routine: fuel selectors switched to full tanks; fuel mixtures to auto-rich; props at twenty-one hundred rpm; gun switches, "ON"; gun sight, "ON"; bomb-bay doors open; bombs armed; shoulder harness locked; and so forth. After clearing the ridge we pitched down and followed the contours of the terrain, picking up speed as we followed the flight ahead of us. The town was a bit off to the right and the airfield straight ahead—a perfect approach for our purpose of sweeping the length of the strip with .50-caliber fire and parafrags.

The lead flight's guns kicked up dust in wide tracks in front of each ship and then the parafrags began to blossom out over revetments and some trees where the enemy planes were likely hidden. Our approach was in line with the length of the runway and our airspeed about 275 miles per hour as we descended in a shallow dive. When we were about three hundred feet over the ground and still descending we were within range to begin strafing the few planes in evidence and some suspicious looking lumps and buildings. The six nose guns barked in unison when I squeezed the trigger on the wheel and the instrument panel vibrated with their recoil.

Suddenly there was nothing. *Nothing!* Just total darkness and complete silence—no roaring engines, no barking guns, no wind whistling past the cockpit's open side windows. My brain was still working, though, for with the silence my instant thought in reaction to this strange event was: So this is how it is. I've been hit and I never even felt it. No pain. No noise. Just like turning off a switch. I'll be damned!

As suddenly as it had stopped, the roaring of the engines was back and I could feel the wheel trembling in my right hand. However, I could still see nothing. Now, my brain said: I must be blind! But we're still flying; pull up before we hit the ground. I eased back on the wheel and the pitch of the engines changed as the plane began to climb. Still unable to see, I held the wheel steady and then relaxed the pressure somewhat to avoid a stall when the controls began to feel slack but I felt we were still climbing a bit. I had not changed the throttle positions and, not being able to see, left them where they were. Since we were still flying my next thought was: Maybe we can somehow get out of this mess yet. There was some hope but how?

About three or four minutes after the incident began I started to squirm in the seat. There was a faint glimmer of light on each side, but nothing identifiable. Straight ahead remained very black indeed. The engines were still turning smoothly at high rpm, so I concluded we could not have been too seriously damaged. Now, however, I could feel a sharp pain across the bridge of my nose. Whenever the controls began to feel sloppy some forward pressure on the wheel would change the engine pitch and should avoid a stall, but there was no way of telling how high we might be above the ground or water. I cautiously tried to let the plane fly itself back to level or whatever attitude the trim and power settings settled into. I was confused and could not fathom just what had happened.

Several minutes and several erratic oscillations must have passed before I began to get an idea of what might have taken place, unlikely as it might have seemed. The thick armor glass panel on top of the cowl above the instrument panel was hinged at the bottom and had two sliding latches holding it into fittings at the top. This arrangement permitted the glass to be easily lowered for cleaning. Somehow, the framed glass panel had fallen and caught me squarely on the nose, wedging the wide, black metal frame against my eyes. I could not see ahead and it had pinned my head in place after jamming my sunglasses down into my cheeks. The glass probably weighed twenty to twenty-five pounds and the black metal frame around it was two and one-half to three inches wide.

That was it! The sliding pins at the top of the frame had somehow worked loose and the vibration of the nose guns beginning to fire had released them. The armor glass panel, which measured about twenty-four inches by eighteen inches, had swung through an arc of about sixty degrees before striking my forehead and nose with stunning effect. With my hand I felt the glass lying horizontally across my nose and, with an upward push, pulled my head back away from the wide black frame so I could see ahead somewhat. It took several tries before I was able to push the glass up far enough for me to see to get the plane leveled out. Shoving it back into place and latching it took still more effort while the plane, on its own, was not flying exactly straight and level.

Wilfred Boyd was not flying with me as gunner that day or he might have concluded that this latest antic was just too much. Hoping that the gunner had not already bailed out, I called, "Sergeant, are you okay back there? I'm having a little trouble up here, but all is under control. Will get back to you shortly." I was relieved to hear a laconic, "Roger, Lieutenant" in response.

My Ray-Ban sunglasses had not broken, which was a wonder as the frames were firmly pinched over the bridge of my nose and gouging into my cheeks on either side. The other planes were a thousand or more feet below and far ahead of us—little wonder, considering that I had been wandering blindly all over the sky. I called the flight leader and advised him we were having a bit of trouble but would catch up shortly. I then told the gunner what I was doing and dropped the parafrags over the sea before closing the bomb-bay doors. It was standard practice to dump the parafrags (which had instantaneous fuses) once the automatic racks had been armed as it was too dangerous to unload them back on the ground.

My nose felt as if it might be broken and a large goose egg was rising on my forehead. Afraid to chance breaking the glasses by attempting to pry them off, I left them pinching my cheeks and nose and peered over the frames. The flight leader, of course, had seen nothing of my abrupt, erratic climb as we approached the target. The left wingman had noticed and assumed that we had been hit someplace. How low we might have been before I regained enough presence to pull back on the wheel is an unknown, but at the angle and speed we were going it must have been a near thing.

We landed after five hours and forty-five minutes in the air and there was time to pry the glasses carefully loose (the lenses were not even cracked) and relate the story of the problems to the gunner and Ernie Koch. Strangely, the sliding pins on the armor glass panel's latches had no holes for safety wires, yet one should have expected that vibration would cause them to work them loose over time. Ernie drilled holes in the pins and thereafter I always checked the catches as part of the routine before starting the engines.

The dropping armor glass panel could easily have been fatal and in my view it could also have been the cause of some accidents. On several occasions planes had flown straight into the ground while firing at targets and the assumption was that enemy fire must have brought them down. Then, there were cases where a plane had seemingly made a perfect ditching in the sea but the pilot was lost—never made it out of the cockpit. The jolt of a water landing would be much greater than the vibration from the nose guns. A falling armor glass panel thus became a prime suspect in my mind when deaths caused by ditchings could not be explained.

There was another unusual incident while we were based at Tanauan, although I was not directly involved in it. We were just leaving the target after a low-level mission one day when a garbled call came over the radio. It sounded as though someone was hurt, but the call was not directed to any of our flight leaders and it was not repeated. None of the planes seemed to be in any difficulty as far as I could tell and we proceeded back to Tanauan. The brief call that had broken the usual radio silence was all but forgotten.

After we landed, however, one of the gunners in a plane ahead of us on the taxiway had his head and shoulders up out of the escape hatch behind the turret and was waving and yelling, pointing toward another plane to attract the attention of the ground crews. After we had parked on our hardstands, the excited gunner was finally able to make his message understood. Soon an ambulance was pulling up next to a plane parked nearby. Doc Walsh and one of the medics were there and an obviously injured man was soon removed from the rear compartment. The ambulance pulled away headed for the hospital while those of us watching from a distance wondered what had caused all the excitement.

We later learned that the short, unclear radio call had been an unsuccessful attempt by the injured gunner to call his pilot while the communications control box was set for the command radio rather than the intercom. A gunner in another plane had recognized the man's voice and understood enough to know the man was in serious trouble. Only after we had landed did the pilot learn from the gesturing gunner that something was amiss in the back end of his plane. The injured gunner had a .45-caliber bullet wound through one of his hands and had lost considerable blood before we got back to Tanauan.

As the story was told, the victim was always apprehensive on missions, particularly at the prospect of being captured by the Japanese. He had adopted the practice of dropping out of his turret just before a run on a target, bracing himself on the floor, and holding his .45-caliber automatic pistol at the ready. In the event the plane went down he was prepared to commit suicide rather than face capture. On this particular mission the gun had mistakenly discharged and shattered his hand. It is the only such case of extreme torment that I can recall.

One of the pilot additions to the 389th Squadron shortly before we left Hollandia, it may be recalled, was Second Lieutenant Osborn. His first name now escapes me, but Osborn was an interesting fellow, small in stature and with a rather disheveled look about him. His expressive black eyes opened wide to express surprise, amusement, or for emphasis, and this caused Owen, always with an apt name at hand, to dub Osborn "Popeye."

Popeye Osborn had been a flying sergeant early in his career, the enlisted rank being available for pilots before and early in the war. These men were rated as "service pilots" and normally were assigned to fly transports or tow targets for aerial gunnery practice and perform other tasks short of combat. Flying sergeants became flight officers (equivalent to a warrant officer) when that grade was introduced for flying personnel. Shortly before reporting to the 389th, Osborn had been promoted to second lieutenant.

Popeye had many tales to tell about flying P-36s and P-40s while towing targets at gunnery school, although he was rather quiet on other subjects. I enjoyed his stories and occasional recitations of ribald poetry. He had a strong affection for the P-40, which he had flown most recently in a fighter group. His background in the A-20 escapes me and perhaps Ed Valentine had checked him out after he joined us. Osborn was a good pilot, notwithstanding his harum-scarum stories about flying this or that plane at some unspecified time in his career.

One afternoon while we were on Leyte, Osborn and I were flying a mission as Cal Slade's wingmen. We were coming over the Samar Strait returning to Tanauan when Popeye's right engine quit without apparent warning. He was flying Slade's right wing and I saw the prop slow down and start to windmill. He quickly feathered it. Popeye then adjusted the trim and power for single-engine flying while practically holding his position on Slade's wing, an expert performance. Popeye looked over at me and flashed a wide grin as he pointed to the stationary prop and then at Slade in anticipation of the double take our leader would do when he noticed only one fan turning on Osborn's aircraft.

As we passed opposite Tacloban approaching the Tanauan strip, Slade checked his wingmen and gave the hand signal to go into right echelon before we peeled off to land. Much to Popeye's disappointment, Cal failed to notice the stopped prop on his right wingman before signaling the formation change. Popeye shrugged as I prepared to cross over to the right, pointed down, and flashed me another grin as he dropped out of formation for a straight-in approach to the airstrip. I then crossed over and took up position on Slade's right wing.

Cal, who apparently did not hear Osborn's radio call to the Tanauan tower declaring an emergency or his being cleared to land, was properly startled when he turned and saw me sitting in Popeye's place and the other plane nowhere in sight. I pointed down and made a motion like a plane peeling off; Cal looked mystified and shook his head. After landing without incident, Osborn had pulled off of the runway into the parking area on the side toward the water to await the other planes. It was impossible to taxi an A-20 any distance with only one engine because the nosewheel was not steerable and the brakes would soon overheat.

Popeye was waiting for us at the end of the taxiway as we started back to camp after we had landed and parked. Without comment, he climbed into the back of the jeep. Cal, who was driving, was very obviously perturbed. Before moving the jeep he said, "Osborn, don't you know enough to stay in formation until we peel off?" Popeye's smile faded. He looked hurt and his eyes opened wide as he replied loudly, "Jesus Christ, Captain, I only had one engine. What in hell did you expect?" My laughter did not help, but we finally convinced Cal that Osborn's story was true, that he had indeed been flying in formation on a single engine for ten or fifteen minutes. Popeye Osborn remained an enigma as long as he was with us, but in my book he was an amusing one.

Only occasionally did we meet up with pilots of the RAAF, although they were very much a part of the effort on New Guinea and other islands in that area. The RAAF's responsibilities remained generally south of the equator after the Philippines invasion. We did, however, see their Beaufighters on Morotai as noted earlier. We had worked with a squadron of RAAF Beauforts once or twice when bombing Atape east of Hollandia the previous summer, but we had had no direct contact with our Aussie counterparts. The general impression seemed to be that the Aussies were uninhibited flyers and inclined to exercise less caution than our leaders demanded. The flight south from Hollandia Mel Kapson and I had made in the rainstorm in that tired C-47 is a good example. An incident at Tanauan confirmed the Aussies' reputation for relaxed and understated behavior.

Each day, an officer from the group was assigned to serve as "airdrome officer" at the airstrip, acting as liaison between the control tower and flight operations. It was usually a boring assignment, because the officer assigned the duty had to remain at the airstrip constantly while the field was open. I drew the assignment one day, but aside from being in the tower when the 312th's mission went out in the morning and again later when it returned, there was little to do. Doc Walsh was also on duty with one of our ambulances, parked near the crash crew's truck in front of the control tower. It had been a typical overcast day with periods of rain and, after checking with the tower operator about traffic expected, I joined Doc, who was keeping dry in the ambulance.

The Australians had two squadrons equipped with A-20s, but as far as we knew they were both operating down in New Guinea. It thus was unusual to see an RAAF A-20 approaching Tanauan from the north that afternoon. The pilot touched down on the wet strip and rolled down the runway past us—a bit fast perhaps, but nothing unusual. Doc and I watched the landing and then continued our conversation, but only for a moment before the crash alarm sounded and the tower operator yelled down from above, "He crashed on the end of the runway!"

The ambulance followed after the crash truck. When we arrived on the scene we found the A-20 and three navy F4U Corsair fighters tangled up in the parking area at the end of the airstrip. The A-20 pilot, realizing that the end of the runway was fast approaching, had clamped down hard on the brakes, which caused the plane to slide on the wet pierced-steel matting. It wound up in the parking area used by the navy F4U fighters.

In the resulting smashup, the A-20 first lost its nose section with six guns mounted in it. It continued sliding into a second F4U, losing most of its right wing before slamming into a third fighter, the right wing of which stabbed through the A-20's cockpit area and out the opposite side of the fuselage. There was fuel, wreckage, and ammunition scattered everywhere. By the time we arrived, several navy crew chiefs were already up beside the cockpit trying to rescue the Aussie. The F4U's wing had sliced through the fuselage like a knife, just missing the pilot's legs and torso, trapping him in his seat.

After a few minutes, the stunned Aussie began to move. When he finally was able to speak, he reported that no bones seemed to be broken. He did, however, have a large, bleeding gash on his forehead. Doc Walsh looked him over briefly before pronouncing that the bleeding was not serious. Doc reassured the pilot that help was at hand and reassurance was very much needed in view of the yells and strings of curses coming from the would-be rescuers:

"Christ! There's gas everywhere!"

"Watch that ammo!"

"Put out the light! *No* goddam cigarettes!"

"Get a cable around this fucking wing and bring a truck."

"Give me an axe; I'll chop the bastard off!"

The crash crew worked furiously to cut the wing tip from the F4U before the spilled fuel caught fire. I was not sure they were going to win the race. Eventually, with much profanity accompanying their efforts, they managed to cut through the wing and pull it out of the way. The pilot, at last able to climb out of the remains of the cockpit more or less on his own, was helped down and over to the ambulance. Doc Walsh pulled the edges of the wound on his forehead together with tape before wrapping a turban of gauze around the pilot's head. He was badly shaken, but the cut on his forehead was the only outward injury.

After retrieving his blue uniform cap and a briefcase from the mangled cockpit and surveying the wreckage of the four destroyed planes, the Aussie rendered his assessment: "Bloody poor show. Thanks, mates." The ambulance driver gave him a ride over to the operations shack to close his flight plan while the dejected navy men looked at the remains of their F4Us. The engineers soon arrived to gather up the several pieces of the destroyed A-20.

The exalted airdrome officer was neither consulted nor seemingly needed. I do not even recall having to fill out a formal report on the incident during my tour of duty.

Maury Owen returned from his extended stay in Sydney toward the end of the month, well after Jim Rutledge and I had finished the major work on the house. Mosquito netting was in short supply and we had not been able to screen all around the tent frame as Owen had directed, so we had mosquito bars over our cots like everybody else. Owen approved of our work in general and did not kick about the cost in booze, but he objected to the mosquito bars. He no doubt had been spoiled by his life in the fleshpots of Sydney. Drawing on his ample liquor stocks, Owen donated another bottle of genuine bourbon to pay for all-around screening. He begged off going out and trying to buy or scrounge the netting himself, however.

The compound for the Seventh Fleet headquarters was still under construction down the coast toward Dulag. We figured they surely would have screening there—and better than any the army might have. The navy always lived well. I wrapped the bourbon in a GI towel and placed it in the jeep's glove compartment, then drove down the coast to the construction site. After locating the Seventh Fleet headquarters, I drove up to a substantial looking building with a raised concrete floor, clapboard siding, and screened windows where work was in progress.

A petty officer of some description watched me pull up and then sauntered over to inform me that they were building the admiral's galley. I looked around and noted for future reference that there was an ice cream machine. The petty officer looked blank when I inquired about the possibility of getting a roll of that beautiful nylon screen the navy used for its tents. As we continued exchanging pleasantries with a hint or two as to what items I could use. The chief soon got the picture that there was whiskey someplace about and that it might be exchanged for say, a sixty-four-foot roll of canvas and nylon screening, a bundle of lath, and a keg of nails.

"Lieutenant," he offered, "why don't you take a walk around and look at the other side of the galley."

"Sounds like a good idea, Chief," I replied. "There's a towel in the glove compartment in case you want to dry your hands." We thus obtained full screening for our house, plus nails for trading to others who were working at making their living conditions more civilized. The nylon screening in one big roll could easily be wrapped around the sixteen-by-sixteen-foot pyramidal tent and just as easily taken down again. It was far superior to the usual practice of cutting up mosquito bars and piecing them together over the tent frame.

We completed our improvements on January 25 and, before the evening meal, Owen, Rutledge, and I relaxed to enjoy our handiwork. It was worth all the labor and Owen's booze we had expended. We had a solid floor, screen all around, and the darkroom cubbyhole in the corner for future photo projects. Owen blew cigarette smoke toward the ceiling as he rested on the cot in his usual horizontal position and observed, "Wouldn't it be hell if we had to move?"

"Christ!" replied Rutledge with feeling as he sprawled in a chair he had fabricated out of bomb crates. He took a deep drag on his cigarette and shook his head at the thought.

No sooner had the idea been uttered than Tom Jones came through the door, beaming like a cherub. "Hey you guys, did you hear the news? We're moving to Mindoro day after tomorrow." He continued to beam and prattle as the three of us profaned everybody connected with such a decision, from the commanding general down to Jones himself—who obviously enjoyed being the messenger and seeing our reactions. Owen became furious as Jones continued to profess amusement that our building efforts were about to be nullified and finally erupted: "Sweet Ass, you are one miserable sonofabitch. Get out!" The pious and somewhat artistic interests that Jones displayed at times had earlier earned Owen's nickname of "Sweet Ass," but this may have been the first time he called him so to his face. Tom looked hurt, but he was still giggling as he exited our palace. Meanwhile, we continued to rant and rave. After all that work making a livable situation in the midst of the Leyte rainy season and we would get to enjoy it for such a short time. Our profanity was justified, absolutely.

Our language in this incident was not uncommon. Profanity of various degrees of invention seemed to be natural with the average GI, whether for emphasis or in ordinary conversation. Officers, most of them at least, showed a little restraint in their choice of profane words and eschewed the most foul—at least most of the time. Owen's outburst on this occasion was unusual in that his delivery was vehement, not just idle chitchat, and evidenced his low opinion of Jones and his idea of a humorous situation.

There was a sense of serious business in the mess hall the following morning, January 26, when the briefing officer started talking to the assembled crews before the day's mission. The 388th and 389th Squadrons were assigned to make a low-level attack on the coastal defense batteries located on Grande Island at the entrance to Subic Bay. Subic Bay was a well-protected harbor on Luzon's west coast north of the Bataan Peninsula. It had been a U.S. Navy base before the outbreak of the war, although apparently not of the same scale as Cavite on the eastern shore of much larger Manila Bay.

The mission briefing outlined a desperate effort against a heavily fortified target, but the coastal guns blocking this strategic harbor simply had to be neutralized. Subic Bay had to be opened for navy use and to bring in supplies by transport ships since Manila Bay would not be available until Corregidor and other harbor defenses could be taken, which might take months. The war would be held up pending the taking of Grande Island. Everything rested with the valiant crews of the 312th Bomb Group—or so it sounded. The briefing officer did not quite end by shouting, "It's do or die, men!" but the importance and danger of this operation was evident in his tone and we took him at his word.

Each squadron would send six planes with the 388th leading. The target's small size dictated that the attack could only be made by successive three-ship flights. Our approach was from the sea and, after overflying the island, the survivors would make a sharp turn to the right toward the hills on Bataan to avoid the antiaircraft batteries lining the inner harbor.

The bomb loads would be five-hundred-pound parachute demolition bombs (parademos) with two parachutes each to give us time to escape the bomb blast. Several times the briefing officer said, "And stay low!" That admonition was hardly necessary, however. My flight would be the last across the target. By then either all the opposition would have been eliminated or it would be a hornet's nest. Oh well, "Ours not to reason why. . . ."

Rutledge was on my right wing but before we had gotten far from Tanauan he reported engine trouble and turned back. Gordon Gerould was flying the spare ship that day, so he moved in to fill the space that had been vacated. A spare ship was dispatched on most missions. It would follow along for the first half-hour and fill in if a plane developed mechanical problems and had to return to base. After crossing Manila Bay and the Bataan Peninsula, our leader took us down to about five hundred feet just south of the mouth of Subic Bay and then circled back north to launch the valiant attack on Grande Island. The navy was depending on us.

The flights circled low over the water and we waited our turn as flight after flight went after that stopper in the mouth of Subic Bay. Grande Island was a rocky protrusion rising out of the water perhaps a hundred feet. It had a few trees on top and concrete parapets all around, masking the coastal defense guns. We had been told what to expect and, although the gun emplacements we could see dated back almost fifty years, the island did look potentially lethal.

Finally, it was our turn. We headed for the fort where smoke and dust from the bombs dropped by the other flights smothered the few trees. We were just over the water and, hopefully, below the depression angle of the heavy antiaircraft batteries as we approached. Our airspeed was well up so as to minimize our exposure time. Our trio of A-20s flew on in close formation, bomb doors open and nose guns blazing to keep the Japanese gunners down. Nevertheless, we all expected to feel some heavy hits at any moment. Like the famed charge of the Light Brigade, we continued on toward the Valley of Death—but we were only three, not six hundred.

At the last minute we pulled up over the island's shore, skimmed across with just enough altitude to dump the parademo bombs, and then plunged back down over the water for our getaway, turning toward the east. My ship had seemingly not been hit and the formation ahead was reforming as I cut inside the 389th's leader to slide into position. Both wingmen also seemed to have survived that boiling caldron of smoke and wreckage on Grande Island. Our escape had been a miracle, no doubt about it.

As we climbed away I looked back at the scene and laughed out loud. All of the big guns that appeared in the reconnaissance photos looked like leftovers from the Spanish-American War. Several of them were not even mounted in emplacements or on carriages. The splashes on the water that had looked so ominous as we approached the island must have been bomb shorts from the flights ahead. Photos of the strike provided fine views of the outmoded ordnance on Grande Island—and there was not a soldier in sight. We had done our job, desperate though it had been. The way was clear for the U.S. Navy to take Subic Bay.

Years later, Gordon "Gerry" Gerould sent me a copy of his personal listing of missions flown with this note: "Mission #51. On my last A-20 mission I finally flew on your wing. I'm grateful you brought me back." After the attack on the deserted fortress of Grande Island, Gerry took over flying the group's C-47 from Don Dyer, who returned to flying A-20s. The flying time was five hours on our heroic, fearless, and successful attack on Grande Island.

On January 27, 1945, the 389th Squadron left Tanauan, its rain and mud, and our plush house to fly to San Jose on Mindoro. The stay there would be only temporary, until a new airstrip and bivouac area could be made ready for us at Mangaldan, Luzon, on the Lingayen Gulf.

Chapter 10

MINDORO AND ON TO LUZON

BY THE TIME THE 312TH BOMB GROUP reached Leyte in early January, 1945, the island was largely secured, although ground fighting would continue in the central mountains for some months. The Lingayen Gulf landings on January 9, following our big raid on Clark Field, marked the beginning of the drive south through central Luzon to Manila and our planes were needed. We were also needed to neutralize the Japanese airfields on northern Luzon and elsewhere from which enemy planes continued to operate and Leyte was simply too far south for effective missions to that area.

The 312th was also hampered at Tanauan by the continuing wet season with the attendant operational problems for both planes and men. Luzon, for the most part, was dry at this time of year and U.S. troops made quick progress following the Lingayen landings and within a week had a beachhead some thirty miles deep and equally wide. Construction crews quickly began enlarging the Japanese airstrip just off the beach at Lingayen town and building a new medium-bomber strip inland at Dagupan, soon relocated to a better site farther east at Mangaldan village. The 312th's planes, aircrews, and crew chiefs left Tanauan on January 27 for a short stay on Mindoro until the field at Mangaldan would be ready.

San Jose on Mindoro was the same airstrip where some of us had landed after the Clark Field mission. We made our temporary home there with the 417th Bomb Group. The 417th's camp area was on top of one of the low hills in back of the airstrip, high enough to avoid most of the mosquitoes and other flying insects. My recollections of this campsite for the short period we were there are entirely favorable: breezes blew across the hilltop from the South China Sea, the sun was shining most of the time, and in all ways it was an improvement over the very damp climate we had experienced on Leyte.

The officers lived in one big tent, as we had done at Hollandia, and we went about raising the two-pole squad tent as if we knew what we were doing. However, after considerable struggle without much success, some of the boys from the 417th came over to show us how it should be done. There were indications that our hosts thought we were tenderfeet when it came to bivouacking and volunteered the usual reminder, "You should have been here when it was rough!" The 417th's A-20s had been at San Jose since December 29 and had experienced several serious enemy air raids until January 9.

The area around San Jose had been a large sugar plantation with a sugar refinery before the war. There were narrow-gauge rail lines with diamond-stack locomotives and flatcars for hauling the cane from the fields. Shortly after we arrived, the U.S. engineers extended a rail line down to the beach to haul supplies coming in by ship. The sound of steam-locomotive whistles gave a touch of civilization to San Jose. The Mindoro landings had involved little ground fighting, so most of the buildings in the village and at the sugar mill were relatively undamaged.

Many of the pilots in both the 417th and 3d Attack Groups had come from Class 44-A and I had known them at La Junta or later at Charlotte. A particular friend in the 417th was Wilburne "Zoot" Morrow from Long Beach, California. Bob Mosley and Bill Morgan were still with the 3d Attack Group and living somewhat south of us. It may have been that the 3d Attack was based on Hill Field while we were on Elmore Field, which had been named for Lt. Col. Howard Ellmore (*sic*), the CO of the 417th who was killed on January 2. Zoot and I visited with Mosley and Morgan a couple of times and they did not fail to remind me, "You should have been here when. . . ." My response was to remind them of how tough it had really been in the merciless rain on Leyte.

Our Christmas mail caught up with us at Mindoro. Nancy in Charlotte had thoughtfully sent me four books. They shipped better than cookies and we were all hungry for books. Nancy had particularly recommended, *The Robe*, which at the time was a best-seller. For some reason, however, I started reading another of the books she had sent. Word of my wealth in books soon spread and those who were not blessed with a perceptive correspondent such as Nancy immediately borrowed the three that I was not then reading. Maury Owen confiscated *The Robe* right off with the promise that he would quickly return it. Soon, however, it was traveling from hand to hand. *The Robe*, which I understand had some religious basis, disappeared, never to return. I thus was unable to report my reaction to this uplifting work, which probably disappointed Miss Nancy.

The books had come through in reasonably good shape, surviving days in the rain on the beach at Leyte and being thrown on and off ships, trucks, and planes. Some of the newspapers and magazines arriving at the same time had been reduced to wet pulp. My folks had tried to be selective in their Christmas gifts, but in packing them had wrapped toothpaste, shaving cream, chocolate bars, and a fruitcake around a fine hunting knife I had requested. It required considerable effort to peel the gooey mess away from the much-desired hunting knife. Even in the distressed condition many were in when they arrived, Christmas packages were a welcome reminder of home.

While we were living in the big tent on Mindoro, the enigmatic Popeye Osborn surprised us again. Word came down from group headquarters that V Bomber Command needed a volunteer with an engineering degree and combat experience. The assignment called for some involvement in choosing future airstrip sites and their layout. The request elicited no response from the pilots, except for Osborn, who remarked, "What the hell, I'll go talk to them just to see what kind of a deal it is."

Osborn's history was still vague to most of us, although he had been in the squadron for six weeks or more and he and I had adjacent cots. Others in the big tent had dismissed most of Popeye's stories and expressed surprise at his audacity in thinking that he was qualified for the advertised position. However, he had seventeen missions under his belt by then and he ignored the negative comments, quietly saying to me as he left for the orderly room, "I've got a degree in civil engineering. That ought to count for something." It was another piece in the puzzle that was Popeye Osborn.

A day or so later, Popeye came into the tent with a smile spread all over his face. In his usual laconic way he announced that he was moving to V Bomber Command to fill the engineering position. He began packing immediately while answering questions about his new job from the now curious former doubters. "Treat me with respect," he said jovially, "'cause I'll be picking your next goddam base." Osborn threw his few belongings into a duffle bag, gave a final wave to the still somewhat astonished group in the big tent, and made his farewell speech: "So long you sonsofbitches. I'm going where the living is easy. Good luck!" With that, a most interesting character was gone; I never saw him again.

It was during our temporary stay at Mindoro that I observed the power of Chaplain Father Clatus Snyder, who was widely known for speaking out whenever he saw the need, sometimes to the discomfiture of the senior brass. Father Snyder's ability to intercede for his men in the case of Tom Jones's love life, however, was amazing at the time—and still is in retrospect. It all began when one of the pilots on leave in Sydney had by chance shared a cab with two others who turned out to be Jones's young friend/fiancée Pat Kenny and a GI companion with glider-pilot wings. Noting the 312th Bomb Group patch on the 389th Squadron pilot's jacket, the GI inquired if he knew Tom. However, there was little more conversation with the young lady or her friend.

Tom somehow learned later that his supposed fiancée was cavorting about with unknown GIs and this put him into an emotional slump. He talked to me about the reported sighting in Sydney since I had spent Christmas with the Kenny family and squired Pat to the beach on several occasions. I had duly reported the family's appreciated hospitality to Tom, of course, and the behavior of the attractive but very young Pat had been altogether proper. I reassured Tom that it sounded innocent enough. Besides, I added, maybe the girl with the GI was not even Pat. Tom seemed satisfied with my viewpoint.

However, being a good Catholic, Tom took up his problems with Father Snyder. Tom became more and more obsessed with the possibility of losing Miss Pat as time passed. Eventually, Father Snyder arranged a ten-day compassionate leave for Tom to go down to Sydney, much to the amazement of those of us privy to the circumstances. We were at last in the Philippines, badly needed, and there was no excess of pilots in the 389th at the time. When there was a much bigger problem to be faced with each mission, Tom's obsession with his personal romantic problem was difficult for us to understand. At the very least it seemed sophomoric.

Tom came to see me the night before he went on leave and asked to borrow my dress shoes. They were the only pair of Florsheim shoes I had ever owned. I kept them encased in a waterproof bag and dutifully polished them each week to keep the mold at bay. "Sorry Tom," I said. "My twelve-Bs won't fit your eleven-D feet. Pat will still love you even in your boondockers." But Tom would not be put off. "It's just for ten days," he pleaded. In the end, I succumbed to his appeals. I had no illusions that after ten days on Tom's paddle feet the shoes would ever be the same, but we were friends, so I let him have the Florsheims. There were larger concerns than a pair of shoes.

After taking care of whatever romantic business there was with Miss Pat, Tom found that there was little transportation coming back north. There was great urgency to move equipment north where the retaking of the Philippines was proceeding apace, so those on leave in Sydney were left to their cruel fate. Tom and what was left of my shoes did not get back to the 389th for six weeks, by which time the uppers had separated from what was left of the soles. My Florsheims went directly into the trash. Tom's romance went into the trash a little later, but you cannot say that Father Snyder did not have some strong clout with someone, misapplied as it may have been in this instance, considering that there was a war in progress.

We were on Mindoro from January 27 until February 11, during which time I flew four missions to Luzon. One of the missions was to the airstrip at Mariveles, a small harbor and village located near the tip of the Bataan Peninsula facing Manila Bay. There was a narrow valley leading from the high ground down to the water and after strafing the airfield in three-ship flights and clearing the harbor we had to bank sharply to the right to avoid overflying Corregidor, which lay just a few miles offshore. It was a poorly led mission and the leader took us over the airstrip much too fast. We had little opportunity to pick out targets—if there even were any left.

We flew north to our new base at Mangaldan, Luzon, near the Lingayen Gulf on February 11. It was a temporary airstrip that had been constructed by knocking down the dikes surrounding several large rice paddies between the villages of Dagupan and Mangaldan. The landing area had been coated with oil and was three hundred feet wide by five thousand feet long with taxiways on each side. Since it was the dry season, the oiled surface was satisfactory. However, because of the high water table, the field would have to be vacated before the rains came later in the spring.

Mangaldan Field was a crowded place. There were two Marine Air Groups (MAGs) flying SBD Dauntless dive-bombers, several PB4Y Catalina search planes, a B-24 (F-7) photoreconnaissance squadron, and the 3d Air Commando Group, which flew P-51D Mustang fighters. Marine Air Group 24 was in charge of operations and had set up camp in a nice palm grove alongside the main road at the south end of the field. The 312th was assigned an open rice paddy area about a half-mile north of the runway. There was no shade and lots of dust. The temperature got up to a hundred degrees Fahrenheit during the day, but the nights were comfortably cool. Breezes blew in from the gulf and there were few bugs, so, everything considered, it was not a bad campsite.

The ground echelon had set up camp before we flew in with the planes, so it was all very orderly, with tents in neat lines, by the time we arrived. Owen, Rutledge, and I bunked together for a short time, but made no move to improve our quarters since rumor had it that we would be moving again soon. After a week or so, Rutledge went on leave. Then Owen and Don Dyer decided to join up in another tent while Len Dulac, the 389th's intelligence officer, and John Edmunds, our communications officer, invited Gerry Gerould and me to join them. Dulac and Edmunds both had jeeps assigned and soon collected enough fragmentation bomb boxes for us to build a raised floor above the dusty dirt and rice stubble.

The water table in the area was no more than eighteen inches below the surface, so we obtained bathing water by digging shallow wells beside each tent. Our tent was next to a paddy dike and the bathing routine was to scoop some of the brackish water from the well with your helmet, sit on the dike, and attempt to wash your face, hands, and feet with that one helmet full. The black earth became a sticky mess as soon as water hit it, so it was a mistake to splash around the well too much. For shaving, we carried another helmet full of water into the tent and placed it on a crude stand. Later, an existing artesian well located in a field about three hundred feet from the squadron's tents was improved with several showerheads over wooden slatted duckboards. With towels wrapped around our waists we trooped out into the field and stood under the pipe to shower in the open. It was a big improvement over the well-and-helmet routine.

Major James Moffitt Wylie was assigned to the 389th while we were still at Mindoro. Major Wylie was a youthful looking, slim fellow about twenty-four or twenty-five years old who had grown up in Clover, South Carolina. Anxious to get home after having spent the previous year at Fifth Air Force headquarters, he had asked to fly combat missions so he could qualify for rotation. Owen sized up this newcomer to our ranks and promptly dubbed Wylie "The Flying Bellhop." It was a very apt nickname considering his youthful appearance and friendly manner.

It was unusual to have two majors assigned to a squadron, but Jim Wylie was a down-to-earth fellow and he quickly made it clear his only aspiration was to fly his missions and go home. He was a graduate of Flying Cadet Class 41-B as I recall, had considerable flying time that included antisubmarine patrols in B-18s early in the war, and had no trouble checking out in the A-20. He summed up his attitude with the statement: "You guys are the ones who know what this is all about. I'm going to fly wing, so forget about my rank." At Mangaldan, Majors Suiter and Wylie roomed together with our flight surgeon, Doc

The 312th relocated to Mangaldan on Luzon near the Lingayen Gulf on February 11, 1945. The camp was laid out in military fashion in dry rice paddies. The 389th Squadron's orderly room and Doc Walsh's dispensary are above.

Walsh, and although their tent was much like the rest, it also had a kerosene-powered refrigerator to keep beer cold—a valuable perk.

I became a flight leader on January 11, 1945. The other members of my flight were Austin Ayotte, Bob Foreman, Tom Jones, and one or two others. While members assigned to a flight usually flew together, there was no fixed rule that a pilot always flew with the same flight leader. Pilots were scheduled to fly wherever they were needed to fill out the squadron formation. The operations officer, who by then was Ed Valentine, made up the flight assignments for a particular mission on the basis of experience and rotation, so there were instances when I flew as a wingmen on a leader with greater or equal time rather than leading a flight. On February 6, a number of us who had joined the 312th Bomb Group the previous summer were promoted to first lieutenant.

On February 15, Cal Slade and I took the group's B-25 on a courier flight to Tanauan. The 312th was still in the process of moving equipment from Leyte by C-47 while needed small parts and personnel were often hauled on frequent B-25 flights. We picked up three newly assigned pilots and their crews at Leyte that day. The three officers— Lieutenants Hummell, Stone, and Wilson—had been instructors in the

The village church at Dagupan, Luzon, near the Mangaldan airstrip on February 22, 1945. The tag end of the Washington's Day parade is moving across the plaza.

A Filipino "transporter" near our airfield at Mangaldan, Luzon, in 1945. Japanese occupying forces confiscated civilian cars and trucks during the war. Patient water buffalo like this fellow were the reliable motive power for all work.

A water buffalo team powers the crusher at this farmer's sugar mill near Mangaldan. At right, Cal Slade walks back to the boiling vats in search of Kentucky-style sorghum for his morning GI Toast.

A-20 Replacement Training Unit at Florence, South Carolina, so they were old hands at flying. However, the sight of Manila burning as we crossed Manila Bay caught their attention: It was their first exposure to war. Chet Hummell was up in the cockpit taking it all in as we looked at the smoke hanging over the city; Manila burned for two weeks before the Japanese were finally driven out. After the war, Hummell and I lived in the same small town near Columbus, Ohio, and became good friends.

The following day, February 16, paratroopers from the 503d Parachute Infantry Regiment landed on Corregidor. The island was something of a symbol for the United States, particularly General MacArthur, who President Roosevelt had ordered out of Corregidor to take command of U.S. forces in the Southwest Pacific Area. Lieutenant General Jonathan "Skinny" Wainwright remained in command of U.S. forces in the Philippines and surrendered the fortress to the Japanese in May, 1942. The island was the stopper in the mouth of Manila Bay and had to be taken before the port could be opened to shipping. The attack plan called for B-24s at medium altitude over the island at about 8 A.M. and the A-20s of the 312th and 417th Bomb

Groups to follow with low-level strafing and bombing to keep the defenders' heads down before the transport planes carrying paratroopers came over immediately afterward.

The entire 312th Group flew this mission with Colonel Strauss leading. The morning was clear as we came down from the north and crossed over the bay some miles west of Manila. The medium-altitude bombing by the B-24s was under way and we could see the red flashes and black puffs of smoke as the sticks of bombs walked across the island's rocky surface. The A-20 groups began their runs as soon as the B-24s finished. The 417th's planes were in view crossing the island's short axis as we dropped down to hit at about the midpoint and cross the high ground on the island's long axis. A six-ship 389th Squadron flight led by Major Graber was assigned to make strafing runs on nearby Caballo Island (Fort Hughes) to suppress the flak batteries there before and during our runs.

There was some minor ground fire as we roared low over Corregidor, but it seemed that most of the buildings had been shattered by previous bombardments. The troop-carrying C-47s approached from the southwest right on time as we finished strafing and banked away out over the bay to watch the paratroopers drop.

The lines of transport planes and the blossoming parachutes trailing behind them as they passed over the island was a never-to-be-forgotten sight. A number of the paratroopers became casualties when they missed the small drop zone and were helplessly blown by a twenty-five-mile-per-hour wind against the cliff on the south side of the island. I did not envy the paratroopers' their assignment. General MacArthur watched the well-executed assault on the badly battered fortress from a lone B-17 orbiting above us.

The attack on Corregidor was Col. Robert Strauss's 126th and last mission. He had been the 312th's CO since it was organized at Savannah, Georgia. He would turn leadership of the group over to Lt. Col. Selmon Wells before going home in March.

The majority of our missions from Mangaldan were in direct support of U.S. Army ground troops, but we also went out at times to help the Filipino guerrillas. We flew two such missions on February 17. That morning we flew up Luzon's west coast to San Fernando Point in support of a guerrilla force. In the afternoon we bombed and strafed Japanese troops dug in on a ridge in the hills west of Fort Stotsenburg. The afternoon effort was an opportunity to see the army's infantry close up as the opposing lines were well defined on the bare ridges.

As we came in low over the friendly lines we could clearly see the GIs in their holes watching us, waving and pointing to the next hill to the west. The area had been fought over for a week or more and a rain shower had just passed, leaving the hills like bare piles of sticky clay or, given the composition of the Philippines, volcanic goo. Ahead of us were the Japanese. They occupied similar holes dotted along the summit of their ridge, and looked like ants as they scurried to get into position for the attack they knew was coming. The enemy directed rifle and machine-gun fire at the planes approaching in three-ship flights, but without visible tracer ammunition we could more easily ignore it.

We were carrying 250-pound demolition bombs with parachutes attached to slow their fall and thus allow us to get clear before the bombs exploded. There were several flights ahead of us and we could see their bombs dropping from the bomb bays toward the target area, the parachutes opening in a line behind. This day, however, something unusual occurred: about every third bomb was exploding in the air as soon as its parachute snapped open. There was a wicked red glare, a ball of black smoke, and then the *keerumph* of the explosion just below our flight level. We managed to hold our course as we passed through this self-made flak. Luckily, the only damage was a few holes caused by bomb fragments. The unexpected explosions were startling because they were close to our level and so clearly visible. Would the next bomb dropped be the one to explode? Were we far enough behind the lead flight to avoid the blast?

At first the armament officers doubted our reports of these airbursts, declaring it impossible. However, there were too many sightings and complaints to be ignored. The ordnance people finally conceded that the tail fuses, usually set for a slightly longer delay, must have been faulty—or incorrectly partially armed—so that they were set off by the opening shock of the parachute. Thereafter, our ordnance techs applied different fuse settings when we dropped parademos.

Life at Mangaldan turned out to be generally pleasant as far as I was concerned. Although the pace did not slacken, the missions were shorter and the targets all different. There was something new to face each time we went out, a new piece of scenery. The campsite proved to be reasonably comfortable and the food improved noticeably as supplies began reaching us through the nearby port of Lingayen. Fresh meat was often available and bully beef or the infamous Spam (baked, diced, fried, or cold) appeared on the menu less frequently. Staff Sergeant Augustus Yelles ruled our mess hall with an iron hand and he and his crew did an admirable job with the supplies available. Our mail had also caught up with us and now came in almost every day.

Dulac, Edmunds, and Gerould proved to be good tent mates. The four of us seemed to have enough in common to get along well. As the intelligence officer, Dulac had all the latest news. I enjoyed stopping by his office and reading the latest "Blue Book" reports on enemy equipment and tactics. Edmunds, a lawyer from Hopkinsville, Kentucky, was a student of history, a quiet fellow with a good sense of humor. In addition to his duties as communications officer, Edmunds served as defense counsel at courts-martial and thus often found himself at odds with the brass. Gerould, who now flew the group's C-47, usually had an adventure to recount after his trips down to Hollandia and farther south. Gerry was from Warren, Pennsylvania, on the Allegheny River. I had visited the town several times, so we had some things in common.

Leaves to Sydney had resumed and a few of the pilots and gunners came up on the roster from time to time. There was still a transportation bottleneck for people returning north, however, as planes were needed to bring supplies up to support the Philippines campaign. It was unlikely that I would have another leave in Sydney, but that was of small moment now. Flying was still mostly enjoyable for me and I felt a growing sense of satisfaction at the number of missions being added to my record. By flying practically every day beginning on February 13—and with two missions each on February 17, 18, and 24—my total reached fifty by the end of the month.

On afternoons when we did not fly, John Edmunds and I sometimes walked over to the beach on the Lingayen Gulf for a swim. We had to go about two miles across some rice paddies, through several palm groves, and a couple of small Filipino barrios, but it was a pleasant walk, with evidence of the prewar American administration located here and there in the form of public wells and substantial village schoolhouses. Most of the thatched-roof houses contained a Singer sewing machine visible through the window that provided the best light, indicating to me that life was not quite so primitive as a first impression of the little houses might suggest. One town had a sizable commercial garage with a Ford sign over the door, but there was little evidence of any recent business.

The wide, palm-fringed beach on the Lingayen Gulf had fine white sand and sloped gently into the water. It was an unspoiled tropical scene. Sometimes, as we baked on the beach or lounged in the shallow water, we could hear the rumble of artillery in the distant hills to the northeast where the war was still going on. The flashes of the guns and the puffs of smoke when the shells landed on the bare hillsides showed that the poor dogfaces were still trying to move the Japanese out of their holes on the ridge tops. I was always struck by the contrast between our peaceful beach where we were and the deadly shelling going on just a few miles away.

Major Suiter got into trouble on February 20. We had been assigned to bomb and strafe Japanese troops holding up the U.S. advance north from the central valley through the mountains toward the town of Solano on the main highway. Although we flew missions to several remote villages in the general area on both the nineteenth and twentieth, a review of the available records suggests it was the mission to Calamba that resulted in Major Suiter's downfall. As I recall, it was the first time Major Suiter was entrusted with leading the entire group rather than just our squadron. Perhaps that is why Colonel Wells was above us in his A-20, overlooking the proceedings from on high.

Major Wylie, who had been flying wing since joining the 389th, now had about fifteen missions, so Ed Valentine judged that he was ready to try leading a flight. Jim had flown with me on several missions and now I would be flying on his right wing. Valentine quietly said, "Keep an eye on him, Joe." Typical of Wylie, he asked me to let him know right away if he was doing something wrong. Ed Wootten was on Wylie's left wing.

It was a short hop—only sixty or seventy-five miles—from Mangaldan, across the central valley, to the area of hills and narrow valleys north of San Jose where the assigned target was located. The village of Calamba was not an easy place to locate, but we had attacked targets in the vicinity previously, so we were familiar with the general layout of the terrain. The ground troops had been pushing north slowly on the highway for several weeks so there should be some signs of the approximate front line visible from the air. Major Suiter led the group, twenty-four planes in all, eastward across the valley and then over the low hills toward Calamba. Whether or not there was a ground controller Suiter could contact is not known, but he was obviously unsure of his identification of the target. He led us around in a wide circle for another look at a small village in a valley but, from the quick looks that I could make while maintaining position on Wylie's wing, the valley seemed too narrow and unlike the description at the mission briefing.

Others in the air that morning also had doubts about our position. As we circled once again at about five hundred feet over the hills several calls came over the radio. "Wrong target, Major!" Then, "Next valley, dammit!" One of the voices sounded like Colonel Wells's, but Major Suiter was not deterred. He had picked out a village that looked to him to be the target and that was where he was leading us. While it seemed to be the wrong place to several of us, there was also the possibility that the major, who could see the big picture better than we who were following, was making a different approach for some reason. Our flight dutifully circled around again, taking our cue from the flight in front of us.

The bomb-bay doors on the planes ahead opened and we started down into the valley toward the small village for our strafing and bombing run. There was a concentration of troops there all right, but they were GIs! Straight ahead, several Sherman tanks were sitting in a clearing, their distinctive silhouettes with the big white stars painted on them plainly visible. The planes in the flight ahead of us started strafing and the parademos began tumbling from their bomb bays. Seeing the mistake, I tried to call Wylie. I was not flying 958 that day and as sometimes happened, the throw-over switch on the command radio's control box was set on "Receive" rather than safety wired in the "Remote" position. My call to Wylie to pull up did not go out, but I managed to get his attention and stop the strafing by pulling ahead and wiggling my wings.

The formation pulled up and reformed as Colonel Wells called to Suiter to follow him. Wells led the group over the next range of steep green hills to hit the proper target. I regretted failing to warn Wylie that things did not look right. Fortunately, although there had been some strafing and a few bombs had been dropped by several of the flights, we later found out that there were no friendly casualties. The tankers had seen us coming and were able to button up before the strafing started. Moreover, the bombs had failed to detonate because they had been dropped too low for the fuses to arm. The tankers and infantry were understandably upset and let the top brass and the 312th Group know about it.

Major Suiter did not fly with us again. He was gone from the 312th in a day or so. It was a sad ending for Suiter, but most of us had judged early on that he was unsuited by age and experience to serve as CO of the 389th Squadron. With Colonel Wells observing the entire incident there could be no second chance for Suiter—nor did any of us flying that day think there should have been. Jim Wylie, who by that time had accumulated twenty-one missions, replaced Suiter as CO of the 389th on March 4. Wylie, Owen's Flying Bellhop, proved to be a fortunate choice. He had ability, an easy-going manner, and common sense, characteristics that earned him our respect.

In late February we experienced our first enemy air raids at Mangaldan. There had been alerts at both Leyte and Mindoro, signaled by three quick shots from an antiaircraft gun, but they had amounted to only a half-hour or so of blackout. No bombs were ever dropped. Occasionally

Mangaldan airstrip was a wide mat on rice paddies from which the surrounding dikes were removed. My aircraft was an A-20G-45, serial number 43–21958. A-20s went by the radio code name "Sugar"—hence Sugar 958. Here it is shown parked on the 389th's flight line, just off the runway. All was fine until the spring rains came, and then the water table rose, forcing the group to hurriedly move to Floridablanca.

we heard the far-off sound of a plane, but it usually turned out to be one of ours coming in with his Identification Friend or Foe (IFF) transmitter turned off. The ground echelon had experienced several air raids when it first landed on the beach on Leyte in November, but the serious raids had ceased by the time we arrived with the planes in early January.

Altogether, four or five raids were directed mainly at shipping in the Lingayen Gulf anchorage and the nearby Lingayen airstrip. However, on at least three occasions Mangaldan Field was the target, although when the raids first began they seemed to be a show—that is, when the enemy planes were some distance away over Lingayen.

We were professionally interested in how the P-61 night fighters would handle the enemy. The twin-engine P-61 was relatively new. It had twin booms like a P-38, but it was bigger, with a pilot and a radar operator. It was interesting to listen to the radio chatter between the ground controller and the night fighters as we tried to pick out the planes in the searchlight beams or against the somewhat lighter sky.

One night we were sitting outside the tent with a radio set up on a table, listening as a ground controller talked to a P-61 pilot. We had been unable to pick out either the enemy bomber—with its distinctive, unsynchronized engines—or the P-61 flying overhead and by now had become a little cynical about the ability of the night fighters. Some of the kibitzers made disparaging remarks as the controller attempted to guide the plane toward the target. Suddenly, there was a big burst of flame out over Lingayen Gulf and we cheered. Then the P-61 pilot was heard to call, "I'm pulling out! An engine just caught fire." We cheered again. The P-61 might have been a good airplane, but our skepticism, based entirely on its ungainly looks, was now confirmed.

The first raid that directly touched us in the 312th Bomb Group camp occurred one night when a single bomber neatly planted six or seven bombs on the west end of the runway and the overrun beyond. The bombs did not explode for some reason and the next morning we took off over them. Each had been carefully marked and sandbagged until it could be removed. When we returned from a mission in the afternoon a P-51 from the 3d Air Commando Group was sitting out among the un-exploded bombs. It had experienced engine trouble on takeoff and the pilot, unable to get off the ground, chopped the throttle and wound up in the overrun area. Fortunately, none of the bombs detonated. The Japanese planes were thought to come from the island of Formosa more than four hundred miles north of us, but there were also some operable enemy aircraft operating from fields in northern Luzon at the time.

The night of March 1 brought the raid that made the big impression upon me. Rutledge had moved into the tent with us temporarily and he, Gerould, Edmunds, and I were on our cots when the antiaircraft battery at the airstrip sounded the alarm. There was no question that this was the real thing, for the distinctive moaning sound of twin-engine Japan-ese bombers was loud and coming our way. The moon was still up, showing the lines of tents and the outline of the distant hills to the west as searchlights probed for the elusive planes with their unsynchronized engines. We went outside dressed only in our underwear and took up seats on top of the dike by our tent to watch the show.

To the northwest, in the vicinity of the Lingayen airstrip, we could see the flashes of bursting shells and streams of tracers from the 40-mm and .50-caliber guns marking the planes' approach. Occasionally a search-light would catch the distinctive twin-boom P-61 night fighter in its beam and quickly shifted away. It invariably generated comments about how ineffective the night fighters seemed to be. There was a lull in the antiaircraft firing and only the uneven throb of the Japanese engines above indicated the location of the raiders.

As we sat on the dike, straining to see the planes against the clear night sky to the west, we caught a sound that was different—a dull, flat, whistle-like sound building steadily in pitch. Without saying so, we knew that the *"Wa—,wa–, wa-, wa, wa, wa!"* came from falling bombs. The four of us immediately dove for the safety of the tent. Rutledge and I wound up on top of each other under Dulac's canvas cot as the bombs began to hit several hundred feet away. A shower of mud clods rattled on the tent's roof. We burst out laughing at the picture of us diving under the flimsy cot for protection and laughed even louder as Gerould and Edmunds came out from under their respective cots. All of the bombs missed the 389th Squadron's camp area but several water buffalo grazing in an adjacent field were killed. I had never heard the sound of falling bombs before, but I needed no explanation of that wavering whistle.

The distinctive moaning of the raiders' engines died away as they headed for home, unscathed by the flak or the P-61s. The searchlights stopped sweeping across the sky. Small groups of men sat around discussing the raid and a few walked over to where the bombs had hit. The night was quiet again. Although the lights had not come back on, the raid seemed to be over.

Then we heard the sound of another plane in the distance, this time coming fast and low from the direction of Lingayen town to the west. In the moonlight off across the airstrip, just above the tree line along the main road, a single-engine fighter could be seen approaching, bright red flashes winking from the 20-mm guns in each wing. The roadway was probably very visible to the pilot under the moon's light. The fighter, the sound of its guns audible above the purr of its engine, flew directly over the marines' camp and disappeared into the shadow of the hills to the northeast. The Japanese pilot's performance—coming in undetected and strafing down low at night—had to be admired from a flyer's professional viewpoint. The marines were not as fortunate as we had been: they reportedly suffered thirty-five casualties from that single pass by the lone fighter.

We were scheduled to fly the first A-20 mission to Formosa the following morning, March 2, and after the air raid there was every reason to believe that the Japanese air forces were still up there and active. The 312th Bomb Group was to attack the Kagi airdrome, which was located on a railroad line about one-third of the way up the island from the southern tip. Although by this time I had become a little blasé about whatever target we were assigned, the prospect of going to Formosa was a little forbidding. It was a big league mission, no question about it. Intelligence reports emphasized that the enemy still had a number of operational airstrips and reserves of planes on Formosa and stressed that the Japanese were continuing to build up their strength on the island. There was also the long overwater flight north and then back again to think about.

Formosa had been under Japanese domination since 1895, so we could expect the natives to be unfriendly should we be unlucky enough to go down. The Formosan troops in the Japanese army and marines were a select group: big guys who had been well trained. "Mean sonsof-bitches," or so said the always-accurate latrine gossip. To escape capture, downed crews would have to head for the mountains on the east side of the island. The primitive people living there supposedly were still resisting the civilizing administration of the Japanese, but nobody could be really sure. For all we knew, the primitives might be cannibals. Still, it was the only hope. The more we heard at the morning briefing, the tougher the Formosa mission sounded.

There was a lot of water between the northern tip of Luzon and Formosa, about 250 miles of it, but a submarine would be waiting off the southern tip of the island in case we had to ditch. There was an air-sea rescue unit with PBYs stationed at Mangaldan, but the Formosa area was still considered too hot for a pickup by a Catalina, given the assumed Japanese air strength. I remember wondering how to tell a U.S. submarine from a Japanese one. They looked pretty much alike to me and trying to find *any* submarine when you might need one did not sound very reassuring.

The mission called for twelve planes, three from each of the four squadrons. A captain from the 386th was the mission leader and I was assigned to fly right wing on Cal Slade (at least I think it was Cal). The 38th and 345th Bomb Groups' B-25s were also going to Formosa that morning. We would fly north with them before separating to hit different airdromes. These were more than the usual unpaved surface or grass airstrips we were accustomed to hitting and there should be lots of planes around.

The weather was fine as we formed up over Lingayen Gulf and joined the B-25s, which were coming up from the south right on schedule. We swung onto a north heading at about a thousand feet and followed the 345th Group just off the west coast of Luzon. The small twinges of anxiety I had felt earlier about going to Formosa disappeared as soon as we were on our way. However, the weather soon became overcast and the ceiling began lowering as we passed the north tip of Luzon. We encountered low scud and scattered rain as we approached Formosa and, as promised, saw a submarine on the surface moving slowly toward the northwest. Looking down at the sub, I again wondered how to tell if it was ours: they certainly were not flying the Stars and Stripes.

The formation turned northwest, staying well off of Formosa's coast and continued along under a darkening ceiling. Kagi airdrome, our target, was about a hundred miles in a direct line from the southern tip of the island, but we flew somewhat farther, staying offshore until the Pescadores Islands showed up in the rain and haze to our left. We had dropped down to just above the water to stay below the enemy's radar before turning onto the northwest heading, but as the weather continued to deteriorate we began to wonder if we would be able to get far enough north so as to be opposite our target before turning east. The 345th was to hit Toyohara airdrome, some seventy-five miles farther north, and its B-25s continued on over the sea when our leader made his right turn toward the coast. The 38th Bomb Group had made its turn toward the island somewhat earlier.

The plan was to cross Kagi airdrome in three-ship flights from north to south and then head for home before the alarm was raised. We headed for the island and its unknown quantities just above the wave tops, but almost as soon as we crossed the coast it became evident that our leader was not in the same class of navigators as Colonel Strauss. The landmarks did not look right according to the briefing information. Then, instead of turning south as expected, the formation made a sweeping turn to the north.

We were all now on auto rich, engines turning at twenty-one hundred rpm, gun switches on, and ready to open the bomb-bay doors and go to work as we followed the lead squadron at minimum altitude. We changed direction several times and I was cursing every turn that failed to bring us onto the target. Admittedly, a wingman flying in formation at low altitude with rain falling is not in the best position to locate landmarks, but it surely appeared that our leader was lost.

By taking quick glances I could see that the Formosan villages all had tile-roofed brick buildings and generally looked much better developed than was typical of the Philippines. There were numerous power lines crossing the fields, straight paved roads, and a modern-looking railroad, but we saw no sign of the Kagi airfield. With each of the turns the formation had spread further out. However, we were still down on the deck, ready to start strafing, as our leader continued to look for landmarks. I wondered how long it would take the enemy to wake up to our presence and launch some fighters.

After roaring around over the countryside for what seemed to be half an hour, or at least much too long, we finally struck out on a south heading. The bomb-bay doors on the planes up ahead snapped open and they began strafing and dropping parafrags. Then an airfield of considerable size suddenly materialized in front of our flight. However, it most definitely was not our target. This airfield was still in the early stages of construction. Rollers, bulldozers, and other pieces of heavy machinery were standing around on the partially graded airstrip. The raw mud was collecting puddles in the falling rain and there were no targets in sight. Our flight did not bother dropping its bombs but continued following the group south along the rail line, hoping that we were being taken to the real target.

A voice suddenly broke radio silence with the order to "Attack targets of opportunity!" Those of us who had not bombed and strafed the uncompleted airfield were free to find something worthwhile to shoot at. Kagi would escape our wrath until a later date. Several planes ahead of us were able to get over a cement plant, a couple of other planes made a pass at a large power plant, while still others dropped their bombs along the railroad. None of those targets were going to be much damaged by our little twenty-three-pound parafrag bombs.

To my disgust, several of the planes to our right were flying over the beach, strafing and dumping parafrags into the shallow water among fishermen working their nets. We had been warned against attacking towns on the assumption that not all citizens of Formosa were pro-Japanese and these helpless fishermen were hardly the enemy. We never brought parafrags back once the automatic racks had been armed so, as the planes ahead began to climb and head home, I tripped our load out over an empty field.

As we left the coast of Formosa, the formation tightened up and we gained a little altitude for the long flight home. Again we passed the submarine on the surface. It did not appear to have had any business that day, but we later learned that two B-25s from the 345th had ditched. Not a single Japanese plane had been sighted. The only flak had been some light machine-gun fire from isolated points that the formation wandered over in the vain search for the Kagi airdrome. The unfinished airstrip had been Mato or Mito, about thirty-five miles south of our intended target. *The Army Air Forces in World War II* identifies the field as Shirakawa, but we called it Mato at the time.

The formation settled in at about two thousand feet for the flight home and (to save fuel) we reset the fuel mixtures to "auto lean"; props to 1,650 rpm; adjusted the cowl flaps to hold close to the optimum 205 degrees Celsius cylinder-head temperature; and set the fuel cocks to finish draining the outboard wing tanks. It was now time to eat our fried-egg sandwiches and drink coffee from the thermos, the usual lunch the mess hall gave us for a long mission. We had spent far too much time in the futile search over Formosa and it was still a long way home, but my fuel supply seemed to be adequate. The weather was clearing as we flew south and it was good to be safely away from Formosa and able to enjoy the scenery.

As we approached the coast of Luzon under now almost clear skies, a pilot called his flight leader to say that he was low on fuel and one engine was running rough. One or two other planes also called to report low fuel and shortly after we reached the coast two planes could be seen losing altitude off to our right. A 387th Squadron plane piloted by 2d Lt. Bruce Nostrand was the one with engine trouble. He was preparing to ditch near the shore off of Cape Bojeador.

The sea was calm and I could clearly see Nostrand's A-20 with another plane flying alongside settle into the water in a cloud of spray. He had jettisoned the cockpit hatch earlier and the ditching appeared to be about as perfect as it could have been under almost ideal conditions. The accompanying A-20 called for "Dumbo," the slang name for a rescue Catalina or PBY, and there was other chatter on the radio concerning the incident and its location. It came as a surprise when we learned that neither the pilot nor the gunner, S.Sgt. Lyle Thompson, was recovered although the gunner was seen in the water after the ditching. Motor torpedo (PT) boats responded to the distress call but found only scattered wreckage.

Did Nostrand forget to lock his shoulder harness and hit his head? Did he get hit in the face by the armor glass panel? Had he gotten entangled somehow and thus unable to get out of the cockpit? Did sharks attack them? We would never know.

By the time we landed back at Mangaldan, I had logged six hours and thirty-five minutes and there was still a decent reserve of fuel left in the tanks of dependable Sugar 958. At the debriefing following the mission some expressed the opinion that the long flight to Formosa and the results were worthwhile, but my report was that it had not been. We had wandered over half of the island and had not found our target or any other targets of importance. The pros and cons of this mission (and the leadership) were a source of discussion in the squadrons for weeks. While we had been gone having a look at Formosa, other 312th Group planes had participated in a mission to the village of Echague and its airstrip in northeastern Luzon. That mission seemed to have gone better than our futile effort.

When the film from my ship's oblique camera was developed it revealed a beautiful sequence of parachutes gently dropping parafrags into a rice paddy—not a single water buffalo, building, or even a railroad line in sight. Sergeant Boyd did not know the load was being dumped, so he naturally turned on the camera when the parachutes began to blossom behind us. The photos were posted in the squadron intelligence office, each of the twenty-two frames boldly bearing the number "958." A large caption below the series of the photos pointed out that this was a horrible example of a waste of bombs. The display was just a little embarrassing.

Major Graber, then the group operations officer, was looking at the string of photos when I came into the office a day or two later and asked, "Who did that?"

Somewhat uncomfortably I replied, "Those were mine, Major. We didn't find the target and the instructions were to try and hit the Japs, not the Formosans. I dumped them in the field rather than in a town."

Graber shook his head in disbelief but Len Dulac spoke up, "That's right, Major, those were the instructions." No more was ever said about my patently wasted parafrags.

Perhaps those who were flying at the front of the formation on the mission to Formosa that day found worthwhile targets of opportunity, but those of us bringing up the rear certainly did not. It was mission number fifty-three for me.

Chapter 11

Incidents at Mangaldan

WHEN THE 312TH BOMB GROUP first flew into Mangaldan from Mindoro we were pointedly informed that the marines were running the airfield and we were to defer to them. The Army Air Forces units were not exactly guests, but the marines of MAG -24 were there first, ran the tower, and would set the policies for air operations. Rightly or wrongly, most of us viewed the navy (which trained marine pilots) as bound by very stuffy navy tradition. They even spoke differently, using deck instead of floor, bulkhead when they meant a wall, head for the latrine, flat-hatting for buzzing, and so forth.

It figured that MAG-24 took over all of the available houses and choice camp areas—as any first arrival might have done—but the wisdom of locating on the main highway may have been questioned after the Japanese night flyer strafed them. They probably had nothing to do with the Mangaldan control tower carrying the code name of "Honey" but it seemed in keeping with an outfit that included ice cream machines as standard galley (mess hall) equipment. There was little visiting back and forth between the marines and GIs that I recall. They stayed on their side of the field and the rest of us tenants stayed on ours. They could at least have invited us over for ice cream occasionally, but they never did.

The landing and takeoff area at Mangaldan was a mat of compacted earth about three hundred feet wide and five thousand feet long with an oil-coated runway down the center and oiled taxiways along each side. There were no serious obstructions at either end, but Honey Tower permitted only single-ship takeoffs on the oiled runway even though the areas on both sides of it remained just as dry and solid. The SBD dive-bombers the marines flew were not much bigger than an AT-6 trainer and it seemed a little timid to us that they always took off one at a time rather than in three-ship formations, which would have sped things up. We always had followed single-ship takeoff procedures. However, that was the routine on the narrow runways we were accustomed to using.

The wide, dry surface at Mangaldan seemed made for formation takeoffs, though, and it was not long before the marine practice was being challenged. The 3d Air Commando Group was on the field when we arrived and its P-51s took off in two-ship elements with the apparent concurrence of Honey Tower. This seemed to work all right, so a few days later, when we saw that the SBDs were suddenly making daring three-ship takeoffs, the 312th followed suit. Within a week the P-51s were going off in two-element, four-ship-flights and Mangaldan was becoming an efficient flying operation. There now appeared to be an open competition between the P-51s and the pilots of MAG-24; we watched and waited.

The SBDs were slow compared to our A-20s, but they always flew an excellent formation, including their formation takeoffs with the wingmen tucked in tight as soon as their wheels left the ground. The A-20s looked good on takeoff if, after becoming airborne, you stayed level and sucked the wheels up quickly as the flight picked up speed. Before we hit the end of the field our airspeed would be about 160 and we would execute a dazzling climb in formation for the watching SBD jockeys. The gear retraction could be made automatic by placing the handle in the "UP" position before takeoff so the gear came up whenever the weight came off of the safety switches. You were in trouble, however, if the plane bounced before it reached flying speed and caused an unintended retraction that dropped the plane onto the runway. Austin Ayotte and a few others adopted this automatic retraction practice but it was not for me. Three A-20s in formation ten feet off the ground at full throttle with their gear coming up at almost the same time was impressive enough.

Not to be outdone, the SBDs waddled out one afternoon and lined up two flights, six ships abreast, on the end of the runway. They roared off together in tight formation and it was admittedly an impressive sight. However, the contest, if that is what it was, ended the following morning when a six-ship SBD takeoff was again undertaken with a bit of fog and dust hanging over the rice paddies. The pilot of the plane on the right end of the line lost his heading, veered off to the right, and cut through our line of parked A-20s. The left wing of Owen's 957 was clipped off at the engine nacelle before the remains of the SBD slid to a

The remains of Maury Owen's Sugar 957 after being struck by a Marine Air Group 24 SBD Dauntless dive-bomber that went astray on takeoff.

stop beyond. Nobody was seriously injured, but Owen's plane was "Class 26," not reparable, and junked. Owen was eloquent and profane in attributing the inability of those "fucking gyrenes" to fly properly to their questionable ancestry and moral turpitude. The incident brought an end to six-ship takeoffs.

Going out on missions day after day affected individuals in different ways. Those of us who managed to fly twenty or more missions without something untoward happening seemed to arrive at our own acceptance of the odds and thought little of the chances of big trouble when we set out again. By the time we were at Mangaldan I had come to anticipate seeing new territory and worthwhile targets with often rewarding pillars of black smoke left in our wake. The fact that the enemy was often visibly throwing back missiles similar to the deadly ones we were delivering was just part of the game and accepted as such. The guns were surely aiming at another plane, right? One always had the conviction that bad luck would find someone else. Besides, rehashing the "what ifs" afterward was pointless.

Unfortunately, not everyone could reach that accommodation between doing what had to be done and the instinct for self-preservation.

There was always the option for flying crews, pilot or gunner, to request being taken off of flying status should the apprehensions become overwhelming. However, for pilots, voluntary grounding was the end of the line, a step not to be taken lightly. One of the 389th Squadron's young replacement pilots grounded himself at Tanauan and although we all tried to understand his feelings, we really could not—he had only flown a mission or two before submitting his request. We tried to talk him out of his drastic decision but without success. We then went on with our lives after observing, "That poor bastard will be here until the goddam war is over." He wound up being given responsibility for the men and equipment left at Tanauan while we flew on to Mindoro and Mangaldan and saw a thousand sights.

Sometimes a specific experience rather than cumulative incidents resulted in a loss of confidence. A dramatic example occurred one afternoon on a ground-attack mission to assist Filipino guerrillas pushing a Japanese force back from the port of San Fernando on the coast north of us. My right wingman that day was Lieutenant Stone, one of the experienced instructors from Florence who had joined us in the middle of February. He demonstrated that he could fly a tight formation, although an air show performance was neither required nor desirable when trying to keep a bead on the target and an eye on the flight leader during a low-level pass.

We were the second flight on this mission and our strafing passes were made from the sea toward the hills behind the coastal plain where the enemy had dug in, up over their positions, and then a wide turn to the right for another run if so directed by the ground controller. On the first pass, the leader in the flight ahead climbed out at 150 miles per hour—much too slow for my liking when flying in a loaded A-20 close to rising ground. On the second pass I dropped farther behind the lead flight in order to stay low and then climb out at 160 or even a bit faster and catch the leader beyond a narrow gap in the ridge.

As our three-ship flight finished its run and started into the gap as planned, something caused me to look back on the right-hand side to check on my wingman. He was nowhere to be seen. I looked down below and found him there, being squeezed toward me by the rising ground and the narrowing gap. Looking back at me through the top of his A-20's canopy was the face of the frantic pilot. He had held his plane in tight formation across the target but then somehow got trapped below rather than being above, even well above, the lead plane. With full throttle applied, I climbed as steeply as possible to open up some space for my trapped wingman to slide off to the side and escape, which he was able to do. After this unexpected excitement we continued making another pass or two without incident.

It had been a close call, but there seemed to be no need for me to say anything to him about it after we landed. The mistake of flying under rather than above the leader had been graphically demonstrated and, as an experienced pilot, Stone would recognize how it had happened. It was therefore a surprise when he followed me into my tent and began belaboring me for my stupidity as a flight leader. His tirade included some irrational threats and while his agitation was understandable, the mistake had been his—he had in fact been very lucky. I made the point that it was the wingman's place to fly *on* the leader rather than *under* him: "What the hell were you doing down there?"

Our heated conversation continued and could be heard several tents away, the tenor of Stone's intemperate remarks clearly understood. Shortly afterward, Stone stopped flying and became the squadron's personal equipment officer. Not until years later did I learn from others that, at times, facing a mission made Stone physically ill. The stress was there for all of us, of course; we each had to handle it in our own way.

On March 6 I again accompanied Cal Slade on another B-25 courier flight to Tanauan. These flights were an interesting break. We were able to study the picturesque islands along the way, although even at this late date we kept an eye out for any suspicious specks in the distant skies. When we made a stop on Mindoro to drop off a crew chief and some parts to repair an A-20, I surprised myself by making a clean approach and smooth landing on Elmore Field from the right seat of a B-25. After all, I had flown them very little in the past year. "Do you always land 'em like that?" Cal joked. "Rarely!" I replied. It was just another enjoyable day in the Philippines.

A big review and award ceremony was to be held on March 10 for the departing Colonel Strauss. Brigadier General Jarred Crabb, the V Bomber Command CO, would be on hand to pass out medals and honor Colonel Strauss for his long leadership of the 312th, all to be capped by a group fly-by. The more senior pilots in the squadron were slated to receive Air Medals, so responsibility for the 389th's part in the show came down to me.

The fly-by was first proposed to be a low pass of the four squadrons together, but the problem of stacking thirty-six planes without extensive practice caused a quick rethinking of the plan. It was decided that we would go over in our individual squadrons led by the 386th and with the 389th bringing up the rear—in air well disturbed by the twenty-seven planes ahead. At low level, prop wash was not a pleasant experience, but

we were all urged to put on a good show for our well-respected departing leader. Moreover, the critical eye of the new group commander,
Lieutenant Colonel Wells, could not be overlooked.

When we got out of the trucks at the flight line on the morning of the
review, Owen surprised me by grabbing my arm and warning, "Now
look, Rut, we don't have anything to prove today, so keep us out of the
goddam prop wash."

The group put on a textbook demonstration of takeoffs by flights and
a smooth join-up over the field while the 312th's ground echelon stood
in formation watching. Whoever was leading in the 386th Squadron did
a good job, first taking the group over the assembled troops at about
eight hundred feet and then making a graceful clockwise turn so we
could space each squadron for the low-level pass. The sight of our
thirty-six planes in tight formation stepped down from eight hundred
feet should have been impressive enough—the 389th was certainly low
enough—but if they wanted *low*-level passes by squadron, then they
would get them.

Watching the 388th up ahead as we spaced ourselves onto the heading to go over the field again by squadrons, it was obvious from the way
the A-20s were dancing around that there was plenty of turbulence. Flying formation in that disturbed air would be no fun for those of us in
the lowest flight, so I eased farther to the left to avoid following in the
388th's flight path. We easily held a tight and low formation in the un-
disturbed air—still technically over Mangaldan Field, albeit a bit distant from the gathered troops watching the show. Nevertheless, I figured it was good enough for the nonserious purposes of the review.

Ed Valentine and Babe Young, who had been on the ground receiving
heroes' decorations, afterward greeted me with broad smiles and said,
"Rutter, the 389th was so far over toward the Lingayen Gulf we could
hardly see you!" My reply was, "Yes, but there wasn't any prop wash over
there." Maury Owen, who was coming along as we walked toward the
trucks to go back to the squadron area, overheard the comments made
by Val and Babe, and said, "Thanks for the nice flight, Little Joe." Several others commented in a similar vein; it was a good day for me *and* for
the 389th, I think.

The only mission I was forced to abort occurred on March 17. We were
to bomb Baguio, the summer capital of the Philippines, located up in the
mountains beyond the Belete Pass. Owen was flying my right wing and
we had almost completed one turn around the field after takeoff when
he called, "Rut, you're throwing oil on the right side." One glance at the

plume of black smoke streaming back from the engine showed that he was right. Another glance, this one at the instrument panel, showed that the rpm on that engine was dropping. After making the appropriate motions to the left wingman and a radio call to Owen to take over, I pulled up and moved to the right as he slid smoothly underneath into the lead and continued the turn around the field.

The sick engine continued to put out some power—it was showing about twenty inches of manifold pressure rather than the normal twenty-eight to thirty inches—and there was no sign of fire or dropping oil pressure. An engine should never be shut down as long as it is doing some good. With full fuel tanks and a load of bombs, any power was preferable to none and we were not going very far. I alerted the gunner that we were going back to land because of the sick engine and assured him that everything was under control.

After calling Honey Tower and advising the operator that we had an emergency and were coming in against the traffic, it was time to turn onto the base leg, drop the gear at the turn onto the final approach, and see how we were lined up. No planes were coming at us on takeoff, but for some reason, the tower operator asked if I could go around again. Having witnessed several unsuccessful attempts to go around on a single engine, I declined. The flights still waiting to take off were ordered to hold their positions and Honey Tower cleared us to land. The landing without flaps was routine and the smoking engine continued to run until I pulled off the runway opposite our parking place.

Ernie Koch had watched our takeoff and was on hand to wave us back in, although he had no idea what the reason was for the very short trip. However, one look at the oil dripping from the trailing edge of the right wing when the engines were shut down was enough evidence for Ernie to know that 958 was in need of serious attention.

Almost as soon as we parked, Ed Valentine, the squadron operations officer, drove up and inquired—in what I took to be a somewhat cutting tone—why I had aborted the flight. Never having turned back before, I took umbrage at his manner and, although we were friends, we wound up having a sarcastic exchange. Just then, Leo Brashier, the engineering officer, came up. He quickly stopped the discussion when he noted the dripping oil and pronounced that the problem was a blown cylinder, maybe two.

Aborting missions for frivolous reasons was not unknown and a few pilots had a deserved reputation for finding mechanical excuses for turning back. When a mission was thought to be particularly tough, the faint of heart would report, "Rough engine," "Low hydraulic pressure,"

"Generator out," or some other problem. However, a thorough check on the ground always proved unable to confirm these malfunctions. Such characters quickly became known to the crew chiefs, who would never have reported their plane "available" in the first place if there had been any indication of mechanical trouble.

For most pilots, completing missions as they were assigned was a matter of integrity, a point of honor to support the others who were also flying the mission. We had volunteered to fly, accepted the training, and valued our officer's commission. Most recognized that we had a duty in return. Those who were known for frequently aborting were very much in the minority, but there seemed to be one or more in every squadron who earned such a reputation. We gave them little respect.

Several crew chiefs pitched in to help Ernie remove the cowling and pull the bad cylinders. It took more than four hours to disconnect the plumbing and wiring, pull the two cylinders and their pistons, and replace them with a new matched set. A broken piston ring or blown valves would cause the cylinder to pump oil, as had occurred in this case, but by the next morning the plane was ready to go on a mission to Osboy.

The crew chiefs and other personnel who kept our planes going deserve more credit than they are given in most accounts of wartime flying. Ernie Koch and his compatriots in the 389th Squadron were as concerned that our planes performed flawlessly as were the pilot and gunner. He was apologetic if something gave us trouble during a mission. Most of the things a pilot wrote up on the Form 1A were usually caused by the bits and pieces picked up over a target rather than by any maintenance oversight. Only after everything had been done to assure that 958 was ready to go would Ernie relax. He did, however, have a basically laid-back personality.

One afternoon, Sergeant Boyd and I arrived on the flight line to go on a mission and found Ernie asleep on a cot in the shade of a wing. Four bottles of beer were hanging on wires under the fuel tank drips, being cooled by the evaporation of the high-octane gas trickling gently over them. "Hey, Sergeant Koch, we have to go flying!" As he awoke, surprised by our presence, Ernie covered his embarrassment by grumbling back, "Jesus Christ, Lieutenant. My beer isn't even cold yet." I have been forever grateful to Ernie Koch for his dedication. He was the one who kept those fans running on a smooth-flying A-20. Had it not been for the conscientious crew chiefs, many more of us might not have seen the States again. Ernie and I remained close friends for fifty years, until his death in 1995.

By mid-March my attitude toward missions and life in general seems to have become somewhat detached. I had the feeling I had seen or done

Crew chiefs of the 389th Squadron, 312th Bomb Group. *Back row, from left:* Gallo, Bowman, Buddy Powell (maintenance chief), Jarrett, Hartman, Wolf; *Front row, from left:* Butler, Robert Keller, Ernest Koch, William Freitag. They were a dedicated group.

everything at least once before and that there could be few surprises left. I still enjoyed flying, but the challenge now was to do things smoothly, as a competent leader, rather than with some attention-getting flourish.

Whether we realized it or not, or showed it outwardly or not, the uncertainties in our life caused some strain as we flew day after day: Rutledge was quieter; Owen could be more sarcastic; Valentine took longer naps. Taking a nap ("catching some sack time," as we called it) was a daily ritual for many pilots, but it was never my habit—although maybe it should have been. There were times when I recall feeling so tired on a hot, humid afternoon that throwing the parachute up onto the wing was barely possible and the climb up the side of the A-20 to get to the cockpit took unusual effort. However, the tired feeling always disappeared once I was in the pilot's seat and busy with the familiar preflight routine.

At lunch one day, several of the young and eager new replacements engaged in a conversation about their observations of the habits of different formation leaders. They first critiqued how easy or difficult they found joining up on a flight leader and then boasted about how a hot pilot could cut inside the more leisurely leaders "Right on the deck and

Crew chiefs pitched in where needed to assist with major repairs. Here, there is a major problem with the right engine of a 389th Squadron plane. *From left:* Jansky (389th line chief), Lydic, Gibson, William Freitag.

catch him in the first turn." We old-timers had perhaps had similar thoughts six months back, but we had since learned a thing or two. Operations Officer Valentine listened to all of this and caustically commented, "It would be nice if you flew decent formation once you get there."

A few days later, two of these young fellows were flying with me in the lead flight and their earlier remarks came to mind as we approached the field in right echelon for landing. Are they really as hot as they think? I wondered. Here's a tight pattern for them! At the precise midpoint of the airstrip I peeled off abruptly to the left as steeply as I dared and held the turn constant in a descending spiral. The gear dropped as I peeled off, half-flaps as the gear snapped into the locked position, throttles to twenty inches of manifold pressure, and the props to low pitch—all the while keeping the speed well above a possible stall until rolling out on final approach with the runway just ahead. Dropping full flaps and simultaneously flaring out, the plane touched down (if a bit fast) just beyond the end of the packed-earth mat.

I felt a bit smug. "You wanted tight?" I said to myself. "That's tight!"

However, as we rolled merrily along on the dirt with the nose still high to kill off speed I realized that I had gone a little overboard with my demonstration. Instead of being near the oiled landing strip, I was well off to the left side, whizzing closely by the tall tails of the 312th's parked planes. Fortunately, the mechanics' solid toolboxes were mostly close to the planes and only a few engine tarps lay on the ground ahead, to be scattered as we rolled over them at about sixty miles per hour. Several perplexed crew chiefs watched my performance and probably thought one of the new pilots had gone astray again. The 389th's area was coming up and, seeing no need to roll by to the end of the mat and come back, I tapped the left brake pedal and turned 958 neatly into its parking space, albeit just a bit fast.

Sergeant Koch came out from the shade of his tent a bit faster than usual. He looked up at the cockpit disapprovingly and said, "Jesus Christ, Lieutenant, is something wrong?" I felt a little sheepish about landing off the runway so close to the parked planes, but passed off the tight descent and expeditious parking as just another landing. If my two wingmen recognized that the performance was for their benefit there would be no comment. I already recognized that I had made a mistake by rising to the bait. Fortunately, no harm had been done. We went back to our usual way of doing things on the next flight.

On March 19 the group was taken off operations for the first time in several months and given a free day. Many of us were interested in seeing how the infantrymen we tried to assist lived and fought on the ground. Charlie Schoner, one of the newer pilots, was game for a trip to "The Front." It was about thirty miles from Mangaldan to the Kennon Road, which went up into the mountains to Baguio from Rosario. Baguio, which was at an elevation of about thirty-five hundred to five thousand feet, had a more temperate climate than down on the central plain and had been the Philippines' summer capital before the war. At the time, Baguio was an enemy army headquarters and the Japanese resisted tenaciously for several more weeks before the city was finally captured at the end of April.

Dressed in our green flying suits, we strapped on our .45-caliber pistols, packed some K rations, and Schoner and I set out hitchhiking. We had no trouble catching a truck going east and we were dropped off beyond Rosario at a crossroads where the road toward the mountains headed north. We walked a couple of miles, passing through several burned out villages, but we encountered no traffic going our way and began to have doubts about our knowledge of the geography. The area was desolate and silent. Just as we were about to turn back, a truck came along and picked us up and after fording several streams we reached the first checkpoint on Kennon Road.

A sentry manning the checkpoint directed us to a nearby tent that served as the headquarters for an infantry company working its way up the road ahead. As we entered the tent, a clerk pointed to a bird colonel dressed in faded green fatigues and seated at a cluttered desk. He listened somewhat quizzically as we explained that we had been on several missions supporting the advance up Kennon Road and wanted a closer look at what was going on. He gave us permission to proceed, but he seemed astonished that someone who did not need to be there would want to visit such a place. As Schoner and I were about to leave the tent, the colonel commented dryly: "You two better take those bars off. The snipers will spot them every time."

We waited with the sentry until a jeep driven by a courier who had business up the road came along. The forward command post was about five miles on up the river's gorge and the driver said he could take us almost that far. The curving mountain road was lined with burned-out cars and trucks, piles of mines that had been dug out of the roadway, and stacks and stacks of abandoned Japanese supplies, including canned food and ammunition. We tried to take in both the wreckage and the rugged beauty of the narrow valley as the driver, obviously familiar with the road, took us upward.

The jeep stopped just before a sharp right-hand curve in the road and the driver announced that this was as far as he could go because the enemy continued to lob shells at every vehicle trying to drive beyond the bend. We would have to walk the short distance up the road to the command post. He left after warning us not to walk too close together as the enemy gunners could not resist such a target. After the courier disappeared on a narrow path leading up the steep hillside on the right side of the road, Schoner and I stood there sizing up the curve, debating whether to run or crawl.

Our debate ended when we heard a tremendous crack made by some kind of gun almost at our elbows. We both jumped for the ditch, sure that the enemy had spotted the jeep. Then we heard American voices just over the berm at the top of the downward slope on the opposite side of the road. We peered cautiously over the edge and saw a mortar crew making adjustments before dropping another shell into the tube. Not having heard a mortar fired at close range, it seemed to me to be a very loud noise indeed. The crew was firing onto the high hill on the opposite side of the ravine. It dawned on us that if they could see a target, it was likely that the enemy could see us. We quickly decided we had better move.

One at a time we walked around the curve in the road and a short distance beyond found a couple of dugouts in the bank above the roadside ditch. A dozen GIs were lounging inside. We could see an artillery spotter in a covered dugout farther down the hillside trying to fix the location of an enemy 75-mm gun across the valley.

After telling the GIs who we were and what we were doing in their territory, they still eyed us with some curiosity. It was hot, we were sticky with sweat, flies were everywhere, and we hardly felt like eating the rations we had brought along. The low-level bombing and strafing we had done in these hills in support of the drive toward Baguio prompted one of the fellows to volunteer that he wanted nothing to do with that flying business. The bodies of two Filipino guerrillas who had been working with the GIs lay covered in the ditch near the dugout. They had been killed that morning, but our hosts seemed to take the loss rather matter-of-factly. We broke out our K rations—the same fare as the GIs were eating—exchanged some small talk, and probably asked some dumb-sounding questions.

A battery of 105-mm guns was located in back of the ridge above us, perhaps where our jeep driver had headed. We were able to follow the shells in flight as they sailed directly overhead. The shells would burst on the opposite hillside and the forward observer would call for adjustments after each barrage. Finally, there was a puff of dust and several timbers flew into the air at the mouth of a cave hiding the Japanese gun. Until that moment, neither Schoner nor I had spotted the target. Now that the gun had presumably been knocked out, the GIs eyed the ruins of a bridge up ahead and speculated how they would get around it and onto the road beyond. The problem seemed to give them little concern, it was just part of the job. To us, however, it seemed much more risky than flying.

After our frontline visit, which lasted only a couple of hours, I wanted no part of infantry life—not even that of the colonel in the decrepit tent back down in the valley. The dirty war being fought on the ground made most of our gripes about conditions in the 312th seem very petty. Our life was safe and comfortable compared to that hot, dusty, fly-infested valley and Kennon Road, where the infantry faced the prospect of advancing around one sharp bend after another with the enemy contesting every move. After wishing the GIs good luck, we caught a ride back down the highway.

Schoner, who had done some trading with booze and combat photos he brought along for that purpose, was now carrying two Japanese rifles and wearing a wristwatch removed from a deceased enemy officer. After walking a half-mile or so toward Rosario and wading across a stream where the bridge had been blown, we were picked up by a courier in a weapons carrier. He was going all the way to Lingayen and, like a salesman traveling a daily route, had located some favored stopping places. He took us to his favorite mess hall for chow and then dropped us off at the 312th's area shortly after dark. Schoner's souvenirs inspired several others to make an expedition to the same area the following day, but one trip was enough for me.

The mission we flew up Luzon's west coast to San Fernando on March 20 proved to be the most frustrating of the war for me. It had tragic results—and for no good reason. We were sent to provide ground support for our infantry trying to clear the area south of the small port, which was just fifty miles north of Mangaldan. One of our newest pilots, flying my left wing, was the archetype of the "hot rock" then being portrayed in the movies and comic strips. He was a nice enough fellow, but not quite as hot as he thought. Another of the participants on this six-ship mission had joined us at Hollandia and had a goodly number of missions. He followed his own interpretation of instructions—or maybe he just did not bother to listen.

It was a bright afternoon and the trip to the target area was short. Half an hour after takeoff, I contacted the forward air controller who would direct us to our targets. The controller was located in a good-sized house with a thatched roof located beside an east–west road that provided a good landmark. The Japanese positions were in a bowl of hills a mile or more south of the road but visible to the controller, who asked that we make single-ship strafing and bombing passes over the locations he identified.

It looked like an ideal setup for making accurate attacks. After making each pass we would circle clockwise toward the coast and then go back for another run from north to south. The controller would give us corrections or mark a new target with a smoke shell after each run. I relayed the instructions over our air-to-air frequency to the rest of the ships, emphasizing that we were to bomb only south of the road.

We went into line-astern formation and made the first run on the smoke marking the approximate location of the dug-in enemy troops. After a couple of strafing passes on spots where ground fire had been observed, the controller asked that we each drop a 250-pound demolition bomb on the next pass. After we completed this bombing run I glanced over and saw our hot-rock wingman had his wheels down and the bomb-bay doors still closed. It was not an easy mistake to make. The distinctive landing-gear handle was mounted on the bulkhead behind the pilot and the bomb-bay door control was on the floor to the left of the seat. Everyone could hear my radio call: "Number Three, pull up your gear and open the bomb-bay doors!"—which should have deservedly embarrassed our hot rock.

The next two runs went smoothly, with the controller becoming more enthusiastic about our accuracy with each pass. Then came a radio call from our maverick pilot: "Yippee! I got the house!" Looking back, I could see that the bomb had exploded much too close to the road. Suddenly, I felt sick. We circled around outside the immediate area, waiting for the controller to respond to my calls. After a while there was a garbled transmission from someone on the ground saying that the house had indeed been hit and that no more assistance was needed.

We pulled off over the water and formed up for the return to Mangaldan. Although it was only fifty miles, it felt like a much longer flight to me. I had no way to relieve the frustration of a mission gone terribly and needlessly wrong. Reading the riot act to the offending, irresponsible pilot after we landed did nothing to alleviate my feelings of disgust.

Luckily, none of the people in the house were killed. However, it was reported to us the following day that the controller had lost an arm. The pilot who could not follow directions was quiet for a few days, but soon back in character. The hot shot who dropped his landing gear was killed with two others in a mid-air collision on May 19, when he came up under another plane while trying to join his formation. The gunner aboard his plane, Pat Reitmeyer, was the only survivor.

On March 21, the day after the mistakes at San Fernando, we were sent out to bomb troops and supplies at Pattao in the Dugo area. The mission lasted three hours and twenty-five minutes, but I cannot recall the once-familiar Dugo's exact location on the island of Luzon. March had been a busy month up to that point, with missions flown just about every other day—a total of nine thus far for me. Then there was a lull and I had six days off while the replacement pilots picked up the load. During the entire month, the 389th Squadron flew seventy-one missions totaling 337 sorties, compared to only 231 sorties in February. (One plane on one mission constitutes a sortie.)

John C. "Porky" Jones—the officer in charge of the motor pool, among other things—provided an excursion boat for the squadron to use while we were at Mangaldan. With the help of his truck mechanics, Porky was able to salvage a Higgins boat (LCVP) that had been disabled and abandoned after the Lingayen landings in January. The LCVP, which was made of plywood, had been patched up to be seaworthy without too much effort and then put into operating order. It was largely treated as Porky's personal yacht, but he occasionally invited groups to go fishing or on swimming outings in the bay off Binmaley. It was on one such excursion that I first saw the recently developed Sikorsky YR-4B helicopter in operation. The strange looking aircraft was equipped with large rubber pontoons and at the time was flying from a barge in the harbor. Although interesting, it did not impress us much at the time.

By way of entertainment, Father Snyder instituted occasional bingo nights after we had gotten settled at Mangaldan. Players paid thirteen pesos ($7.50) for a card and the top prize each evening was several hundred dollars cash or an item of approximately equal value, such as a diamond or other piece of jewelry. The good Father had somehow managed to contact church people in Manila who had access to valuable Filipino crafts and prewar works of art suitable for prizes. Sometimes I attended these bingo nights. It was good entertainment for an hour or so, and I once won a linen damask tablecloth with a dozen matching napkins.

On another bingo night, the featured prizes were three silk mandarin coats from prewar China, hand embroidered and trimmed with gold and silver thread. They were indeed works of art, hidden away during the Japanese occupation. A blue one, more elaborately decorated than the others, was deemed the top prize. The last game of the evening, which was for the big prize, was a "coverall." The numbers were called and, at just the minimum needed to cover the card, I yelled, "Bingo!" The anticipation and suspense had not lasted very long and I felt a little sheepish as I went up to collect the beautiful grand prize. Father Snyder did not seem very enthusiastic about the outcome, nor did some of the other regular players.

The following day, one of the chaplain's assistants stopped by our tent and inquired if I would consider contributing the mandarin coat back to be used as a prize again. The chaplain's assistant made the pitch that since I was not married it was the generous thing to do for, after all, many of the men would love the chance to win such a garment for their devoted wives pining away back home. I crassly declined; the coat really was beautiful and it would look good on either of the two young ladies I knew. The chaplain's emissary came back a day or so later, this time to offer to buy the coat for $125. It was a surprisingly large sum for 1945, but I was not tempted and the blue silk coat eventually made it back to the States.

Another incident that occurred while we were at Mangaldan also bears telling. It was a social commentary that amused most of those who witnessed it. With so many U.S. troops in the Lingayen area, it was not long until some Filipinos saw a business opportunity in organizing the rather informal prostitution trade. A couple of low resorts, sporting houses, or pleasure palaces—take your choice—with stables of nubile young ladies were established in the nearby village of Dagupan. The army, being realistic, took a tolerant attitude and had assumed de facto, if not actual, control over the inevitable situation. These service establishments attracted a rather considerable clientele. Once, while I was taking some photos in Dagupan, an MP warned me not to include the line of waiting clients in my composition of the street scene.

At breakfast one morning, John Edmunds, our legal-eagle and defender of the GI in trouble, looked up from his plate and asked in his quiet way, "Did you hear that the cathouse was robbed last night?" Only John seemed to have heard this news. Perhaps it was because one or more of the suspects had already retained him. "There's going to be a lineup at ten o'clock to identify the culprits," he added. "Maybe some of you flyboys will want to volunteer for the morning mission so as to be unavailable." Then John, with a sly smile, went back to his dehydrated eggs and diced potatoes.

Several masked soldiers had indeed held up the house of ill repute and made off with a sizable haul of the accumulated receipts. The indignant owner demanded justice. In the interest of local relations, the commanding officers of several of the units in the area launched an investigation and did, in fact, hold an in-ranks inspection. Several men from the 312th were among the suspects. Sure enough, a formation was held behind our tent area later that morning and the house madam and several of her soiled doves checked the lineup. It was a most unusual review of the troops, given the nature of the business, but no perpetrators were identified in the 312th's ranks. If the culprits were ever brought to justice, we never heard of it. Nevertheless, witnesses recalled the incident for years afterward.

The military experience proved to be an education in so many diverse subjects!

Chapter 12

WINDING DOWN

ON MARCH 27 WE HAD A MISSION to Mankayan to bomb and strafe troops. The target was a mining town located up in the mountains about thirty miles north of Baguio and, as I recall, we made single-ship passes because of the confined valley. The stepped terraces climbing the mountainsides in these narrow valleys in northern Luzon were a marvel of engineering. They created level fields permitting rice farming where no other suitable land existed. When flying, there was always something of interest for the curious tourist.

The Japanese still held most of the area north of Luzon's central valley and they were putting up a stubborn resistance. The strength of the forces holding the mountains and the valleys beyond was sizable, the terrain was excellent for defense, and there was still the threat that the Japanese could somehow break out into the lowlands toward the south and cause havoc. The enemy had also retreated into the mountain areas a hundred miles to the south of Mangaldan and east of Manila, from which they still controlled the city's main water supply. The conquest of Luzon was still months away. In fact, sizable Japanese army units were still in the northern mountains when the war ended.

The U.S. 25th and 32d Divisions had been trying for a month to push the Japanese back north toward Belete Pass near Santa Fe on Highway 5. The objective was to get into the Cagayan Valley, which extended for –almost 150 miles through northern Luzon between the central mountains and the Sierra range along the eastern side. In addition to troops, the enemy had several airfields that could be used for sorties against U.S. positions and shipping from time to time.

Just back from another mission in March, 1945, are (from left): Pat Reitmeyer, Iron River, Michigan, gunner; Joe Rutter, Sewickley, Pennsylvania, pilot; and Ernie Koch, West Hazelton, Pennsylvania, crew chief.

Something new in the way of missions to assist with the drive up Highway 5 came on March 31 when our squadron drew the assignment of providing night harassing cover for troops trying to move up to Balete Pass. The following day, April 1, was supposed to be some kind of Japanese holiday and intelligence officers guessed that this might prompt a major assault against our lines in celebration of the event. The 389th was to provide a plane over Highway 5 from dusk to dawn, ready to drop illuminating parachute flares over the Japanese lines whenever requested by a ground controller. The idea was to keep the enemy awake all night and to light up his positions if there were any indications of an attack.

The 312th Bomb Group had not flown any night missions in the Philippines, nor to my knowledge in New Guinea. Ed Valentine, our squadron operations officer, presented this novel assignment to us at lunch. When he asked for volunteers, four or five thought it sounded unusual enough to make it interesting to us. I drew the 2 A.M. to dawn shift following two others who would provide the cover during the earlier periods beginning at dusk.

The group officers' club had been built near the 389th's area and a party celebrating something or other was planned for the evening of March 31. There would be a variety of potables ranging from brand-name whiskey brought up from Australia to "gonk," a vile concoction made of our Halazone (a water purifying agent) flavored water, synthetic lemon powder, and Gilbey's London Dry Gin. A Filipino dance band had been hired to play should anyone be so fortunate as to be accompanied by a Red Cross girl or a nurse. It was supposed to be a big time, but missing the party was not a real sacrifice for me: drinking gonk was *not* my idea of a great evening.

One thing that I do recall from attending the very few organized parties held by the 312th was listening to a fellow from headquarters who had a really fine voice. He sang without accompaniment and must have had a repertoire of ballads, but the one that sticks in my mind was "Diane." Or was it "My Diane?" After more than fifty years, whenever I hear that tune I think of that unknown GI in faded khakis, leaning against the bamboo bar singing in a strong baritone voice for an appreciative audience.

I turned in shortly after dark with the sounds of the Filipino combo playing and the occasional roar of laughter as the conversation became oiled with gonk. Before drifting off to sleep I wondered a little about the challenge of night flying after not having done any for almost a year. There was no light-line for guidance out here. I figured it might be a little tricky, but what the hell?

Ed Valentine shook me awake sometime after 1 A.M. "Out of the sack Little Joe!" he said loudly. "Let's go make like a bird!" The band was still playing and it was evident from his manner that Ed had been enjoying the party. He was not, however, neglecting his duties as operations officer. After I pulled on my clothes, strapped on the regulation .45-caliber automatic, and picked up a packet of maps, Ed drove the gunner and me down to the flight line. Sergeant Boyd had dealt himself out of this night mission, instead, sent one of the new men to fly with me.

The moon was still up and the sky at Mangaldan generally clear overhead, although I could see some scattered clouds over the distant mountains to the west. Ernie Koch was dozing on his cot under 958's wing and was only a little grumpy about having to stay up all night for this unusual mission. The plane that had been out covering Highway 5 earlier was just landing and we waited to hear the pilot's report before starting the engines. He told us that the clouds covered all of the mountain valleys to the east and north and that he had been unable to find the controller's marker lights. Without a fix on the ground, he was unable to drop the flares. He ended up spending three hours riding around above the clouds. He said the first pilot had reported the same conditions.

Ed became impatient with my continued questioning of the just-returned pilot. Anxious to rejoin the party, he urged, "Let's go, Joe! You can find the damned place." The reports did not sound encouraging, but I figured maybe we could do better—after all, those guys on the ground deserved all the help they could get. We had some trouble raising Honey Tower on the radio to advise that we would be taking off shortly and would need runway lights. The extended delay noticeably irked Ed, but the tower eventually responded and the mission proceeded.

At the east end of the runway, ready to take off toward the dim horizon, I could hear Lt. K. I. Gunnarson, my instructor back at Marana almost two years earlier, introducing us to night flying: "Get on the instruments until you're high enough to see the horizon." The outline of the mountains off to the west would serve as a guide as soon as we got a little altitude. The lightly loaded plane was off the ground quickly in the cool night air. The runway lights blinked off as soon as we cleared the line of palm trees at the end of the field in the event some stray Japanese bomber was lurking out there somewhere. I watched the instruments until we had climbed past five hundred feet before looking around, identifying the horizon, and beginning a turn to the left to take up a course east across the central valley.

Flying at night quickly felt natural again, even after an extended absence. After gaining a little altitude, the ground features such as streams, roads, and fields stood out in the moonlight and the mountains toward Baguio on the left showed up very clearly. It was a short flight of about fifty miles, twenty minutes or less, to pick up Highway 5 north of San Jose.

The ground controller answered my first call and reported that the valley in his area and beyond to the north was cloud covered but that there was a fair ceiling above the ground. I hoped that this controller thought, "a fair ceiling" was on the order of five hundred feet or more and that he was a good judge of height as we followed Highway 5 toward the mountains. Soon we were under the layer of clouds the controller had mentioned. He had been right about the ceiling: Visibility was good and we could easily identify the highway below.

With the moon now obscured by the cloud deck and landmarks on the ground more difficult to identify it took two attempts before I was able to get far enough up into the valley to locate the controller's position. He had marked it with two open-top fifty-five-gallon drums with lights inside. The ceiling was about eight hundred feet. When the controller called for a flare drop, we were supposed to hold at 180 miles per hour for sixty seconds after passing over the marker lights before dropping the flare. This would assure that we illuminated the enemy's lines rather than our own. Bursts of gunfire going both north and south marked the approximate battle line two or three miles beyond the marker lights. To me, the front looked very active, indeed.

We circled around to get lined up over the highway for the first drop and, as we roared into the narrowing valley about five hundred feet over the checkpoint, the controller commented, "You're the first one I've seen tonight." We were unable to go the full sixty seconds before the cloud cover forced me lower than I felt comfortable flying and I had to make a tight turn between the dimly visible hills and retreat. At that point, at least, there was enough room to turn around safely. However, it was difficult to judge distances in the gloom under the clouds. It took more faith than I had to continue farther up the narrowing valley, but it did not appear that we came too close to the hillsides in making the 180-degree turnabout.

I made two more tries, but failed to get farther than forty-five seconds up into the valley before chickening out. The controller listened to each pass, trying to judge the distance to where I made my turns, and decided that dropping a flare at that point would be too close to his lines. On the next attempt we skimmed just on top of the cloud layer and dropped the flare. Unfortunately, by the time it drifted down through the cloud it was almost burned out and did not provide much illumination.

Closer examination of the problem showed that there were actually two layers of clouds separated by probably a one-hundred- to two-hundred-foot gap. Trusting that there would be more room between the hills at the higher elevation, I flew on a compass heading for the full minute, dropped the flare, and made my turn on instruments without disaster. This flare broke through the lower clouds soon enough to illuminate the countryside and the controller was enthusiastic. Unfortunately, within fifteen minutes the two layers of cloud had closed. The controller, having decided that the front seemed quiet, announced that he was going to get some sack time. He asked that we come up over the valley about every twenty or thirty minutes, kick out a flare, and fire our guns in an attempt to harass the enemy.

I continued to make circuits out over the central plain and then back up Highway 5 toward Balete Pass until the sky in the east became pink with the tropical sunrise. The clouds in those valleys would not burn off until the sun was high in the sky, about midmorning. The gunner and I talked occasionally on the intercom just to make sure the other was awake. It was refreshing to be out alone, with no formation to worry about. The calm, cool night air was also a welcome relief. The moon illuminated the light and dark patchwork of fields and rice paddies and the bright white ribbon of Highway 5 disappeared under the white blanket filling the valleys to the north, making for an easy mission. April 1, 1945, was the morning our troops landed on Okinawa far to the north of the Philippines. It was also Easter Sunday.

There was one incident that quiet night that enlivened things for a time. The radar station at Lingayen called about an hour or so into our patrol and inquired if we had seen any other planes in the area. Neither the gunner nor I had seen anything unusual, but the radar man reported that he had two blips on his screen and requested that I turn on my IFF transmitter. It was customary to turn off the IFF when we departed on a mission and not turn it on again until we approached friendly territory on the return trip.

The radar operator called back after a few minutes and said he had us identified and that there appeared to be another plane a few miles behind us going in the same direction. The report added spice to the flight, but the gunner scanned the sky behind us and reported he could see nothing. The radar sighting of a second plane may have been an electronic glitch of some sort or the other plane was not a hunter or simply had not seen us. Japanese planes, probably transports, had passed over Mangaldan at night on several occasions as they came down from Formosa on their way to the large island of Mindanao, which was still in enemy hands.

The outlines of the hills to the east became more distinct as the sky gradually lightened with the sunrise and the ground features became separated from the shadows. The ground controller came on the air again and released us. He commented that the night had proved to be quieter than anticipated and thanked us for standing by.

I contacted the radar station at Lingayen and requested permission for an approach to Mangaldan. I again switched on the IFF so we could be positively identified. Dawn was a favorite time for hit-and-run raids by lone Japanese fighters operating from the fields in northern Luzon, so the cautious operator instructed me to make successive turns and hold a specified course before he cleared us to head for Mangaldan.

"Honey Tower," I called as we approached the field. "Sugar Nine-Five-Eight five miles south for landing. Over." There being no other traffic, we were immediately cleared to land toward the east. The sequence for landing was by now automatic: Gear down, half-flaps, booster pumps on, check mixtures, check rpm. The gear came down with a solid thump and a quick glance at the indicator on the instrument panel showed "three green," meaning all three wheels were down and locked into place. As I turned onto the final approach the flaps went to full down and the throttles back to fifteen inches of manifold pressure. We were almost home and everything was routine when the runway ahead suddenly disappeared into a fog bank.

"Kee-rist! Where did that come from?" I quickly added power to go around again and started milking the flaps up when I discovered the source of the fog: the warm, humid air at the lower altitude had condensed on the cold plate of thick armor glass and cut off my view to the front.

"Tower, Nine-Five-Eight going around for another try. No emergency."

I swiped a hand over the outside of the glass to clear the fog away and the night mission to Balete Pass was over. It had been three hours and forty-five minutes flying time for us, but the ground troops would not get through Balete Pass for another six weeks, until May 13.

The morning sun was burning down on the flat, dry rice paddy in which the 389th was camped by the time the gunner and I were able to get a ride from the strip. I knew Sergeant Yelles would have some bacon to go with the scrambled dehydrated eggs in the mess hall, but first Len Dulac wanted full details of the mission for his intelligence report. Dulac expressed surprise at the news that we had found the controller and gotten close to the target area. The two pilots who had gone out earlier had given him only negative reports. By the time Dulac was satisfied, breakfast was about over. The remaining scrambled eggs were cold and had the consistency of sponge rubber, and crumbs of burnt bacon formed an unattractive blob in a corner of the greasy pan, but at least the coffee was still hot.

The group, meanwhile, was going off on another mission while I looked forward to hitting the sack. Jeeps and trucks departed for the airstrip and a little later I could hear the aircraft engines bark and roar in the distance down on the line. In a short time the engines sounded a deeper, thundering note as the group took off, three by three, and then a rumbling wave of sound passed overhead as the formation began to fade into the distance. It was comfortable in the deep shade inside the tent and quiet in the camp as most of the ground crews were standing by at the airstrip until the planes came back a few hours later. It had been an interesting night and, with no thoughts of a mission coming up, I was soon asleep.

Ed Valentine woke me up in the early afternoon. It seems that two of our pilots returning from leave in Sydney had called from Clark Field to request transportation to Mangaldan. They had found rides as far as Clark but were stuck there now, or so they said. I suggested that they try walking or hitchhiking or even stay overnight and try another day—I did not care, I needed my sack time. Besides, I told Val, there must be another pilot available to go get those fat cats. Val returned my protests with good-natured wisecracks, so I finally agreed to go down to Clark. I dressed and fished out a D-ration chocolate bar for lunch.

My plane had gone out on the early morning mission, so I was given the plane crewed by Sgt. Robert Keller, a close friend of Ernie Koch's from the same area of northeastern Pennsylvania. Bob Keller was about my age and a friendly, clean-cut sort of guy with a big smile. He asked if he could ride along to Clark and back, so we removed the five-man life raft from the shelf behind the cockpit. A passenger riding on the shelf was not in the safest position: he was not strapped in and a sudden stop would propel him into the pilot's head and possibly beyond. Riding on the shelf was neither uncommon nor forbidden. Moreover, since we would not be over water there should be no need for the life raft.

Several airstrips with their own identities made up Clark Field and I was familiar with none of them since I had had no occasion to land there. As soon as I was in the vicinity, I asked one of the several towers operating there to direct me to troop carrier operations, which turned out to be a field with a prewar concrete runway. The runway had an advertised length of thirty-three hundred feet, as I recall, and had been extended a hundred yards or so with loose gravel on the east end. It was shorter than I was used to but probably adequate for the C-47 and C-46 cargo planes. It was the designated place to pick up our passengers. The tower operator responded to my request for landing by saying that this was a troop carrier strip and short for Sugar aircraft, but he cleared us to land. He cautioned that the gravel overrun was soft and should not be used.

There was rising ground at the west end of the runway and when landing toward the east for the first time, the approach over those hills was a bit deceiving. I touched down too fast and too long, farther from the end of the too-short length of paving than intended. I should have pulled up and gone around, but I did not. Instead I dropped the nose at once and tromped hard on the brakes. The plane was slowing satisfactorily without heroic measures on the brakes, but we still were going thirty to forty miles an hour when the concrete ended and we hit the soft gravel. It seemed doubtful that the nosewheel strut would withstand the shock, but it did. The plane quickly slowed. The tower operator's reluctance to clear an A-20 to land on his field was well advised. Fortunately, we had been lightly loaded.

Keller stayed with his plane (no doubt to check it carefully for possible damage from my hard treatment) while I walked over to operations to find our two passengers. I was not surprised when those particular characters were nowhere in sight. After waiting around for most of an hour, the only conclusion was that they had caught an earlier flight north, after all. My mood was not improved by this inconsiderate treatment after requesting a special flight from Mangaldan just to get them. A navy ensign and a GI were waiting for a ride to Mangaldan, so I invited them to ride in the back of the plane in place of my missing prima donnas.

Another A-20, this one from the 417th Bomb Group, was now parked beside ours. It, too, had been sent to pick up a passenger who was not yet in sight. Although the pilot had avoided the gravel at the end of the runway, he seemed somewhat concerned about getting off from that short strip and asked what I thought about it. "No sweat! Thirty-three hundred feet is ample," I replied. He said he would see how (or if) I made it out and wait a bit longer to see if his passenger would show up. Keller stowed our two passengers in the gunner's compartment in the rear before climbing back on the shelf behind me.

A new dimension to the short airstrip was added when the tower advised that there was no suitable taxiway, so we would have to take off toward the west and the hills beyond with about a ten-mile-per-hour tailwind. I taxied over to the east end of the runway and lined up close to the end of the pavement. It might have been an optical illusion, but it appeared that the runway ran uphill toward those rising hills. This seemed to be an occasion for using short-field takeoff techniques something like the carrier takeoffs demonstrated by the frustrated B-25 instructors at La Junta who were not selected to fly in the Doolittle raid on Tokyo in 1942.

The drill was: flaps down full, throttles advanced to their stops and the wheel held well back before releasing the brakes. The nosewheel came off quickly, as in a B-25, but I did not try to stagger off the ground the way those La Junta boys had demonstrated. I just tried for a very short takeoff. We clawed into the air well before the end of the runway, but we were not yet at our customary flying speed and the ground was rising rapidly ahead of us.

The speed picked up slowly and the rising foothills ahead made it difficult to reduce the rate of climb to gain airspeed. The controls felt sloppy below 150 miles per hour and the weight of our two passengers in the rear contributed to the feeling that the plane was precariously balanced on a point as I cautiously milked up the flaps and began a shallow climbing turn to the left, away from the hills. It was a strange sensation. Although it lasted only a short time, until the airspeed crept higher and we got away from the rising ground, it was uncomfortable. As we circled back over the runway it looked to be much shorter than thirty-three hundred feet.

Half an hour later we were looking down at the wide and long mat at Mangaldan, which appeared comforting after that short Clark Field strip. Honey Tower acknowledged my call for landing instructions and directed me to land to the east. The tower operator added that there was a thirty-mile-per-hour crosswind from the southeast, but that posed no problem for an A-20. With Keller observing closely, alert after watching the end of the concrete runway rushing up a little earlier, I rolled into the landing pattern but allowed a little longer approach to judge the effect of the strong crosswind. As fellow pilot and friend Vern Schrag once related at Charlotte, "Joseph, I was holding right aileron, opposite rudder, and bottom engine for a perfect approach!" With more luck than art I leveled out precisely as the wheels began to rumble on the dirt. It was an unexpected grease-job to cover up for my poor performance at Clark Field.

As we taxied back to the 389th's Line, Bob Keller asked with mock innocence, "Was that a rough landing, Lieutenant?" We both laughed. I hope that Keller reported it with proper awe to his buddy Ernie Koch, for it turned out to be the last landing I made in an A-20.

A day or two later, Doc Walsh stopped by our tent and started a conversation about my possibly going home. He indicated that with my combat hours and mission tally, he would look favorably on a request to be grounded. Doc may have taken this same approach with others who had completed their allotted time, but it seemed a bit strange to me then— that is, asking me to request to be sent home. He did not mention there being any evidence in my demeanor that indicated fatigue. I expressed honest surprise at the suggestion of going home—I had not given any thought to it.

We talked some more and maybe my mixed feelings about going home confirmed whatever Doc's assessment of my mental condition might have been. My response to the proposal was: "Well Doc, some of the others have accepted a promotion to captain and stayed another six months. That would suit me fine, too." I thanked Doc for dropping in and, as he left the tent, he said, "Take the opportunity, Joe, go home while the going is good."

My correspondence with Harriett had continued steadily throughout my overseas tour. We had agreed when we parted the previous June that serious decisions about our future, given the uncertainties of the war, would await my return. I had reached no conclusions about what to do after the war and I found it admittedly strange that it should have caused me any hesitation about going home. I did not want to make the military a career, so gaining another rank was not a real goal—it was simply justification for postponing making any serious decisions for another six months.

The unexpected visit by Doc Walsh suddenly focused my attention on going home sooner rather than later. Going back to being a file clerk shuffling papers at the FBI field office was not attractive and I did not consider it. Rubbing shoulders with Maury Owen, John Edmunds, and others older and wiser, not to mention Nancy in Charlotte, had made a college degree a logical goal for me. The recently passed package of benefits known as the "GI Bill of Rights" made college financially possible as well as obviously desirable. I had broached no future scenarios for "us" in my correspondence with Harriett. Until Doc's unexpected visit, my return home was assumed to have been many months away and there was still an element of luck involved.

The Allies were moving faster toward Japan, but the best guesses we had heard pointed to another two years of war and a bloody invasion of the Japanese home islands. Perhaps the 312th's next move would be to Okinawa, where the battle was still going hot and heavy, with no early move possible. The group had become my home. Perhaps there was a little self-torment involved in delaying going home when it was offered—a savoring of delightful anticipation.

Two nights later, Doc again stopped by our tent. My attitude, even after thinking about the possibilities, had not changed. We talked pleasantly for a while. Finally, Doc said, "You know Rutter, Colonel Wells says you can stay here six years and you will never make captain." Doc had been rooming with Colonel Wells when I first joined the 389th Squadron in Hollandia, so his message carried some weight.

"That's what he said, Doc?"

"Yes!"

The promotion was the only valid reason I had to stick around. After briefly reflecting on his answer, I replied: "Well, I guess that changes the picture. Go ahead and ground me."

Had Doc Walsh *really* talked to Colonel Wells about my situation? The message was not unlike the colonel, at least as I thought I knew him. Doc, however, was an interesting character who liked the sauce and could stretch a story when need be. Still, he undoubtedly had my best interests at heart. My record stood at sixty-four missions and 215 combat hours. The smooth landing in Bob Keller's plane on the morning of April 1, 1945, had been a fitting climax to life in an A-20.

It turned out to be an excellent time to hang up my parachute. Unknown to most of us then, the 312th Bomb Group was being phased out as a light bomb group and was slated to be converted into a Very Heavy Bomb Group flying the new Consolidated B-32 Dominator, comparable to a B-29, but without some of the trimmings. The big four-engine bombers were slated to begin arriving in mid-May with full crews and the A-20s would be replaced as each squadron in turn was outfitted with the new equipment. The 386th Squadron would be the first to change over. The remaining A-20 pilots would be shifted to the other squadrons until the entire group was designated "VHB" and had a full complement of B-32s.

Besides, who on April 1, 1945, would have guessed that the war with Japan would be over by September? Even Vice Pres. Harry Truman, who would succeed President Roosevelt when he died less than two weeks later, did not know anything about the atomic bomb at the time.

My friends had not understood my initial diffidence to Doc's offer to ground me. Jim Rutledge was wistful and wishful as he thought about his family in Culver City, California. Maury Owen mumbled that he would give back those pleasant leaves in Sydney if he could go home too, then added, "Anyone who volunteers for a night mission needs to be sent home."

Cal Slade asked how many bottles of gonk it took to get Doc to recognize my serious case of combat fatigue. Don Dyer smiled and said: "What a lucky sonofabitch! I can see you now, Rutter: a goddam hero surrounded by women while your buddies are still here fighting the war." Bob Foreman lost no time in asking Valentine to assign 958 to him. It was a plane he particularly enjoyed flying.

Chapter 13

HOMEWARD BOUND

NO DATE HAD BEEN SET for the next shipment back to the States, but it probably would be within three or four weeks, if past experience was any criterion. The processing for shipment home was handled at a transit camp near Tacloban on Leyte and transportation could be by either sea or air. While waiting for orders home, I felt a strong curiosity to see what the city of Manila was like and how badly it was damaged.

We had watched it burn for two weeks or more as the Japanese defenders were rooted out. John Edmunds had a friend who was an officer in an antiaircraft company stationed on the southeast side of the city, on the road leading south to Cavite, so I would have a place to stay for a few days. Marty Sobel, the assistant squadron adjutant, and another ground officer were driving down to Manila in a jeep on some sort of official business so, with Major Wylie's blessing, I went along and spent most of a week wandering about as a GI tourist.

The dry and generally pleasant weather on Lingayen Gulf was changing. Most days were overcast and there was an occasional shower. It did not take much moisture to change the black, cracked soil into a slick mess and we knew that any extended rainfall would raise the water table and turn the Mangaldan airstrip back into a rice paddy. Several hard rains during the second week of April left pools of standing water in low spots and the field had to be closed until the sun came out and dried the mud.

Another airstrip was being prepared for the 312th at Floridablanca, twenty miles south of Clark Field, but the advent of the wet season made it imperative to get all planes out of Mangaldan as soon as possible.

The Tarlac, Luzon, railway station in April, 1945. The trains were running between Lingayen and Manila when the 312th moved to its new base at Floridablanca. The narrow-gauge, wood-fired locomotives came from Germany and the passenger cars behind the freight cars were from England.

There was a break in the weather on April 16 and the marine SBDs, 3d Air Commando P-51s, and our A-20s scattered to new, dryer locations. The 389th Squadron brought up the rear, departing in the late afternoon with the soggy runway just passable enough for the last planes to get off and head for the not quite completed facilities at Floridablanca.

The ground personnel and equipment were moved south by railroad. We loaded up early on the morning of April 18 for what turned out to be a long, slow trip over the rickety narrow-gauge railroad. The coaches had wooden seats, which were in no way conducive to sleep, but we survived on them for two days and a night. Here and there along the way we stopped and spent more hours stationary than moving. Although the eighty-five-mile journey was hardly a pleasure excursion, it was a great way to see the countryside with its towns, farms, and livestock. The nearest station on the railroad to Floridablanca was at another San Fernando, where we arrived the evening of April 19.

The airstrip had been a Japanese base of some importance and when the 312th was forced to move the engineers were still busy clearing away

Although Manila had been declared an "Open City" when Allied troops pulled out in 1941, the Japanese tenaciously defended it until the end—and then destroyed it—in 1945. Note the remains of the State Theater in downtown Manila, April, 1945.

The gutted Metropolitan Theater on P. Burgos Boulevard, Manila.

wrecked planes and rebuilding and extending the runways, building taxiways and hardstands, and so forth. The mountains rising a few miles to the west sheltered the area from the winds bringing moist air in from the South China Sea. Foridablanca was dry under the shadow of the mountains and the airstrip under construction was very dusty.

Almost as soon as our camp was set up we had visits by the Negritos, a very short primitive people who were usually naked and lived up in the mountains. Starving, these people were anxious to retrieve garbage from the mess hall and wandered through the camp daily looking for food. There were wandering groups of Japanese troops in the highlands to the west and the Negritos had been forced to move to the lowlands to survive.

My faithful A-20G-45, serial number 43–21958, made its last landing when Bob Foreman brought it into Floridablanca after the hasty departure from Mangaldan on April 16. In the early dusk and with the dust swirling, Bob had run over a piece of junk that was thrown by the prop and passed through the lower right side of the fuselage near the cockpit. The jagged piece of metal had cut a number of hydraulic lines and

Remains of Manila's general post office.

caused other damage that would take longer to repair than was deemed worthwhile, so the plane was declared Class 26, suitable for salvage of parts. I paid a visit to my old friend and sat in the cockpit one last time. Some miscreant had already removed the clock from the instrument panel and also the Douglas "First Around the World" emblem from the center of the control wheel. They were the only souvenirs I was interested in keeping. I might have taken that damned plate of armor glass, but it was too heavy to consider lugging home.

There were a number of wrecked and abandoned Japanese planes around the airstrip, including some obsolete, fixed-gear Mitsubishi Type 96 fighters that appeared to have been abandoned where they sat for a year or more. Strange planes, particularly the enemy's, are a curiosity for most pilots, so we spent several afternoons looking and poking around the Japanese equipment. The design of many of the aircraft seemed crude, particularly in the case of the bombers, which lacked power-operated turrets and still had hand-held guns. The fighters—such as the Oscar, Zeke, and Tony—had clean designs but were of lighter construction than our comparable planes and carried 20-mm automatic cannon mounted in the wings whereas the U.S. standard was a half-dozen of the smaller .50-caliber machine guns. (Japanese planes were identified by code names, with boys' names for fighters and girls' names for most bombers and reconnaissance types.) The few examples of newer Japanese fighters looked to be the

The entrance to Intramuros, Manila's inner city, which was still off limits in April, 1945, when I finally had a chance to play tourist.

equal of our latest designs. Fortunately, we never encountered them in the air.

My only duty assignment while waiting to go home was to act as "Atabrine Officer." Each man was supposed to take a yellow Atabrine tablet daily to prevent the onset of malaria and there were a few who resisted taking the pills. Rumors of bad things resulting from the shots and pills the army administered were commonplace. Atabrine, for example, allegedly caused sterility and permanently yellowed one's skin. However, the alternative was the fever, aches, nausea, and potentially more serious effects of malaria, so I supervised the taking of a pill at the evening meal. My presence at the chow line was mostly symbolic; there was little resistance to gulping down the pill.

The camp area at Floridablanca was located on a grass-covered plateau some distance from the airstrip. The climate was so pleasant that for several days I slept on a cot out in the open. Jim Rutledge and I decided to share a tent for the short time I would be around and we contracted with one of the enterprising Filipinos to build a raised bamboo floor and tent frame. The cost was a reasonable thirty pesos. While Jim was out flying missions, I served as the overseer on the project and broke out our jointly owned navy nylon screening to wrap around our new quarters. The green split-bamboo flooring was limber, so we had to be careful to place boards under the legs of our cots to keep them from breaking through. Nevertheless, we had a comfortable house.

As a result of the sudden move to our new base, the incoming mail was delayed for several weeks. I had, however, written to my correspondents to let them know that my war was over and that I would eventually be coming home. No date had been announced for my leaving the 312th and traveling to the transit camp. Men reportedly waited up to a month at Tacloban awaiting shipment, after which they were assigned to travel either by sea or air. The method of transportation really did not matter to me. Besides, a couple of weeks on a ship might be enjoyable. Still, I preferred hanging around the 389th Squadron rather than waiting in a transit camp.

When one of the ground officers made a trip up to Clark Field one morning, I rode along to have a look around, particularly at the collection of captured planes. The Japanese had spread several hundred planes around the dozen airstrips at Clark Field and, although our air raids had destroyed or damaged most of them, many had been found hidden and in good condition. The Air Technical Intelligence Unit (ATIU) had gathered up a large number of Japanese planes for study and the more interesting newer examples were being shipped to Wright Field outside Dayton, Ohio, for further analysis.

It took some inquiry and hitchhiking before I located the ATIU airstrip. There I enjoyed myself walking along the line of flyable planes. It was an outdoor museum and some of the new types of fighters were being flown against our service types. The fighter code-named Jack (the Mitsubishi J2M) was one we had not seen earlier. It was rather hot looking, and I visited with a navy pilot who was flying one against our Grumman F6F Hellcat carrier fighter. He thought the comparison was close. Several other pilots were rubbernecking around the plane collection that morning, but the ATIU people kept us at a distance—no souvenir picking was tolerated.

The wrecked hangars that had been my guiding point during the low-level mix-up on January 7 were still in much the same condition they had been in that morning. I walked through one of the derelict hangars, looked up through the bare girders and pieces of tattered metal roofing at the sky, and mused that there was no question luck had been riding with me.

The 35th Fighter Group mess hall was not far away, so I went there for lunch. The walls were decorated with various pieces of Japanese aircraft, in keeping with scenes from the western front in World War I as depicted in the movies *Hell's Angels* and *Dawn Patrol.*

By the time I finished eating it was time to see about getting back to Floridablanca. I walked back to the main road and flagged down a truck heading in the right direction and the driver took me eight or ten miles south and dropped me off before turning off and heading east. I stood beside the road for perhaps ten or fifteen minutes in the hot sunshine, but there was no traffic coming by from either direction. It was an area of old, overgrown fields with no signs of habitation nor evidence of a military presence, so I moved across the road and took a seat under the shade of several large trees to await some southbound traffic. The only sounds were from a few birds flitting about overhead or in the nearby shrubbery.

After another fifteen or twenty minutes a cloud of dust appeared around a bend in the direction of Clark Field. Crossing the road and sticking out my thumb brought the jeep to a quick stop. A Military Police colonel and his driver eyed me with interest.

"How long have you been here, Lieutenant?" the officer asked.

"About half an hour, Colonel. A truck going to a quartermaster outfit down that road back there dropped me off here. There hasn't been any traffic since."

He motioned for me to get into the backseat and we started down the dirt road. "You didn't see anything at all?" the colonel asked.

"No, nothing's come by."

"Maybe you're lucky. This road has been closed. About two hundred Japs are reportedly moving down from the hills out into the valley and they have to cross the road somewhere along here. You sure you didn't see any people?" That casual trip could have been a lot more exciting! The good colonel, concerned about one guy standing out there hitch-hiking, took me all the way back to the 312th.

Military regulations prohibited taking undeveloped film back to the States and any such discovered in our possession would be confiscated at the transit camp. I thus attempted to process the dozen or more rolls of film I had stored in condoms. One dark night we organized an impromptu photo lab: four helmets with developer, water, fixer, and wash water were set up on the floor of the tent, all in a row. Then, taking the rolls of film with me, I crawled under two GI blankets draped over the "lab" while Rutledge sat outside with a watch and called out the time for developing while I blindly maneuvered the strips of 120 film through the four baths. Two or three of the rolls were lost because moisture had

C46-48 386BS. LT. RUTLEDGE II MAY '45

Nose art designed and executed by Jim Rutledge for his plane "Ravin' Rachel," the oldest A-20 in the 389th Squadron. The paint was hardly dry when the plane was lost in a midair collision on May 19, 1945.

caused the paper backing to adhere to the film and I could not work them apart by feel. There were some pieces of paper backing sticking here and there that damaged some frames but Jim and I eventually got the job done. The results were far from professional as there was no way to judge the temperature of the developer and the five-minute time we used produced grossly overdeveloped negatives, for the most part. However, there were at least some images to take home with me—and no undeveloped film for a zealous official to confiscate. There were, of course, some ribald comments the next morning when a dozen used condoms were observed around our tent.

On April 29, those of us who were slated to return home received orders to move to the transit camp on Leyte. After four weeks of relaxing, I was ready to leave and I thanked Doc Walsh for his advice to "Go home while you can." Our trim A-20s were still down on the flight line, but the word was out that the group would be receiving its B-32s soon and that would change everything. Those big four-engine trucks might be the latest in technology, but flying them held no attraction at all. Operating alone in an A-20, except for the gunner in the rear, down on the deck dealing out mayhem to an enemy, had been the most challenging and at times exciting life and could not be repeated.

Owen and I spent a good bit of time talking about going home and what we would do after the war. He urged me to take advantage of the GI Bill as an opportunity not to be missed. During one of our discussions I expressed regret at not having been in the Pacific somewhat earlier, when there had been even more serious opposition and excitement. The older and wiser Owen responded, "Well, Rut, this way you're going home alive." The remark caused me to realize my good fortune. It *was* the right time for me to go home.

It was customary, at least in the 389th Squadron, for those not so lucky to ask someone who was going home to send flowers to wives, girlfriends, and mothers. Some of the returnees actively solicited flower orders of $10 to $20 apiece from the homesick and lovelorn parties and thus collect sizable wads of cash. On more than one occasion nothing was ever heard about the flowers; there were no letters of gratitude or expressions of love acknowledging receipt of the unexpected remembrances. I never asked anyone to send flowers on my behalf because the chance that the courier would never carry through seemed all too likely. It therefore came as a surprise when I found myself importuned to send flowers. I wound up with a list of about twenty addresses and more than $450 in cash.

Transit camps were one of the poorer experiences of military life. The camp at Tacloban had a reputation no better than the average and some who had spent time there later reported a dismal experience. We were fortunate, however: the troopship *General John Pope* was at anchor in the harbor when we checked in and would be leaving soon. While most returning pilots hoped for air transportation, I was content with idea of a relaxing sea voyage home. Besides, since nobody was expecting my arrival on any certain date, it made little difference if I traveled by air or by sea.

We were at Tacloban long enough to take in the first performance of a USO troop fresh from the States performing the musical *Oklahoma!* The show was staged out in the open, the Seventh Fleet band provided the music, the costumes were colorful, and the girls were pretty, fresh, and enthusiastic. The corny plot did not detract from the magic of that performance under the stars and the audience of tired, thin, Atabrine-yellow returnees in faded khakis ate it up. Seeing that lively bit of state-side fluff would have made anyone anxious to get home—even jaded types like me. Hey! Those girls!

We loaded onto the *General John Pope* on May 2 and that same afternoon joined a convoy headed south. The *Pope* was an 11,450-ton P-2 transport owned by the navy and operated by the Military Transport Service. She could carry about five thousand troops, but on this trip the ship was perhaps only half full.

Officers were assigned to cabins with bunk beds, mattresses, and white sheets, whereas the enlisted men were quartered in the troop holds with the typical four-high, folding canvas bunks. Company grade officers (lieutenants and captains) were assigned to a large inside cabin measuring about twenty by thirty feet. With sixty assigned, it was crowded and stuffy to say the least. The navy crew was very particular to follow its own rules and priorities, including no water available in the washroom until 6 A.M.—not even saltwater. There was always a crowd trying to shave, shower, and brush their teeth when the water was finally turned on, so our accommodations were not that much better overall than in the troop holds.

We army types had the perception that life in the wartime navy was downright decadent, perhaps even sissified. That impression was confirmed when we entered the officers' dining room for lunch the first day and saw the tables covered with white linen, set with shining silverware, sparkling glassware, and real china. Colored mess men dressed in jackets and ties stood by to serve. We, on the other hand, in our well-worn army khaki, faded by dozens of scrubbings with GI soap and brush, hardly fit into such surroundings. Yet why should the navy not have been comfortable? After all, they had the means of transport and there clearly was plenty of room on this ship for decent facilities. Nevertheless, the scene was unexpected. We soon adapted to the civilized conventions and quickly forgot about eating from mess kits and drinking from tin cups. Although the menus were not too elaborate, they were certainly a much-appreciated change from C-ration stew, Spam, and bully beef.

It was interesting to look out at the variety of ships in our convoy, the *General John Pope* being one of the largest. There were a number of the ubiquitous Liberty ships, a few of the newer Victory types, and some tankers. Several of the freighters appeared to be Hog Islanders built during World War I. A small ship that had the lines of a yacht, including a clipper bow, probably had been owned by an Astor, Morgan, or one of the Dodge brothers in her civilian days.

After two days in the convoy and with no alarms of submarines or aircraft the *Pope* broke away alone and zigzagged on a southeast heading for the island of Biak. This was not exactly our idea of a direct course toward the States, but there were more passengers to be picked up. We anchored in the harbor off Biak, just below the equator, early in the evening on May 7. It had the same familiar hot and humid air we remembered from nearby New Guinea. Many of us slept on the hatch covers under the stars that night.

The following morning, May 8, 1945, the ship's newspaper announced Germany's surrender. That ended any speculation I might have had about eventually going to Europe. There were a few typically laconic GI remarks, but the announcement of the end of the war in Europe, so far from our world of the SWPA, did not cause any noticeable excitement—our focus was going home. The Pacific war continued and guesses as to when it would end ranged upward of two years, even allowing for the help of outfits in Europe that would be redirected to the Pacific theater. None seemed to see much chance that the Japanese could be defeated without an invasion of Japan itself.

There was a large general hospital at Biak from which the *General John Pope* was to pick up convalescent cases and take them home. We watched from the deck all day long as LCVPs and barges brought litters out to the ship, a forceful reminder of how lucky most of us had been. Many of the patients were in heavy casts or sheathed in bandages. It would be a long time before their particular overseas tour would finally end. We lay in Biak Harbor all day; the number of hospital cases that came aboard was sobering.

The *General John Pope* sailed for home on the morning of May 9, first heading east across Geelvink Bay until the coast of New Guinea was close off the starboard side. I stood by the rail and looked at the unbroken jungle, a line of tall palms along the shore with dense foliage behind and the green mounds of the mountains rising on the southern horizon to touch the layers of gray clouds. It was a contemplative last look at that primitive island with its exotic birds, strange animals, and stone-age natives living under the jungle's lush green canopy. Along that shore were unseen villages of thatched huts raised up on stilts and eyes undoubtedly watching and wondering about our purpose. The thought crossed my mind that I would never even have seen these unspoiled tropics if it had not been for the war and the chances of fate that had placed me there—and now permitted me to go home.

Curtains of rain began to fall from the leaden clouds over some of the higher ranges off to the south, just as it did every day in New Guinea. Moreover, there were still thousands of Japanese troops in those green hills, scattered in bases we had bypassed and left to exist as best they could until the war ended. Soon the coastline disappeared behind a sheet of silver-gray rain and the ship heeled over as it took one of its long zigzags, steering a new course to the northeast. It was unlikely I would ever see New Guinea again; an interesting and sometimes exciting chapter of my life was closing.

As we left New Guinea behind, twenty of the junior officers elected to move down into the empty forward troop hold in the bow of the ship. We gave up our places in the crowded "officers' country" room with its beds and mattresses in exchange for space to spread out. The pipe-framed canvas bunks were at least as comfortable as the cots we had used for most of the past year. There was a good-size head for the troop hold with saltwater showers available, although the saltwater soap took some getting used to. We also soon learned that the heaving of the ship was more noticeable up in the bow when the sea was running, but overall it was worth these minor inconveniences to escape the claustrophobic junior officers' quarters. Those who remained in officers' country were probably pleased to see us go, so everybody was happy.

We had few duties beyond a day or so of assigned responsibility for the enlisted spaces down in the holds. The cramped troop areas had to be kept reasonably clean and neat, with the latrine and floor-mopping details assigned by a senior sergeant. The duty officer was expected to put in an appearance in the hold several times a day and make a cursory inspection. If any problem arose with the men, the duty officer was expected to handle it. However, there were no emergencies on the days I served. The sea voyage was a time for all of us to read, play cards, shoot craps, or swap stories to pass the time from one meal to the next.

Although I was the only pilot going home from the 389th, there were several from other squadrons in the 312th. Halstead Cross, sometimes called Cross Baby, from the 386th, was one of the La Junta gang. There were several others from this "club" on board, including Wilburne Morrow from the 417th Group. There were also several B-25 pilots from the 345th Group down in our exclusive forward hold, so the great mix-up on the Clark Field mission was debated at length with no opinions changed.

The *General Pope* traveled alone across the Pacific day after day, constantly zigzagging to foil any enemy submarine that might happen across our path, but there were no alarms. There was a blackout at night and at sunset the public address speakers routinely announced, "The smoking lamp is out on all weather decks." This was matched by another call two or three times a day that became familiar: "Now hear this! Clean sweep-down fore and aft on all decks. Sweepers, man your brooms." Navy orders were indeed different.

For the most part, the weather was pleasant with only a few days under clouds or with the wind stirring up the chop on the water. Flying fish accompanied us most of the way. We also occasionally saw porpoises keeping pace with the ship. Aside from the Spartan quarters, this could have been a pleasure cruise. I much preferred it to spending hour after hour in a hard seat in a cargo plane, or being part of a crew flying a war-weary B-25 or B-24 back to the States.

We passed close enough to one of the Hawaiian Islands to see it briefly through some rainsqualls, but we made no port calls during the trip. On the morning of May 21 we passed a group of rocks, the Farallon Islands, which poke out of the sea several miles outside the entrance to San Francisco Bay. Rumors had been flying about for three days as to the precise hour we would arrive in San Francisco and the decks were crowded with men watching for the first sight of solid land. Fog and a wan sun kept the coast hidden until we were very close. The ship finally came out from under the low ceiling into the sunshine and there was the Golden Gate Bridge, straight ahead. The deep blue sea and whitecaps contrasted with the steep brown and green splashed hills on either side of the bay, making for an unforgettable sight.

There was little talking on the crowded forward decks as the ship approached the coast and we drank in the sight of the mouth of the bay and the colorful buildings of the city beyond. It was an emotional moment for even the hardest cases and each of us spent time in quiet reflection as we at last passed under the Golden Gate. We had seen few ships during the thirteen days since leaving Biak, but here was a harbor full of merchant and navy ships of all sizes. The white buildings of San Francisco covered the hills on the right while up ahead we could see the expanse of the bay and the city of Oakland beyond. The sudden lifting of the fog was like drawing a curtain to expose a stage of a world we had almost forgotten; the bay was as crowded as the sea had been empty.

Looking down over the bow of the ship from the deck above it was easy to spot the pilots in the crowd. Conditioned by a year or more of flying in unfriendly skies, their heads were constantly turning as they searched for a passing plane, checked ships at anchor or in motion, and eyeballed buildings and bridges, smokestacks, high-tension towers, and radio antennas on the nearby hills. Then they would look back around the scene all over again. The habit was ingrained by hours of searching for targets, checking the sky above, and then taking a sweeping look across the instrument panel before starting over again in constant watchfulness.

Cross Baby stood quietly beside me at the rail as we came under the bridge and the bay and the city opened out before us. My mind drifted back over eleven months to the clearings in the New Guinea jungle, the battered airstrips at Nabire and Utarom, churned mud and shattered trees at Mount Hakko, and then the palm plantations, green rice paddies, villages with always a stone church, and the railroads in the Philippines. There had been the mission to Clark Field, flak over the Marikina airfield and sweating out dropping bombs in those narrow valleys in the mountains, nor would we forget the images of Manila burning. What a contrast to now look at the peaceful harbor full of shipping and the buildings of San Francisco gleaming in the bright sunlight.

We were lost in our own thoughts when Cross suddenly turned to me with a broad grin breaking over his face. "Jesus Christ!" he shouted. "Look at all that stuff! What a beautiful target!"

The same thought had struck me at almost the same time. The scene was the juiciest target imaginable when judged from the perspective of an A-20 cockpit, which had been our life for almost a year. What destruction we could have caused! We laughed uproariously that sunny morning as we sailed through San Francisco Bay. Those around us probably wondered what could possibly have struck us as being so funny. Even fifty years later, I still get a smile when I see some scenic panorama before me and the thought instinctively comes: "What a beautiful target!"

The great adventure was over.

EPILOGUE

THE *General John Pope* LANDED at a pier in downtown San Francisco at about eleven o'clock on the morning of May 21, 1945. This completed a round-trip for the ship that had begun March 26, and included stops at Manila, Leyte, and Biak. There was a military band on the pier and a surprising number of civilians who had somehow learned that the *General Pope* would be arriving that day, presumably with loved ones aboard. The festive welcome with music and flags was appreciated and somewhat unexpected by most of us. We were just happy to see San Francisco again. After all, the half-serious phrase, "The Golden Gate in 'forty-eight" was usually offered when someone asked for opinions of when we might get home.

As we stood there by the rail, Cross Baby looked idly down at the pier, watching the operation as the ship was being tied up and appreciating the several dozen young chicks who were there—awaiting just us, of course. Suddenly, Cross turned away from the rail with a look of disbelief, maybe even shock, on his usually happy face and exclaimed, "Christ! My wife and her mother are down there." The news that Cross Baby was a passenger on the *General Pope* and the date of the ship's arrival—even the pier number—had penetrated to Long Beach, the slogan "Loose Lips Sink Ships" notwithstanding. The unanticipated appearance of a personal welcoming committee forced a change in the bon vivant Cross's touted plans for a delay and some celebrating in San Francisco before traveling south. We observers were amused by his consternation. Was that attractive young lady on the other end of the pier also looking for our boy?

During the passage from Biak five or six of the wounded patients had died. There was also a reported suicide or two, but this could have been another of the GI rumors that seemed to be always floating about. The hospital cases were taken off first and the rest of us who were returning outwardly unscathed waited with not even a mild complaint. In due course we were ordered off and directed to the ferry *Army Queen*, tied up across the pier in the next slip, for transfer to Angel Island.

The *Army Queen* had the look of an old steamboat to me. I had always been interested in riverboats and a quick investigation turned up the name *Isleton* carved above the main cabin door. It was an enjoyable trip aboard the *Isleton/Army Queen* as we made our way across the sparkling, choppy bay that bright spring morning and continued past notorious Alcatraz to Angel Island. We were home at last. During the war, Angel Island had been a processing center for troops shipping out by sea. Now it was the reception center for those returning from the Pacific war.

We went through the usual paperwork and received a briefing explaining how we would be sent on to processing points nearer to our homes. Our stay on Angel Island would be short. Those of us from the East would take a train to Indianapolis or to Fort George Meade near Baltimore. The West Coast boys would go by train down to Santa Ana where the Flying Cadet Preflight School had been converted into a processing center as the flying training program was gradually curtailed.

A briefing officer at Angel Island also informed us: "You will all be sent home for a thirty-day leave. During that time you should make a decision on whether you want to stay in the service or get out." That announcement suddenly shed a different light on things for me. Since a military career was not my ambition, I had best make plans to get on with my life. Attending college was now a closer rather than later possibility and my aim, whatever else I did, should be to get into a suitable school in the fall.

On the second day at Angel Island, Wilburne Morrow and I crossed back over on the ferry to see the sights of San Francisco. We did not look very stylish in our faded and tattered khaki uniforms, boondocker shoes, yellow complexions, and too-long hair, but we considered these to be marks of distinction. We were veterans, after all. We stopped to have a drink in the first decent bar we saw and after downing a couple of beers, Zoot suggested that we hit the Top of the Mark at the Mark Hopkins Hotel and have dinner in style. It was a good idea, but we hardly looked like five-star hotel customers and there was also that wad of money in my pocket covering promised flower orders, which was a first order of business for me.

We picked out a florist shop at random from which to send the love-and-kisses messages from 389th Bomb Squadron members. Zoot took half of the address list and we began writing $20 telegraph flower orders, which was about twice the customary flower order. I suppose the manager of this shop had seen many strange customers during the war years, because he did not seem surprised at the amount of unexpected business we brought to him. The couple of beers we had downed did not help in deciphering the handwritten names and addresses, but in half an hour or so we had completed the job and the florist was something over $400 to the good.

Our next stop was a barbershop in order to get us a little more presentable with shaves and haircuts. We plopped down into two empty chairs and viewed a price list of tonsorial services posted above the mirror. At the top it read, "THE WORKS—$16." That seemed exorbitant, especially considering that a shave and a haircut cost $1.25. Zoot inquired about the scope of services encompassed in "The Works" and was informed that it included a shampoo, massage, haircut, tonic, shave, mudpack, manicure, and so forth. "Hell, give us The Works," ordered Zoot. "Fine! Me, too!" said I.

After an hour or more in the barber shop enjoying all the pampering (an experience I have never repeated) the later events of that evening become somewhat blurred. We did make an entrance into the Top of the Mark and ordered a drink or two but, with no ribbons on our chests, nobody seemed impressed or even interested in where we had been. Most of the loud-talking customers in clean and pressed uniforms were shipping out rather than returning heroes. They looked at us a little strangely—we did stick out in the sophisticated surroundings—and seemed to be wondering why these bumpkins did not know to wear decent uniforms when choosing to enter such a celebrated watering hole. We did not stay there long.

Someplace in the Mark Hopkins, probably the main dining room, we had a big dinner. Our worn clothes and high-top, rough-leather boondockers invited stares from the well-dressed civilians and stateside military types in the room. After another drink, Zoot observed loudly, "Look at those goddam shack troopers; you can always tell one." (Shack troopers were those who had cushy desk jobs and avoided leaving the States.) We observed that the civilian types who were younger than forty were "Probably Four-F draft dodgers" and added, "By the way, bring us another drink." The hostess was undoubtedly wishing she had more potted palms behind which to hide her two crude, uncivilized customers while we savored our steaks and probably talked much too loudly.

Wilburne called a young lady he knew in town who shared an

apartment with two other girls. He may have met her when we were waiting to ship out in 1944. We stopped by for a visit but it was mid-week and while the young ladies were cordial and pleased to see that Zoot had survived the war, they had jobs to go to in the morning. So, we moved on. We managed to miss the last ferry back to Angel Island and wound up killing time in a newsreel theater, drinking a lot of coffee, and eating an early breakfast in a diner while waiting for the six o'clock ferry.

Upon arrival back at the transit barracks we found that the group destined for the East would be leaving around noon that day. The West Coast boys would also be moving out a little later in the afternoon on a troop train heading to Santa Ana. In short order, Wilburne Morrow, Halstead Cross, and I parted company with mutual wishes of good luck, bringing to a close friendships and shared experiences extending back over two eventful years.

Our troop train loaded at the Oakland Army Base after we crossed the bay from San Francisco on a railroad car float. It was a very long train, sixteen cars as I recall, and after loading we waited several hours before the train pulled out. It would take us a full week to cross the country for there was already heavy westbound traffic as troops and equipment were being moved toward the Philippines or the new base on Okinawa. Our low-priority eastbound train was diverted to less used lines or sat on sidings for long periods as we were routed first south toward Los Angeles, then east over Tehachapi Pass and through various small towns on branch lines in California, Arizona, New Mexico, Texas, Louisiana, Tennessee, and on to Fort Meade, Maryland.

The day after arriving at Fort Meade I started back for Pittsburgh on an afternoon train from Baltimore. Rather than sit up half the night, I stopped off at Harrisburg and stayed at the Penn-Harris Hotel, where Bill Neel and I had stayed a little over a year earlier on a flight up from Charlotte. Over a leisurely dinner in the dining room I reflected on all that had happened and changed since my conversation with Bill in that same room. Bill's premonition about returning to New Guinea had been all too correct: he was not coming back. Fate was fickle.

While I was dispatching the flowers from San Francisco I had also sent telegrams to interested parties announcing my arrival from the war zone. It was the middle of the afternoon when I arrived at Way's house in Sewickley—in style, by cab from Pittsburgh at a cost of $7.50 when a one-way bus ticket was probably thirty-five cents. Grace and Fred Way Jr. gave me a big welcome at the back door. It felt good to be back in the familiar surroundings of the house on River Avenue, which had been a second home to me before I left for Aviation Cadet training in March, 1943. We talked long into the night.

I had obtained new uniforms at Fort Meade, but a first order of business to complete my transformation was to replace my only shoes, the well-worn GI boondockers, before presenting myself to Harriett. No military-style dress shoes in my size were available in Sewickley, so I took the train back to Pittsburgh and located a pair at Kaufman's department store. Unfortunately, even at Kaufman's, size twelve was not available. The clerk, Bill Shaner from Sewickley, finally convinced me that a pair of eleven and one-half wide shoes would do fine and he collected my ration coupon. Too short but wide was still too small, however, and after suffering for the sake of appearances for a couple of weeks I gave the shoes to my brother and bought another pair that fit.

Sad to say, that evening meeting with Harriett did not turn out to be the joyous reunion which a year's correspondence had led me to anticipate. A year had been a long time and when we were alone the young lady told me quickly, but gently, that she had met someone and was officially engaged. I now understood the palpable tension exhibited by the rest of her family as we had made conversation in the living room after the initial happy greeting. At least she had spared me by waiting to tell me face-to-face. To receive a "Dear John" letter while camped out in New Guinea or the Philippines and living for the next mail call would have been devastating. In any event, the big romance was unexpectedly over. The dreams were shattered, but the surprise and shock were survivable.

A happier note on my homecoming was finding that my friend Ab Rainbow had arrived in Sewickley at about the same time after completing his tour in Europe with the 366th Fighter Group. We spent many an hour rehashing all that had taken place since we had agreed to join up together in the summer of 1942 "to fight the war sitting down."

With so very few of the young, familiar faces around Sewickley it was time to move on and visit my folks in Massachusetts. My two visits to Wenham a year earlier had both been brief. The only acquaintances I had made were my parents' contemporaries. Gasoline rationing was still in effect, but a compassionate neighbor lent us a car and my ten gallons leave allotment took us on several trips to the beach. It was a strange feeling for me to look out over the calm, quiet sea and contrast that peaceful picture with the one in my mind of the still hostile shores in the Pacific. Gunfire could still be heard on Luzon and men were dying back there, distant in miles but not in memory. While all was now over in Europe and quiet on the Atlantic, the sight of the sea would for years bring up thoughts of all the action that had taken place there and beyond during 1939–45.

I promptly wrote a letter to Maury Owen to let him know how things had gone on the trip home and what he could expect. He should have completed his missions by then. In particular, Owen and the others would be interested in the policy of immediate release after the thirty-day leave. There came a gleeful reply from Owen reporting that several of the pilots who had accepted promotions to captain in exchange for staying another six months were now looking a little sour. He also wrote, "The boys all thank you for sending the flowers; you must be the first S. O. B. who actually did so."

After my thirty-day leave was over I reported to Camp Davis, North Carolina, for reassignment and hopefully a prompt discharge.

One weekend I went to Charlotte to visit Nancy, who greeted me effusively, as did her entire family. The boy who had been in the German prisoner of war camp had returned a few weeks earlier and there seemed to have been a mutually agreeable dissolution of that engagement or understanding.

Nancy and I talked at length about the plans we each had for the future, she aiming for more education while I was looking to begin college someplace and figure out an interesting direction for work afterward. The weekend I spent with Nancy was light and enjoyable, as our association had always been, but we both knew that our shared affections did not then go much beyond where we had left off a year earlier. We went our separate ways, but those spring months in Charlotte in 1944 are forever a pleasant memory.

July 21, 1945, was my last day on active duty. My discharge was issued at Fort Dix, New Jersey. I spent the next six weeks or so relaxing and explored some college options in a somewhat disorganized fashion, still not having a good idea of an interesting goal or how to go about reaching it. By the happenstance of a chance visit with the dean of Marietta College in Marietta, Ohio, rather than by plan, I enrolled there in the fall of 1945. The choice of a small, liberal arts school proved to be a good one for me and after graduating in 1948 I worked mostly in the engineering area of the property fire insurance industry, first in Ohio and later in Michigan, for more than thirty-five years.

My mother admired the workmanship and beauty of Father Snyder's mandarin coat bingo prize but declined to keep it when I offered it to her, saying, "It belongs on a younger person so you keep it until the right one comes along." Several years later I discovered that the coat fit and suited Fred Way's younger sister, Bee, and it is still around here some-place after fifty-plus years.

My interest in planes and flying has continued by way of a hobby. When our two sons were teenagers we bought a well-used Cessna 140 and flew it for pleasure for five or six years with great enjoyment. Two years of military flying had satisfied my curiosity about instruments and radio navigation, but I still look up when a plane passes overhead.

Fighting the war in a light bomber was an experience that could not be duplicated—the discipline, the training, the pleasure of flying, and exposure to the wider world. It was certainly a turning point for me and the manner in which I adjudged risks, made decisions, and reacted to problem situations would always be viewed differently after those days.

My experiences were admittedly more fortunate in their outcome than they were for many others who had also volunteered or were drafted. Looking back, the discomforts, worries, and outright scares are pushed in the background by the challenges overcome and the sights and smells of exotic places. I would do it all again—in an A-20.

INDEX

Photos and maps are indicated with **bold** typeface.

ISBN 1-58544-289-5

90000

9 781585 442898